Revelations of Chance

SUNY series in Transpersonal and Humanistic Psychology

Richard D. Mann, editor

Revelations of Chance

*Synchronicity as
Spiritual Experience*

Roderick Main

State University of New York Press

Published by
State University of New York Press, Albany

© 2007 State University of New York

All rights reserved

Printed in the United States of America

No part of this book may be used or reproduced in any manner whatsoever without written permission. No part of this book may be stored in a retrieval system or transmitted in any form or by any means including electronic, electrostatic, magnetic tape, mechanical, photocopying, recording, or otherwise without the prior permission in writing of the publisher.

For information, address State University of New York Press,
194 Washington Avenue, Suite 305, Albany NY 12210-2384

Production by Kelli Williams
Marketing by Anne M. Valentine

Library of Congress Cataloging-in-Publication Data

Main, Roderick.
    Revelations of chance : synchronicity as spiritual experience / Roderick Main.
        p. cm. — (SUNY series in transpersonal and humanistic psychology)
    Includes bibliographical references and index.
    ISBN-13: 978-0-7914-7023-7 (hardcover : alk. paper)
    ISBN-13: 978-0-7914-7024-4 (pbk. : alk. paper)
  1. Coincidence—Religious aspects. I. Title. II. Series.

BL625.93.M35 2007
204'.2—dc22
                                                                                       2006012813

10 9 8 7 6 5 4 3 2 1

In memory of
John Mein Main
(1930–2006)

CONTENTS

List of Illustrations ix

Acknowledgments xi

1. Introduction 1

2. Synchronicity and Spirit 11

3. The Spiritual Dimension of Spontaneous Synchronicities 39

4. Symbol, Myth, and Synchronicity: The Birth of Athena 63

5. Multiple Synchronicities of a Chess Grandmaster 81

6. The Self-Revelation of Synchronicity as Spirit: A Modern Grail Story 113

7. Synchronicity and Spirit in the *I Ching* 141

Notes 189

References 233

Index 247

ILLUSTRATIONS

Figure 7.1   Whole and divided lines
Figure 7.2   The four kinds of lines
Figure 7.3   Hexagram 44, Kou/Coming to Meet
Figure 7.4   The eight trigrams
Figure 7.5   Hexagram 43, Kui/Break-through (Resoluteness)
Figure 7.6   Hexagram 35, Chin/Progress
Figure 7.7   Hexagram 12, P'i/Standstill (Stagnation)
Figure 7.8   Hexagram 61, Chung Fu/Inner Truth
Figure 7.9   Hexagram 50, Ting/The Cauldron

ACKNOWLEDGMENTS

I would especially like to thank Adrian Cunningham for his detailed comments on much of the material in this book; David Curtis for many illuminating discussions about synchronicity over the years; and James Plaskett for generously making the accounts of his experiences available for me to study. I would also like to thank the following who commented on parts or drafts of this work at various times: Allan Combs, Philip Goodchild, James Hall, Peter James, Victor Mansfield, Peter Moore, Andrew Rawlinson, Stuart Rose, Sean Ryan, Geoffrey Samuel, Robert Segal, Elliott Shaw, Patrick Sherry, and Bill Thompson. For practical and moral support, I would like to thank my parents, John and Catriona Main, and my wife, Shiho.

Some of the material in chapter 4 was previously published in "Putting the Sinn Back into Synchronicity: Some Spiritual Implications of Synchronistic Experiences," 2nd Series Occasional Paper (Lampeter, UK: Religious Experience Research Centre, 2001).

Some of the material in chapter 7 was previously published in "Synchronicity and the *I Ching*: Clarifying the Connections," *Harvest: Journal for Jungian Studies* 43, no. 1 (1997): 31–44.

CHAPTER 1

INTRODUCTION

The following are four examples of the kind of experience with which this book is concerned.

A professor of biology, Adolf Portmann, was delivering a lecture that he intended to conclude with a story about a praying mantis. Just as he was about to broach this subject, a praying mantis flew into the lecture hall through an open window, circled around Portmann's head, and landed near the lectern lamp, to the effect that the insect's wings cast on the white wall behind him a huge shadow in the form of the arms of a praying man.[1]

In all his years of driving, relates the writer Paul Auster, he has had just four flat tires. These occurred in three different countries and were spread out over a period of eight or nine years. On each occasion, however, the same person happened to be in the car with him—an acquaintance he saw rarely and briefly and in his relationship with whom there was "always an edge of unease and conflict."[2]

One night a man dreamed that he was visiting Australia with his wife and some family and friends. He was being driven in a car around a large town and came eventually to a square where there was a church with three large bells hung at ground level in the open. Some months later he and his wife actually did visit Australia, and on a car excursion from Melbourne with a couple of relatives they ended up in the town of Wangaratta in north Victoria. There they came across a church on the floor of which, just inside the door, were three large bells—with a further five lying elsewhere in the church—waiting for a new bell tower to be built.[3]

An analyst on vacation suddenly had a strong visual impression of one of her patients she knew to be suicidal. Unable to account for the impression as having arisen by any normal chain of mental associations, she immediately sent a telegram telling the patient not to do anything foolish. Two days later she learned that, just before the telegram arrived, the patient had gone into the kitchen and turned on the gas valve with the intention of killing herself. Startled by the postman ringing the doorbell, she turned the valve off; and even more struck by the content of the telegram he delivered, she did not resume her attempt.[4]

These four experiences are highly varied in both their content and the manner of their occurrence. They have, however, an important set of characteristics in common. Each of them involves two or more events that parallel one another in such a way as to suggest that they are connected, and yet the usual way in which such connections are accounted for—in terms of some kind of causal relationship—seems inapplicable. The occurrence of such experiences has come to be called "meaningful coincidence" or—in the term introduced by the Swiss psychiatrist C. G. Jung (1875–1961)—"synchronicity." A full account of this latter term will be given in chapter 2.

There is certainly nothing new about such experiences themselves. Their basic form can readily be discerned in events traditionally described as, for example, answered prayers, successful magic, divine interventions, signs and omens, and moments of good or bad luck. Within the last one hundred years, however, the phenomenon of synchronicity has come to receive an increasing amount of attention independently of its relationship to any specific traditional belief structures or modes of thought. Though the present work refers to traditional frameworks for elucidation, its primary concern is with this recently emerged independent status of the phenomenon.

A considerable body of writing specifically on synchronicity has already accumulated. However, a disproportionately small amount of this writing has been concerned with exploring at a serious level the possible spiritual aspects of the phenomenon. (A full account of what is meant by "spirit" and "spiritual" in this work is provided in chapter 2. Briefly, the terms refer to an aspect of consciousness and reality that cannot be reduced to either the physical or the psychic.) As a contribution toward meeting this lack, the present work is a sustained inquiry into the relationship between synchronicity and spirit. Although the primary aim is to add to our understanding of synchronicity, some insights may also be gained into the more general problem of studying anomalous and spiritual phenomena of whatever kind.

The work is set within the broad field of religious studies. This is a field traditionally very accommodating toward multidisciplinary and polymethodological approaches,[5] and considerable advantage has been taken of this. My specific approach has been to set to one side initially the problem of situating the present study within this or that particular discipline or circumscribed set of disciplines, focusing instead simply on the phenomenon of synchronicity itself, in whatever variety of forms it has seemed most accessible to further scrutiny. In practice, this has meant several things: First, briefly reviewing existing studies mainly within the fields of analytical psychology, parapsychology, statistics, and cognitive psychology. It has also involved invoking theology and philosophy in order to elicit and elaborate on possible spiritual implications within the concept of synchronicity. Again, it has meant looking in detail at a kind of synchronistic case material that has not previously been studied—namely, extensive series and clusters of interrelated incidents all experienced by a single individual. Finally, it has led to a detailed and multifaceted examination of the ancient Chinese Oracle of Change, the *I Ching*.

The majority of the work that has been done thus far on the subject of synchronicity is, not surprisingly, within the field of Jungian psychology. Jung himself, who coined and introduced the term "synchronicity," wrote two significant essays devoted solely to its explication—one extensive essay and the other a more easily digestible abridgement of it.[6] Also influential were the statements on synchronicity contained in his foreword to the Wilhelm-Baynes version of the *I Ching*.[7] The ideas contained in these three sources are repeated, and occasionally modified or extended, in various other contexts throughout Jung's voluminous writings.[8] Practically all of this material will be drawn on throughout the present study and especially in chapter 2, where Jung's theories provide the point of departure for the definition and characterization of synchronicity in this work.

Among Jung's immediate followers, Marie-Louise von Franz has made the largest contribution to the subject of synchronicity.[9] Principally she has pursued certain indications within Jung's work concerning the possible relationship between synchronicity and natural numbers. This has led her into profound and fascinating explorations of the emerging interface between psychology and physics, and has also resulted in some suggestive speculations concerning the operation of divinatory procedures such as the *I Ching*. However, von Franz's primary orientation is toward the scientific end of the spectrum of possible relevance of synchronicity, while the orientation of the present work is toward the religious and spiritual end.[10]

Another Jungian-influenced approach to the understanding of synchronicity is the attempt to view the phenomenon mythically, that is, in terms of the "god" or "spirit" that might be considered responsible for it. Thus, various writers have thought to elucidate aspects of the nature of synchronicity by viewing it imaginatively—or "imaginally"[11]—as the expression of one or other of the gods of the Greek pantheon: Hermes the trickster and transgressor of boundaries; Pan the god of spontaneity; or

Dionysus bestower of the experience of mystical fusion and timelessness.[12] Similarly, the way usually inert matter can appear in synchronicity to be miraculously animated has caused the phenomenon to be imaginatively explored in relation to the figure of the Golem.[13]

Among the numerous other Jungian contributions are studies with a more clinical emphasis,[14] attempts to modify Jung's theoretical thinking,[15] and a miscellany of other studies relating synchronicity to, for example, apparitions, the theories of relativity and quantum physics, typology and hypnotic induction, the Rorschach test, and relationships between adoptees and birthparents.[16] There is increasing interest, too, in the relationship between Jung and Wolfgang Pauli and the significance of this relationship for the development of the synchronicity concept.[17] Finally, there has also been some stimulating recent research attempting to relate synchronicity to processes of emergence and self-organization.[18] Within all of this, however, the possible spiritual aspect of the phenomenon receives only marginal attention.

Indeed, within the Jungian framework there have been very few major studies focusing on the more spiritual or religious dimension of synchronicity. Three notable exceptions are works by Jean Shinoda Bolen, Robert Aziz, and Victor Mansfield.[19] The first of these emphasizes the importance of synchronicity as an experience that can lead to a sense of cosmic meaning and connectedness.[20] It does so, however, in a rather intuitive way, and the book is at its best when dealing with the more practical and psychotherapeutic aspects of synchronicity, before it moves into a consideration of the spiritual dimension. Aziz's book, by contrast, is a scholarly attempt to elucidate the significance of the concept of synchronicity for Jung's own psychology of religion, and engages in an illuminating way both with many general aspects of Jung's psychology and with particular issues relevant to the phenomenology of religion.[21] The main thrust of Mansfield's book is to reveal connections between relativity and quantum physics, Jung's theory of synchronicity articulated in terms of compensation and individuation, and Middle Way Buddhism. In relation to Buddhism, Mansfield skillfully develops the idealist implications within Jung's thinking.[22]

My own previous book-length study of synchronicity is a detailed examination of Jung's writings on the topic.[23] It looks in turn at how the theory of synchronicity fits into Jung's overall psychological model, including a consideration of its apparent inconsistencies; the wide range of personal, intellectual, and social contexts that informed Jung's thinking on synchronicity; how Jung himself applied the theory of synchronicity within his critique of science, religion, and society; and the continuing relevance of the theory for understanding issues in contemporary detraditionalized religion. In contrast, the present work is concerned with elucidating the phenomenon of synchronicity as such rather than Jung's theory of it, and therefore has a wider range of theoretical reference. It is also more focused on the specifically spiritual implications of synchronicity.

Standing alone as a focused, scholarly contextualization of Jung's theory of synchronicity is Paul Bishop's study. This work presents synchronicity as the heir to Romantic notions of "intellectual intuition," the belief in the possibility of acquiring knowledge by a form of direct cognition that bypasses the need for sensory information.[24]

Psychical research and parapsychology played a large part in both the genesis and the subsequent development of Jung's theory of synchronicity. In addition, these disciplines have provided the context for several studies of coincidence that do not center on Jung's ideas. For example, before and independently of Jung, the psychical researcher Alice Johnson published in 1899 a lengthy study based on a large number of carefully reported and documented coincidences, sifting them for possible evidence of the paranormal.[25]

Arguably the greatest impact on the study of coincidences outside specifically Jungian circles was made by Arthur Koestler, who was also writing from a predominantly parapsychological perspective. In the early 1970s he published two books specifically on coincidences, and also accumulated a large collection of spontaneous case material through appeals in the media.[26] In addition to parapsychology, his thinking on this subject was greatly influenced by physics and the other hard sciences. He postulated that there were two complementary principles operating at all levels of reality: a self-assertive tendency, which enables entities to assert their individuality and autonomy, and an integrative tendency, by which those same entities remain subordinate to the demands of the larger whole of which they are a part.[27] His suggested explanation of coincidences is to see them as expressions of his integrative tendency, which he thought could be regarded as "a universal principle which includes a-causal phenomena."[28] However, unlike Jung—and rather surprisingly for a novelist—Koestler shows little appreciation of the psychological and imaginative dimension of the phenomenon.

On the question of whether there might be a spiritual aspect of coincidences, Koestler's theory seems neutral. He points out that the integrative tendency can give rise to a range of self-transcending emotions, that is, "a craving to surrender to something that is larger than society and transcends the boundaries of the self—which may be God, or nature, or a Bach cantata, or the mystic's 'oceanic feeling.'"[29] The integrative tendency, as Koestler presents it, exists throughout reality; if there is a spiritual aspect of reality, then presumably the integrative tendency would also operate within that aspect. Thus, the theory does not seem to have any specific implications for ontology. Of coincidences more specifically, Koestler remarks that certain of them can have

> a dramatic impact which may have a lasting effect and lead to profound changes in a person's mental outlook—changes ranging from religious conversion in extreme cases, to a mere agnostic willingness to admit the existence of levels of reality beyond the vocabulary of rational thought.[30]

However, in spite of this theoretical openness to the idea of the spiritual, the center of gravity of Koestler's writings on this subject is scientific and not specifically concerned with issues of spirituality.

Koestler's work was the inspiration for the first large-scale survey of coincidence experiences carried out in 1989 under the auspices of the Koestler Foundation.[31] A questionnaire that appeared in *The Observer* on December 24, 1989, generated 991 usable responses. Examples of the accounts received appeared in a book by Brian Inglis in 1990,[32] while the entire sample was coded and analyzed by Jane Henry and the results published in 1993.[33] Concerning the types of coincidence experienced, 33 percent of the respondents accepted the characterization "prayer answering," and similar numbers the characterizations "guardian angel" (34 percent) and "library angel" (30 percent).[34] Concerning what factors might have accounted for or influenced the coincidences, 51 percent accepted "Destiny/Fate/Karma" as a possibility, 38 percent accepted "Synchronicity (Jung's theory)," and 36 percent accepted "Divine or diabolic intervention."[35] The survey was not specifically designed to elicit information regarding the spiritual experiencing and interpretation of coincidences, but the preceding figures nonetheless serve to suggest that many experiencers do view them in this light.

Other worthwhile work on coincidence from a parapsychological perspective includes a book by Alan Vaughan and articles by John Beloff, Ivor Grattan-Guinness, Lila Gatlin, and Charles Tart. Also worth mentioning in this context is a study carried out by Stephen Hladkyj which found that reports of synchronistic experiences shared more characteristics with parapsychological experiences than with mystical experiences.[36]

Coincidence phenomena have also attracted the attention of Freudian psychoanalysts with an interest in parapsychology. Freud himself published several papers dealing with "telepathy" and "occultism," as he referred to these phenomena.[37] These papers are collected, along with other contributions, in a book edited by George Devereux.[38] One contributor, Jule Eisenbud, long continued to write interestingly on this subject from the psychoanalytic perspective.[39] Recently, Mel Faber has developed a wholly naturalistic interpretation of synchronistic experiences based on post-Freudian psychoanalytic insights.[40] His explicit aim has been to provide an alternative explanation to that offered by Jung and in particular to challenge the spiritual interpretation of synchronicity.[41]

Other writers address the problem of coincidence from the perspectives of statistics and cognitive psychology. Regarding statistics, George Spencer Brown has suggested that the apparent significance of coincidences and of results in parapsychology may be due simply to a mistaken understanding of how statistics operate.[42] The mathematicians Persi Diaconis and Frederick Mosteller, without calling the basic principles of the discipline into question, have argued that statistical considerations alone are able to explain away the apparent meaningfulness of most coincidences.[43] In response it has been noted that in most real-life cases of synchronicity there are so many imponderables that even approximate evaluations of probability become dubious.[44] Again, it has been questioned whether it is even sensible in principle to try to evaluate synchronicity statistically. For example, Jung and von Franz argue that statistics work precisely by ignoring what is unique about the individual case, whereas synchronicity tries to investigate that uniqueness.[45] Others have drawn attention to problems in the very nature of statistics, including that there is no normative probability theory.[46]

Caroline Watt has reviewed various considerations from cognitive psychology that demonstrate that people are generally very poor judges of probability under the kind of conditions of uncertainty in which most coincidences take place and are also prone to perceive or process information erroneously.[47] She notes, however, that these considerations, which are usually invoked to explain away anomalous experiences, cut both ways and could equally explain why certain events are judged or perceived not to be anomalous when in fact they are.[48]

Awareness of these statistical and cognitive psychological explanations of putative coincidences not only can help sharpen our powers of judgment under uncertainty but also, through preventing us from too hastily abandoning the search for causes, can sometimes lead to the discovery of unrecognized causal factors. As Diaconis and Mosteller point out, "much of scientific discovery depends on finding the cause of a perplexing coincidence."[49] However, the statistical and cognitive psychological explanations would need to be actually proven in each particular case if they were to invalidate the kinds of spiritual explanation or interpretation that are the focus of the present study.

Several writers have suggested that certain heterodox scientific theories, particularly those with an emphasis on holism, may be relevant to an understanding of coincidence. Two theorists whose names crop up repeatedly are the physicist David Bohm and the plant physiologist Rupert Sheldrake.[50] Particularly suggestive is the centrality and flexibility of the concept of information within both Bohm's theory of the implicate order and Sheldrake's hypothesis of formative causation. The concept of information also plays a role in von Franz's speculations on the relationship of synchronicity to number, as well as in several other investigations into the possible modus operandi of coincidence.[51]

Another emphasis in recent work on synchronicity is on narrative. This emphasis has informed both the collecting of accounts of synchronistic experiences and the manner in which they are then analyzed and understood.[52]

In view of the important role played by the *I Ching* in Jung's development of the concept of synchronicity, it might be expected that researchers would already have explored this in some depth. However, apart from Jung's own work and its immediate extension by von Franz, very little of substance seems to have been written on the subject of synchronicity and the *I Ching*. There is an article by Wayne McEvilly that attempts to clarify the relationship from a philosophical perspective; a couple of pertinent sinological articles—very solid and illuminating—by Willard Peterson; and an article by the psychologist and parapsychologist Michael Thalbourne and some colleagues that reports on an experiment suggesting that a paranormal factor may be at work within the *I Ching*. The concept also receives attention in some of the writings on the *I Ching* by Stephen Karcher.[53] Apart from these few studies, the relationship between synchronicity and the *I Ching*—and even more the relationship of synchronicity to spirit in the light of the *I Ching*—has been left pretty much as an open field for research.

A final area that the phenomenon of synchronicity has impacted on significantly is New Age spirituality. In a 1994 survey of subscribers to the largest-selling New Age magazine in Britain, *Kindred Spirit*, 81.8 percent of the sample of 908 respondents reported having experienced some form of "psi," with synchronicity as the joint-fourth most frequently experienced kind of psi (40.6 percent of the sample).[54] Writings that might be embraced by the broad term "New Age" vary greatly in quality, and might include several of those already mentioned here with some favor.[55] Often, however, it seems that references to synchronicity in the context of New Age spirituality are somewhat vague and intuitive, offering little in the way of genuine enquiry or clarification.[56] Certainly, they do little to fulfill the need for a detailed exploration of the possible relationship between the concepts of synchronicity and spirit.[57]

The present study aims to demonstrate that the possible spiritual nature of synchronicity can be explicated more rigorously and to a much greater extent than might have been anticipated. It attempts this by exploring general theoretical issues, by attending to experiencers' responses, by interpreting specific features of synchronicities, and by investigating the synchronistic basis of the ancient Chinese Oracle of Change, the *I Ching*.

In chapter 2, I first characterize and define the concept of synchronicity as I shall be using it in the remainder of this work. My definition of synchronicity is largely based on Jung's but involves some important clarifications and modifications. The discussion therefore involves concisely explicating Jung's thinking about synchronicity and how it fits into his overall psychological model. I then similarly characterize and define the concept of spirit. I consider a wide range of understandings of spirit as found within various religious traditions, as well as within Jungian psychology and transpersonal psychology. Out of this diversity I elaborate a fairly accommodating, largely detraditionalized, synthesis suitable for the purposes of the present study.

An attempt to elucidate the relationship between synchronicity and spirit more systematically is made in chapter 3. This involves eliciting from my characterization and definition of spirit a range of more specific spiritual concepts implied within it. For this I draw mostly on a variety of twentieth-century theological writings from within the western Christian tradition, though in each case the understanding arrived at is by no means restricted to the Christian context. No previous attempt has been made to establish the possible relationship between synchronicity and spiritual concepts in such detail.

In chapter 4, the application to synchronicity of these spiritual concepts is illustrated by means of an extensive case study. The case study consists of material that has been published but, in spite of its extraordinary nature, does not seem previously to have caught the attention of any commentators on synchronicity.[58] Indeed, no previous study has presented and commented on such an extensive series of synchronicities—certainly none has attempted to elicit from the synchronicities a comparable range and depth of meaning. The present study especially highlights that the content of synchronicities frequently involves symbolic and mythic motifs.

Following on from this, in chapter 5, an even more extensive body of synchronistic material is presented, again consisting almost exclusively of the experiences of one individual, whose own responses to and interpretations of the material are reported in detail. At the time of my original work on it (1991–95), the material had been neither published nor seriously studied before.[59] It came to my attention through contacts in the field, and was sent to me directly by the experiencer himself. The presentation of such an extensive body of case material centering on a single individual is again unprecedented within the literature on synchronicity.

Having presented this material and the experiencer's responses to it, I next, in chapter 6, offer my own evaluation and interpretation. My interpretation is attempted using a methodology analogous to that used within Jungian psychology for the analysis of dreams, myths, legends, and other products of the imagination.[60] So far as I am aware, this kind of analysis in relation to synchronicity has not been undertaken before.

Finally, chapter 7 looks at the possible systematization of synchronicity in the ancient Chinese Oracle the *I Ching*. A specific comparison is made between the kind of synchronicities occurring in this relatively controlled context and the kind that occur more spontaneously. I look at those of Jung's writings that specifically relate synchronicity to the *I Ching*; at twentieth-century Western scholarship on the *I Ching*; and at the work of the Eranos I Ching Project in Switzerland (1988–94), which combines Jungian psychological insights with modern sinological scholarship. The discussions in this chapter explore the relationship between synchronicity and the *I Ching* in greater detail than has been done before, and also for the first time use the *I Ching* as a specific framework for elucidating the possible relationships between synchronicity and spirit.

CHAPTER 2

SYNCHRONICITY AND SPIRIT

Synchronicity and spirit, the two core concepts in this study, are not easy to define in a way that is at once precise and comprehensive. The referents of both terms are highly elusive—to the extent, indeed, that they have even been denied to exist at all.[1] In the present chapter, therefore, I attempt to make the referents of the two concepts more visible by offering for each in turn both a broad general characterization and, set within this, a fairly precise working definition. These characterizations and definitions will largely be based on established usage, but modified in the light of my own observations and reflections and, in particular, my critical engagement with Jung's views. For the time being, the two concepts will be treated separately. The understanding of them that emerges will then form the background for subsequent chapters exploring their various interrelationships.

SYNCHRONICITY

Zechariah's Horses

Consider the following incident that happened in 1973 to Stephen Jenkins, a schoolteacher in the south of England and an independent investigator of strange phenomena. As he recounts in his book *The Undiscovered Country*, for some time he "had been pursuing a very remote enquiry, relating to the fact that in certain schools of Central Asian Buddhism prophecies and forebodings exist about the coming of a serious world cataclysm."[2] Being aware of the similar ideas in Christian apocalyptic literature, he was led, he says, "to a lengthy and detailed comparison of the teaching of the two religions in this exceedingly esoteric field." As part of his study he immersed himself in the visions of Ezekiel and Zechariah, paying special attention to Zechariah's vision of the four horsemen with their horses of red, black, dapple, and white.[3] On the evening of August 23, 1973, he and his wife started a holiday at the Garden House Hotel in Cambridge. Jenkins describes how

> at seven-fifteen I went out onto the balcony of our room, having that day completed an exhaustive study of Zechariah, and having noted particularly that the horses reappear as the sinister Four Horsemen of the Apocalypse in the *Revelation of St John*. In the long field below the hotel were quietly grazing four horses: red, black, dapple and white.[4]

Jenkins's response to this incident indicates how improbable he considered it and how powerfully he was affected by it:

> The coincidence—especially when numbers, varieties and possible combinations are considered—was so impressive that I photographed them next day, to prove to myself more than anyone else that they were really there. After all, there could have been five, or two black ones, or a grey, or a piebald or a chestnut.[5]

Furthermore, on July 23, 1974, exactly eleven months after the above incident, Jenkins relates that he was on Okehampton Common in Devon, near Yes Tor, where he had gone with a group of his school pupils to look at, photograph, and survey the area around a curious stone that seemed to have been formed by the elements into a natural sculpture of a crouching bird. While they were involved in this, Jenkins turned and looked behind him

> and there, drifting over the eastern shoulder of Yes Tor, came a small herd of Dartmoor ponies. Ahead of them by a clear 100 yards was a group of four: red, black, dapple and white. I could hardly believe my eyes, and took care to photograph them, too.[6]

From Coincidence to Synchronicity

Uncontroversially, what Jenkins experienced here was a coincidence (or a couple of coincidences, if one considers separately the 1974 sighting of the four ponies). A coincidence, according to the *Chambers Twentieth Century Dictionary*, is "the occurrence of events simultaneously or consecutively in a striking manner but without any causal connection between them."[7] In Jenkins's case, one event was his reading about and reflecting on the visionary image of four horses (or sets of horses) colored red, black, dapple, and white.[8] The second event was seeing the four correspondingly colored horses from his hotel balcony. Since this occurred on the same day as he was reflecting on the visionary image, it might, loosely speaking, be considered *simultaneous* with the first event. In this episode there was also a third event: seeing the four ponies (again appropriately colored) on Okehampton Common. Happening eleven months after the other two events, this can only be considered *consecutive* to them, though again in a rather stretched sense of the term. Regarding the striking manner of the occurrence, this is amply demonstrated by the fact that Jenkins says he found the events so impressive and incredible that he required photographic testimony to persuade himself that the animals really were there as he thought he saw them. As for the lack of causal connection between the events, on a common-sense level this too is evident enough: Jenkins's interest in the visionary texts neither influenced nor was influenced by the presence of the four horses in the field or the appearance later of the four ponies on Okehampton Common.

Thus, Jenkins's experience fulfills the commonly accepted conditions for being termed a coincidence. Its status as something more than just a coincidence—as a synchronicity—depends on the presence of the additional property of meaningfulness. Jenkins himself refers to what happened to him as a "significant coincidence"—implying, clearly, that there are such things as "insignificant" or "meaningless" coincidences, from which experiences like his own can and should be differentiated.

It was Jung whose work first brought into focus the distinction between meaningful and nonmeaningful coincidences and who coined the word "synchronicity" to refer to the former. Jung's own conception of what makes some coincidences meaningful and others not was deeply rooted in his overall psychological theory, in particular his theory of archetypes and the collective unconscious. However, not everyone who acknowledges meaningful coincidences as a distinguishable class of events would necessarily share Jung's views as to what precisely constitutes their meaningfulness. To dissociate themselves from these theoretical undertones, some writers have therefore tended to eschew the word "synchronicity" altogether unless they happen to be referring specifically to Jung's theory, using instead the more neutral term "meaningful coincidence" or even just "coincidence."[9] Nevertheless, a popular and widely current use of the word "synchronicity" has evolved that equates it with meaningful coincidence but leaves open the question of what constitutes the meaningfulness.[10] In the present study, the term "synchronicity" is freely used in this latter uncommitted sense; on occasions where it applies specifically to Jung's theory, this is clearly indicated by the context.

A Working Definition of Synchronicity

An experience such as Jenkins's, then, is more than just a coincidence, it is a meaningful or significant coincidence and hence, in a sense of the word acceptable both to him and to the present writer, it is a synchronicity.[11] Using Jenkins's incident as a primary example, I now attempt first to formulate somewhat more precisely what I take to be the defining conditions of a synchronistic experience and then to show a number of respects in which some potentially misleading assertions within the most influential previous attempt at such formulation—the definitions offered by Jung—have thereby been avoided.

A synchronistic experience, as I understand the term, is one in which

1. two or more events parallel one another through having identical, similar, or comparable content;
2. there is no discernible or plausible way in which this paralleling could be the result of normal causes;
3. the paralleling must be sufficiently unlikely and detailed as to be notable;
4. the experience must be meaningful beyond being notable.

This definition still requires qualification and expansion, and we can conveniently provide these by considering the definition vis-à-vis Jung's attempts to define synchronicity.

Jung on Synchronicity

Jung defined synchronicity in a variety of ways. Most succinctly, he defined it as "meaningful coincidence,"[12] as "acausal parallelism,"[13] or as "an acausal connecting principle."[14] More fully, he defined it as "the simultaneous occurrence of a certain psychic state with one or more external events which appear as meaningful parallels to the momentary subjective state."[15] An example of Jung's will convey what he means by these definitions as well as how the concept of synchronicity fits into his overall psychological model. The example concerns a young woman patient whose excessive intellectuality made her "psychologically inaccessible," closed off from a "more human understanding."[16] Unable to make headway in analyzing her, Jung reports that he had to confine himself to "the hope that something unexpected would turn up, something that would burst the intellectual retort into which she had sealed herself."[17] He continues:

Well, I was sitting opposite her one day, with my back to the window, listening to her flow of rhetoric. She had had an impressive dream the night before, in which someone had given her a golden scarab—a costly piece of jewellery. While she was still telling me this dream, I heard something behind me gently tapping on the window. I turned round and saw that it was a fairly large flying insect that was knocking against the window-pane in the obvious effort to get into the dark room. This seemed to me very strange. I opened the window immediately and caught the insect in the air as it flew in. It was a scarabaeid beetle, or common rose-chafer (*Cetonia aurata*), whose gold green colour most nearly resembles that of a golden scarab. I handed the beetle to my patient with the words, "Here is your scarab." This experience punctured the desired hole in her rationalism and broke the ice of her intellectual resistance. The treatment could now be continued with satisfactory results.[18]

In this example, the *psychic state* is indicated by the patient's decision to tell Jung her dream of being given a scarab. The *parallel external event* is the appearance and behavior of the real scarab. The telling of the dream and the appearance of the real scarab were *simultaneous*. Neither of these events discernibly or plausibly caused the other by any normal means, so their relationship is *acausal*. Nevertheless, the events parallel each other in such unlikely detail that one cannot escape the impression that they are indeed *connected*, albeit acausally. Moreover, this acausal connection of events both is symbolically informative (as we shall see) and has a deeply emotive and transforming impact on the patient and in these senses is clearly *meaningful*.

Jung attempts to account for synchronistic events primarily in terms of his concept of *archetypes*. For this purpose, he highlights the nature of archetypes as "formal factors responsible for the organisation of unconscious psychic processes: they are 'patterns of behaviour.' At the same time they have a 'specific charge' and develop numinous effects which express themselves as *affects*."[19] They "constitute the structure" not of the personal but "of the *collective unconscious* . . . psyche that is identical in all individuals."[20] Also relevant is that they typically express themselves in the form of *symbolic images*.[21] Jung considered that synchronistic events tend to occur in situations in which an archetype is active or "constellated."[22] Such constellation of archetypes in the life of a person is governed by the process of *individuation*—the inherent drive of the psyche toward increased wholeness and self-realization. Individuation in turn proceeds through the dynamic of *compensation*, whereby any one-sidedness in a person's conscious attitude is balanced by contents emerging from the unconscious that, if successfully integrated, contribute to a state of greater psychic wholeness. Relating these psychological dynamics to the example, Jung suggests that it has "an archetypal foundation" and, more specifically, that it was the archetype of rebirth that was constellated.[23] He writes, "Any essential change of attitude signifies a psychic renewal which is usually accompanied by symbols of rebirth in the patient's dreams and fantasies. The scarab is a classic example of a rebirth symbol."[24] The emotional charge or numinosity of the archetype is evident from its having "broke[n] the ice of [the patient's] intellectual resistance." The compensatory nature of the experience is also clear: her one-sided rationalism and psychological stasis were balanced by an event that both in its symbolism and in its action expressed the power of the irrational and the possibility of renewal. Finally, that all of this promoted the patient's individuation is implied by Jung's statement: "The treatment could now be continued with satisfactory results."[25]

While this example and analysis illustrate Jung's overall understanding of the kinds of events that compose synchronicities and what confers the meaning that elevates mere coincidences into synchronicities, Jung finds it necessary to expand his definition still further. His most systematic attempt to pin down precisely what he understands by the term "synchronicity" is with the following three-pronged definition. An event that fits into one or another of these three categories is synchronistic:

1. The coincidence of a psychic state in the observer with a simultaneous, objective, external event that corresponds to the psychic state or content (e.g., the scarab), where there is no evidence of a causal connection between the psychic state and the external event, and where, considering the psychic relativity of space and time, such a connection is not even conceivable.
2. The coincidence of a psychic state with a corresponding (more or less simultaneous) external event taking place outside the observer's field of perception, i.e., at a distance, and only verifiable afterwards.
3. The coincidence of a psychic state with a corresponding, not yet existent future event that is distant in time and likewise can only be verified afterwards.[26]

The second and third prongs of this definition are intended to capture cases in which the coinciding external event occurs either at a distance or in the future (giving "clairvoyant" or "telepathic" and "precognitive" coincidences, respectively). An example of the former is Swedenborg's famous vision in which he "saw" in detail the progress of a fire in Stockholm two hundred miles away at the same time as it was actually happening.[27] An instance of the precognitive kind of coincidence would be the case mentioned by Jung of a student friend of his whose father had promised him a trip to Spain if he passed his final examinations satisfactorily. The friend then had a dream of seeing certain things in a Spanish city: a particular square, a Gothic cathedral, and, around a certain corner, a carriage drawn by two cream-colored horses. Later, having successfully passed his examinations, he actually visited Spain for the first time and encountered all the details from his dream in reality.[28]

However, even this tripartite definition of Jung's does not seem to capture everything that he elsewhere considers important about synchronicity. For example, in each part of this definition the central notion of meaning has been left entirely implicit. Indeed, even if one were to make a composite definition synthesizing all the important features in Jung's various formulations, several major problems would remain. I now examine some of these problems and suggest how they might be avoided by the working definition that I have proposed. In the course of doing this a fuller sense will emerge of what exactly is implied in my working definition.

The Requirement of Simultaneity

A first problem with Jung's definitions is his repeated emphasis on simultaneity. It is true that simultaneity—and even more so, near-simultaneity—is one of the most commonly occurring features of events that are registered as coincidences. However, as the third prong of Jung's three-part definition recognizes, simultaneity is not a strictly necessary feature. I would suggest that the proximity of two or more events in time is simply one of the respects in which they can parallel one another.[29] The more nearly simultaneous the events are, the more that particular detail of their paralleling contributes to their notability. It is quite possible, however, that if other kinds of detail are sufficiently impressive, the absence of even near-simultaneity can have no serious effect on an event's claim to coincidental or synchronistic status. Jenkins's sighting of the four Dartmoor ponies is a case in point. Happening eleven months after his earlier incident, it is certainly not a simultaneous occurrence. However, other details of the event—such as that exactly the same combination of colors of horses was involved, that Jenkins was again engaged in a form of esoteric inquiry, and perhaps that the incident happened on the same day of the month—are sufficiently striking for a coincidence to be registered.

Indeed, in certain cases the very lack of near-simultaneity between events can contribute to their coincidental status. For example, if a person dreams of a detailed series of events that subsequently happens in reality, the likelihood of there being a normal causal explanation for this is often greater when the time interval between dream and actualization is small, that is, when there is near-simultaneity. In such cases it could easily be that the same situation that is about to evolve into the series of actual events has been noticed and then imaginatively carried forward by the dreamer's mind into the apparently precognitive dream image. Such extrapolation is possible by a fairly normal, if unconscious, process of inference. However, if the time interval between dream and actualization were significantly greater, the likelihood of such inference would be less and in many cases extremely improbable. With these kinds of experiences, then, the further one is from simultaneity and near-simultaneity the more likely it is that what one is dealing with is a synchronicity.

Psychic and Physical; Inner and Outer

A second important difference between the definition I have offered and those of Jung is that in the latter the coincidence is said to be between "a psychic state in the observer" and an "objective, external event," whereas in my definition it is not specified what the nature of the parallel events should be. Again, it is true that most events that are registered as meaningful coincidences do meet Jung's requirement. However, it is easy to find counterexamples. I was once having lunch with someone who, while we were talking, casually began making origami models out of a paper napkin—something I had not seen done for several years. Later that afternoon I saw a boy at a bus stop who was looking intently at a sheet of instructions for making origami models, one of which at least was the same as had been made by my lunch companion (who, incidentally, later assured me that he had not recently seen any such instructions but felt he was acting purely spontaneously). This incident has a fair claim to being a meaningful coincidence, but it does not obviously fit Jung's criteria. I was the observer of the two events, yet the first event neither was a psychic state nor took place in me the observer: it was a physical event happening in the environment outside of me. To be sure, by the time I saw the second event, the first one had become internalized in me as a memory, so that in that sense it was "a psychic state in the observer." But the memory was neither active nor in any other way especially prominent in my consciousness until the occurrence of the second event.[30] Again, consider the case in which two acquaintances discovered that on the same night they had dreamed (and recorded—unusually for one of them) the same unlikely image of people involved in synchronized swimming. The possibility of them both having been influenced by a common factor—such as something seen on television the night before—was ruled out as far as possible.[31] Here, to be sure, the process of communication by which the two people learned of each other's dream was, for both parties, inevitably an outer physical event. But the coincidence is clearly between the two independent dreams, which are primarily psychic events.

I would suggest that the first event of a synchronicity could be psychic or physical, inner or outer, and likewise with the second and any subsequent events.[32] However, it has to be borne in mind that with certain possible combinations of events the plausibility of there being a normal causal connection between them is much greater than with other combinations. Thus, it is theoretically possible that two inner events should occur to the same person without them being causally related by any normal process of suggestion or association. Within the space of a few days one experiencer had a dream of a flock of owls, then an impression during meditation of a live owl, and then a daylight vision of a Greek temple with an altar surmounted by the statue of an owl.[33] It is, of course, most natural to assume that the impression during meditation and the daylight vision were causally influenced by the earlier occurrence of the dream, or perhaps that all three appearances of the owl image were triggered by a shared normal cause such as having recently heard an actual owl or seen a representation of one. But it is also possible that the three inner appearances of the image all arose as independent expressions of an archetypal patterning or other form of ordering that does not operate simply from the level of normal psychophysical causation. As Jung acknowledges, "we cannot prove a causal connection in every case of amplification, and thus it is quite possible that in a number of cases, where we assume causal 'association,' it is really a matter of synchronicity."[34]

Furthermore, from the point of view of a specified observer, in all those coincidences in which the primary experiencer is someone else—which obviously includes coincidences that one hears or reads about secondhand—both events are, in an important sense, external. Jenkins's intense interest in the visionary image of the four horses was an inner event considered from his point of view. But from the point of view of persons other than Jenkins, both that interest and the subsequent sighting of the four horses, in other words, the whole coincidence, was an outer event, something that happened in the objective world independently of those persons' subjective concerns and involvement. It is sometimes assumed that when coincidences are meaningful they are so only to their primary experiencer—that person supposedly being the sole authoritative judge of whether a given coincidence means anything or not. However, while this may be true for the specifically subjective meaning of the experiences, it is far from being true of every aspect of meaningfulness of the experiences. A coincidence, no matter to whom it happens, is an event in the collectively experienced world. As such, there are respects in which such an event might be meaningful to persons other than its immediate experiencer. To such persons, however, not experiencing the events firsthand, the coincidence is primarily an external occurrence.

Jung's almost exclusive emphasis on coincidences involving an inner psychic and then an outer physical event may not be entirely due to the greater conspicuousness of this kind of coincidence. There may also be a theoretical agenda informing his emphasis. Jung's writings on synchronicity are much concerned with the possible implications of the phenomenon for our overall view of reality. In particular, he finds synchronistic experiences strongly supportive of a unitary view of reality; that is, the view that psyche and matter, in spite of their extreme differences and seeming incommensurability, are complementary aspects of what at a deeper level is one reality. The synchronicity principle, he considers, "suggests that there is an interconnection or unity of causally unrelated events, and thus postulates a unitary aspect of being."[35] It may be that his eagerness to present evidence in support of this unitary worldview led him to highlight the kinds of coincidences he did at the expense of other possible kinds such as those between exclusively outer events (for example, the origami incidents) or exclusively inner events (for example, the parallel dreams of synchronized swimming).[36]

Relative Acausality

In the definition I have proposed it is required that there should be *no discernible or plausible way in which the paralleling between the coinciding events could be the result of normal causes*. This is a requirement that the paralleling should indeed be "acausal," but it is recognized, realistically, that this "acausality" is relative to the experiencer's or observer's understanding. No cause should be discernible or plausible: this does not rule out the possibility of there being some indiscernible (or at least undiscerned) and implausible cause—a cause that one can neither perceive at present nor readily believe possible, even though it may exist. Again, the kind of cause required to be neither discernible nor plausible is qualified as "normal." This leaves open the possibility of there being paranormal, transcendent, or other kinds of "nonnormal" cause. Obviously, this raises problems of its own regarding how one is to distinguish a normal from a nonnormal cause, but a rough guide can be the definition of "normal cause" as one that would be recognized by practical common sense and/or the current scientific consensus (insofar as these are themselves determinable).[37] The crucial point, however, is the non-absolutist nature of the "acausality" required by the definition: the door is always left open to the possibility that what currently seems acausal may later come to seem causal when viewed in the light of greater knowledge or from the perspective of a worldview that recognizes paranormal and transcendent modes of causation, or even just a hierarchy of levels of normal causation.

Charles Tart, for example, with specific reference to this problem, has proposed four further categories in addition to physical and psychological causality (both observed and presumed). The first is what he calls *state-specific causality* where "things that seem paradoxical and don't make sense in our ordinary state of consciousness may yield to causal analysis by suitably trained practitioners who can enter the requisite ASC [altered state of consciousness]."[38] Next, he recognizes the possibility of *paranormal causality* where "we observe reliable orderings (Smith tries to send telepathic messages to Jones, and Jones picks them up a significant percentage of the time), but by the currently understood laws of the physical [and psychological] world, these orderings could not have come about."[39] Another possibility is that there could be *being-specific synchronistic causality* where "because we can get a partial, albeit inadequate, grasp of some kind of meaningful action at work . . . we postulate that there are causal factors involved, but these factors are either so complex and/or of such a different order of reality than the human mind (and its instrumental aids) that they will forever [or at least for the time being] remain beyond the limits of our comprehension."[40] Only as his final category does Tart recognize the possibility of *absolute synchronicity* where "we observe relationships between two or more events, but even though the events happen in a meaningful pattern, they are not *caused* at any level."[41]

Tart expresses doubt "whether we could distinguish in practice absolute synchronicity from being-specific synchronistic causality."[42] For Jung, by contrast, it is precisely this absolute synchronicity or absolute acausality to which his definitions supposedly refer, requiring that there be "no evidence of a causal connection between the psychic state and the external event, and where, considering the psychic relativity of space and time, *such a connection is not even conceivable* [emphasis added]." Here the possibility of a causal relationship between the events is excluded absolutely; there is no scope for increased knowledge or a shift of perspective to bring causality back into the picture at some point.

Meaning and Content

The final difficulty with Jung's definitions to which I wish to draw attention here concerns the notion of meaning. The definition I have proposed requires simply that "the experience must be meaningful beyond being notable"; the question of what constitutes the meaning is left open. To a certain extent this was probably also Jung's *practical* understanding of the situation. However, the manner in which he tried to bring his ideas into focus on a *theoretical* level generated at least two significant problems. One is the point, already alluded to, that he grounds his understanding of what constitutes the meaning of synchronicities in his overall psychological theory. Inasmuch as many of the concepts central to this theory—the collective unconscious, the archetypes, compensation, individuation—are questionable at a number of points, this questionability inevitably transfers to his understanding of synchronistic meaning.

The second problem is the ambivalence in the way Jung uses the word "meaning." On the one hand, it clearly refers to the significance of the coincidence for the experiencer (and sometimes for other observers) either personally or because of what it might be taken to imply about the nature of reality (for example, that reality is essentially unitary). On the other hand, Jung also uses the word "meaning" to refer to the content that the coinciding events have in common: they have "the same or similar meaning" or "appear as meaningful parallels." This usage is basically neutral with regard to what the coincidence might signify for an experiencer: one could replace "meaning" in this second sense with "content" (that is, the events have "the same or similar content," they are "parallel in content"). It is true that the two senses of "meaning" do not exclude each other—the meaning/content can be meaningful/significant to an experiencer or observer—but it is equally true that they do not entail each other and it is as well to be aware that when Jung speaks of "meaningful coincidence" there can be this ambiguity. On occasion it may even play its part in a form of conceptual legerdemain: a person wondering whether to accept and use the concept of synchronicity might be persuaded differently if given to understand that it refers to a coincidence of two or more events that share the same meaning/content than if given to understand that it refers to a coincidence that has some significance relative to human knowledge generally or to an experiencer's or observer's personal concerns. The source of the ambiguity probably lies in the fact that for Jung the content of any genuine synchronicity must be archetypal and therefore also meaningful in the sense of significant. In my own usage, the meaningfulness of the coincidence refers only to its significance; when I refer to the points of paralleling between the coinciding events, I use the word "content."

Indefiniteness in the Proposed Working Definition

The working definition I have proposed is largely inspired by Jung's but includes some important qualifications and modifications that enable it to avoid the difficulties that have been mentioned. In particular, it makes no assumptions about the simultaneity of coinciding events and about whether those events are physical or psychic, inner or outer. It avoids making absolute statements about the acausal relationship between coinciding events. It distinguishes between the notability required for something to be registered as a coincidence and the deeper meaning required for a coincidence to be elevated into a synchronicity. And it leaves open what might supply that deeper meaning.

Nevertheless, within the definition I have proposed there are several points of indefiniteness: for example, concerning what constitutes an "event" or "paralleling," or who judges what is "discernible or plausible," "sufficiently unlikely and detailed," or "meaningful." I have allowed this indefiniteness rather than aimed for maximum precision in order not to exclude from the outset any experience that might have some claim to being synchronistic. When examining coincidences, there is always scope further down the line for sharper critical evaluation and a separating out of the stronger and more interesting experiences from the weaker and less interesting.

SPIRIT

The task of arriving at an adequate working definition of spirit is, if anything, even more difficult than attempting to define synchronicity. In different traditions, and at different times within those traditions, the terms that would be translated into English as "spirit" have carried widely varying meanings and nuances. In what follows I first illustrate something of this diversity, referring to a variety of dictionary and encyclopaedia entries *sub verbo* "Spirit" as well as to statements drawn from transpersonal and Jungian psychology. Informed but also cautioned by the complexity of the picture that emerges from this brief survey, I then state and explain the specific emphases that I give to my own understanding of spirit for the purposes of the present study.

Various Understandings of Spirit

The *Macmillan Dictionary of Religion* offers about as succinct a definition of spirit as could be made without running the risk of being misleadingly partial: "Originally a metaphor for the 'wind' or 'breath' whereby

God creates and empowers living beings. The term has come to be used of immaterial entities, including the human soul."[43] Here already, at this level of broad summarizing, one can notice two distinct kinds of understanding: spirit seen as an animating principle and spirit seen as a form of entity. Regarding the metaphorical origin of the concept, this is the same in many languages: the Sanscrit *atman*, the Hebrew *ruah*, the Greek *pneuma*, the Latin *spiritus*, the Arabic *ruch*, and the Swahili *roho*, for example, all mean "breath" or "wind."[44] Not surprisingly, there are exceptions to this metaphorical origin, notably the German word "*Geist*" that, according to Jung's research, has connections with Old Norse and Gothic words for "to rage" and "to be beside oneself"[45] and "probably has more to do with something frothing, effervescing, or fermenting."[46]

A fuller characterization of the understanding of spirit as an entity can be gained from the *Concise Dictionary of Religion*. In this work the "spirit or soul" is defined as something that "lives within the body, giving it life and everything that is distinctively human. It is this aspect of the person that is believed to relate to God and the religious realm."[47] The same entry also makes clearer what kind of "immaterial entities" there may be besides the human soul: namely, "various spirit beings" and "the spirit of God or the Holy Spirit."[48]

In the above definitions "spirit" and "soul" have been used virtually interchangeably. Some of the senses in which the terms can be differentiated, specifically within the Jewish and Christian traditions, are discussed in the *Encyclopedia of Religion*:

> The English words *soul* and *spirit* are attempts to represent the two sets of ideas found in the Bible: *soul* is continuous with the Hebrew *nefesh* and the Greek *psuche*, while *spirit* is continuous with the Hebrew *ruah* and the Greek *pneuma*.[49]

Although "the one set of ideas . . . cannot be entirely dissociated from the other," there are notable distinctions, such as that "*ruah* [hence, also the derived New Testament understanding of *pneuma*, spirit] . . . does not have the quasi-physical connotation that *nefesh* [and, hence, also *psuche*, soul] has."[50]

The *New Catholic Encyclopedia* distills a general philosophical characterization of spirit as

> any reality that in its nature, existence, and activity is intrinsically independent of matter, is not subject to determinations of time and space, is not composed of parts spatially distinct

from one another, and is, or is related to, an original source of such activities as are centered on being under the universal aspects of truth, goodness, and beauty.[51]

For various thinkers, the entry continues, "spirit is primarily identified either with reality as a whole in its inner nature (spiritualistic monism), with an objective order of transcendent realities (Platonism), or with impersonal and collective realms of being (values, group spirits)."[52] In addition to and distinction from these more impersonal characterizations, the same work maintains that within Christianity "spirit is always personal and subjective, and all other manifestations of spirit can be reduced to their source in the person."[53] (Hence, in part, presumably, the tendency to coalesce the terms "spirit" and "soul.") However, even within the broadly shared assumptions of this one tradition there has been scope for a wide range of more specific characterizations. Thus, "the radical and essential manifestation of spirit has been variously singled out as: creative activity, self-consciousness, interiority or subjectivity, intelligence, reason, knowledge of universals, love, freedom, and communication (dialogue)."[54]

Attempts have been made by some perennialist thinkers to move beyond the terms of any particular tradition and to find a more universal definition of spirit. On the whole, these thinkers tend to emphasize the more absolutist characterizations and to express themselves in apophatic, paradoxical, and transcendentally colored language. The transpersonal psychologist Ken Wilber, for example, professedly representing the consensus both of the major world religions and of the great mystics and philosophers throughout the ages, Eastern and Western alike, describes "absolute Spirit" as "radiant and all-pervading, one and many, only and all—the complete integration and identity of manifest Form with the unmanifest Formless";[55] elsewhere as "universal . . . beyond body and mind . . . transverbal, transegoic, transindividual . . . a point where the soul touches eternity and completely transcends the prison of its own involvement";[56] and again as "nondual awareness or unity consciousness . . . the height of transcendence . . . also purely immanent . . . present equally and totally in each and every object, whether of matter, body, mind, or soul."[57]

A couple of phenomenologically sensitive discussions of the concept of spirit, recapitulating and extending much of what I have already covered, occur in Jung's two essays "Spirit and Life" (1926) and "The Phenomenology of the Spirit in Fairytales" (1945/1948).[58] "Is not the word 'spirit' a most perplexingly ambiguous term?" Jung asks near the beginning of the first of these essays; then explains:

The same verbal sign, spirit, is used for an inexpressible, transcendental idea of all-embracing significance; in a more commonplace sense it is synonymous with "mind"; it may connote courage, liveliness, or wit, or it may mean a ghost; it can also represent an unconscious complex that causes spiritualistic phenomena like table-turning, automatic writings, rappings, etc. In a metaphorical sense it may refer to the dominant attitude in a particular social group—the "spirit" that prevails there. Finally [and Jung stresses that this is not a joke], it is used in a material sense, as spirits of wine, spirits of ammonia, and spirituous liquors in general.[59]

Later in the same essay he emphasizes that spirit can also be understood as "the image of a personified affect" or as "the reflection of an autonomous affect";[60] and that "in its strongest and most immediate manifestations it displays a peculiar life of its own which is felt as an independent being."[61] He distances himself from the kind of perennialist characterization mentioned above by maintaining that "[t]here are many spirits, both light and dark. We should, therefore, be prepared to accept the view that spirit is not absolute, but something relative that needs completing and perfecting through life."[62]

The opening pages of "The Phenomenology of the Spirit in Fairytales" offer an even more extensive account of the "wide range of application" of the term "spirit," presented in a series of sometimes explicit and sometimes implicit contrasts.[63] Jung summarizes his account as having described "an entity which presents itself to us as an immediate psychic phenomenon distinguished from other psychisms whose existence is naïvely believed to be causally dependent upon physical influences."[64] He identifies the "hallmarks of spirit" as "firstly, the principle of spontaneous movement and activity; secondly, the spontaneous capacity to produce images independently of sense perception; and thirdly, the autonomous and sovereign manipulation of these images."[65]

A Working Definition of Spirit

The preceding discussion demonstrates the extraordinary diversity of ways the concept of spirit can be understood, many of which cannot readily be squared with one another. There are several strategies one could adopt in order to try to account for and orient oneself within this complexity. One could simply favor some understandings of the term and dismiss the others as either wrong or irrelevant to the purposes in hand. More embracingly, one could introduce a concept of the evolution either of the term "spirit" or of the manifestation of the reality of spirit—or indeed of our understanding of either of these—and then attribute different usages to different stages in this evolutionary development.[66] Or again, one could emphasize that spirit transcends and therefore cannot adequately be grasped within verbal concepts—the most one can do being to characterize its various facets and modes of manifestation, accept the apparent contradictions and paradoxes that emerge, and offer the totality of this many-sided characterization as one's best approximation to a verbal depiction of spirit.[67] The strategy adopted in what follows is a combination of the above suggestions. Out of the range of possible understandings and nuances of the term "spirit" I focus specifically on those which best serve the purposes at hand. I do this in the belief that some understandings are indeed—for reasons that one might want to consider "evolutionary"—more relevant than others in the context of contemporary knowledge. And I fully acknowledge that my characterization is only an approximation, limited by the inherently paradoxical and inexhaustible nature of the concept of spirit. This said, I also believe that approximate characterizations can be made that are worthwhile.

My working definition of spirit, then, is the following: *Spirit is one of the major differentiable and experienceable aspects of an overall continuum of consciousness and reality, together with, but of greater subtlety than, the physical and psychic.* A fuller characterization of the term can be arrived at by spelling out some of the implications of this definition—a task that will occupy the remainder of this chapter.

Spirit as One Aspect of a Continuum

Spirit has been defined as an aspect of a continuum. In specifying that the continuum is of *consciousness and reality* it is meant that each of the constituents of the continuum—the physical, the psychic, and the spiritual—is being considered an aspect both of every individual person and of the world as it exists independently of any individual person. For convenience I will henceforth often subsume both of these ideas under the one term "reality." Further, although I have specified three aspects of the continuum, I recognize that subtler distinctions could be made: for example, into five aspects (matter, body, mind, soul, and spirit), or even into seven, nine, or more aspects.[68] In particular, one might want to introduce the concept of the divine, either as itself an additional aspect situated, as it were, beyond the spiritual, or else as the ground of all the other aspects.[69] However, for the purposes of this study the tripartite differentiation should suffice, since spirit can be adequately defined in relation to the psychic and the physical.

On a common-sense level, the physical and the psychic are readily recognizable and distinguishable from each other. One can recognize such physical things as books, rivers, and birds, on the one hand, and such psychic things as memories, feelings, and thoughts on the other; and one can distinguish the two categories as in certain fundamental respects different from each other. Spirit is another such broad category and might include such things as inherent patterns of order, beauty, and intelligibility in reality; moments of creativity, insight, or unitive awareness in an individual; also senses of otherness, freedom, love, and so on.[70]

Though categorially different, spirit stands in continuity with the psychic and physical. Just as there are ambivalent zones of transition between the inanimate and the animate, and between the biological and the psychological, which suggest that these categories phase into one another and therefore may exist as aspects of a continuum; so there are features of psychic functioning that may be considered to phase into the specifically spiritual.[71] For example, it is often very difficult in practice to differentiate between the contributions made to the solution of a critical problem (in whatever discipline or area of life) by the normal psychic processes of deduction and inference and by the (as I understand it) spiritual process of insight. The continuum that is being postulated here—a kind of spectrum: from physical to psychic to spiritual[72]—is characterized by increasing subtlety of "substance" and operation and consequently also by increasing difficulty of observation and quantification. Physical objects can be easily observed and accurately measured, and they are relatively stable. Psychic forms are generally only measurable, if at all, in terms of their frequency and the subjectively evaluated intensity or vividness of their manifestations, and they tend to be evanescent and very difficult to observe. In turn, spiritual contents (for example, moments of insight or creativity) are notoriously difficult to observe or quantify at all. They are as shifting and invisible—and yet as pervasive in their influence—as the root metaphor of the word "spirit" (as "breath" or "wind") might lead one to expect.

Viewing spirit as one of the major distinguishable aspects of a single continuum of reality respects both its similarities to and differences from psyche and matter. It is undoubtedly partly because of the clear similarities on certain points that some thinkers have tried to reduce or assimilate spirit to psyche and/or matter; while it will have been the no less obvious differences that led others to postulate a fundamental separation and opposition, and for this to be sustained by common language usage.[73] The concept of a continuum enables these apparently incompatible positions to be appreciated together.

Some Differentiating Attributes of Spirit

Among the differentiating attributes of spirit one might include the following. First, manifestations of spirit are generally characterized by numinosity, with all the qualities implicit in this term: otherness, awefulness, overpoweringness, urgency, fascination—in general, a distinctive prerational and transrational emotional charge.[74] This was especially noted by Jung who, as we have seen, observed that spirit could be characterized as "the reflection of an autonomous affect."[75]

Another way in which spirit is distinguishable from psyche or matter is in its ability to transgress the usual limitations of these other fields of reality. The activity of spirit, it seems, is not bound by the same "laws" of time, space and causality that generally operate physically; nor even by the more fluid expressions of these principles within the psychic domain.[76] Having said this, I do not believe one therefore necessarily has to go so far as to speak of timelessness, spacelessness, and acausality—except perhaps in a relative sense. After all, there could be orders of temporal, spatial, and causal relationship that, while not comprehensible from the normal psychophysical perspective, would be so from the perspective of a consciousness oriented more fully within spirit. The important point here is simply that spiritual activities are characterized by their ability to transgress some of the apparent "laws" or principles governing events as we normally experience them psychophysically.

This can be further appreciated in terms of the experience of unity. From the perspective of spirit, the division that is usually experienced in consciousness between subject and object, observer and observed, can be perceived to break down and be replaced by a more holistic mode of awareness in which the deeper identity of subject and object comes to be appreciated.[77] It may be that if one were totally centered within the spiritual aspect of consciousness, this observer–observed unity would itself be experienced as total, as claimed by certain mystics.[78] However, there seems no reason why spiritual consciousness of this kind should not coexist with normal psychophysical consciousness so that, while unitive awareness is present, it is not all-absorbing but remains accompanied by dualistic consciousness. One could argue that such simultaneously unitive and dualistic awareness would be a more accurate reflection of the totality of consciousness, more truly holistic, than would be unitive awareness alone.

Another indication of spirit's categorial distinctiveness is its capacity for repatterning or restructuring contents within the fields of the psychic and physical. For example, within a moment of creativity an artist brings into being among his or her materials and ideas an aesthetic relationship that did not exist before and could not have been simply extrapolated from what already did exist. Similarly a scientist, in a moment of insight, will see a way of making greater sense out of existing data and theory—and yet this new understanding could not have been arrived at by normal processes of inference or deduction from that existing data and theory. Or again, a person might undergo an ethical transformation without this discernibly being the result of any conscious effort to control behavior or beliefs. In each of these cases, a factor additional to the recognized physical and psychic contents seems to have entered the picture, providing the new perspective or vantage point and thereby enabling the restructuring of the psychophysical to take place.

The seemingly intelligent, informative, meaningful nature of this creative and insightful restructuring implies that the workings of spirit are, or at least can be, highly purposive.[79] Again, that such moments cannot, in general, be called on at will suggests that spirit is autonomous. As we saw, spontaneity and autonomy have been emphasized as attributes of spirit by Jung. On this point one can observe that the notoriously unpredictable phenomenon of inspiration is designated by a word that carries the same root meaning as "spirit" (that is, "breath," "wind").

Interpenetration of the Psychophysical

Although in various crucial respects distinguishable from psyche and matter and able to operate on them as if from a superior vantage point, spirit can also be characterized as interpenetrating and interfused with the psychic and the physical. This is implicit in the ability of spirit to express itself within the medium of the psychophysical. It also accords with Wilber's definition of spirit as "all-pervading," "present equally and totally in each and every object, whether of matter, body, mind, or soul." However, whereas Wilber also believes that spirit, including one's own consciousness as spirit, can subsist in a state totally independent of psyche and matter,[80] it seems to me unnecessary, and perhaps unwarranted, to make that further claim. As an aspect of a single continuum of reality, spirit may be more or less the center of one's attention at any given time, but even when seemingly dominating one's field of awareness it would probably still be bound up with the other aspects of the continuum. Mystics who claim to have entered states of pure spirit, because of the very fact that they registered the experience and subsequently returned to tell the tale, must have remained connected in some important way to their psyches and bodies. Indeed, it could be the case that spirit, rather than just being *capable of* interfusing psyche and matter, is *incapable of not* being in some sense interfused with them.

Ontological and Epistemological Parity with the Psychophysical

It is sometimes maintained that, because spirit can operate on the psychic and physical and is not reducible to them, in some important sense spirit is ontologically and/or epistemologically superior to the psychic and physical. It is "realer" and gives access to knowledge that is "truer,"[81] since it is situated at a higher level in the "Great Chain of Being."[82] It may be that there are senses in which such a hierarchical understanding is appropriate,[83] but this does not necessarily entail superiority. When one is aware of the spiritual aspect of reality, for example, when one is comprehending something with a degree of insight, one may consider oneself to be in touch with a more universal and enduring level of being and knowledge. However, under a different worldview—materialism, for instance—this priority could easily be reversed, with the greatest degree of reality and knowability being accorded to the physical. Certainly, there are respects in which the more spiritual aspects of consciousness seem to be superior to the more material and psychic aspects (for example, when insight puts order into existing data and theory). Equally, however, there are respects in which the material or psychic aspects might be considered to be superior to the spiritual (for example, in terms of stability, practical utility, and susceptibility to measurement). The spiritual aspect of reality has properties that the psychic and physical aspects lack; but equally the psychic and physical aspects have properties that the spiritual aspect lacks. It may be that the sets of properties are complementary, even mutually dependent; but at any rate I see no reason for elevating one set above the others rather than seeing them all as integral and equal aspects of one reality. In the present study, therefore, I do not wish to align myself with any orientation that gives priority to one aspect of reality at the expense of the others, but rather to respect, as much as possible, the whole field of experience and to accord equal, though differing, ontological and epistemological status to each of its aspects.

Direct Experience of Spirit

Finally, as has already been implied several times, spirit, as I wish to understand the term, refers to something that can be directly experienced. A further idea of what kind of direct experiencing I mean can be gained by referring once again to the experiences of creativity in the arts and insight in the sciences; also to such experiences as the perception of beauty, moments of unitive awareness, or connection with a deep sense of objective meaning or intelligibility in reality. None of these, as experienced, readily lends itself to reduction in physical and/or psychic terms. In relation to one's consciousness, these qualities of creativity, insight, beauty, unity, and intelligibility can be experienced in several ways: as an aspect of one's consciousness; as an aspect of the world independently of (though perhaps including or corresponding to) one's consciousness; or in the form of a seemingly autonomous being (a "spirit"), again independent of one's consciousness.

Jung and the Direct Experience of Spirit

It might be thought that one could easily co-opt Jung as a supporter of the view that spirit can be directly experienced. For he frequently emphasizes the importance of direct religious or spiritual experience as opposed to reliance on dogma and faith.[84] However, when Jung focuses on what are actually experienced in religious and spiritual experiences, he stresses that these are, and must be, psychic phenomena, for "the sole immediate reality is the psychic reality of conscious contents."[85] Nevertheless, I believe that Jung's cautious view of the possibility of directly experiencing spirit is unnecessary even within the terms of his own thinking, as I now hope to show.

"We live immediately only in a world of images."[86] In this brief sentence is contained the essence of Jung's view concerning the epistemological status of matter, psyche, and spirit. Throughout his writings Jung comfortably uses each of these terms: he is not a materialist, denying reality to psyche and spirit; nor is he an idealist who considers material and psychic forms to be transient illusions; nor, in his advocacy of the psychic perspective, does he deny real existence to matter on the one hand or to spirit on the other. He accepts and uses all these terms. "I do not contest," he writes, "the relative validity of the realistic standpoint . . . or of the idealistic standpoint . . . ; I would only like to unite these extreme opposites by . . . the psychological standpoint."[87] However, what this uniting amounts to is the location or centering of human consciousness within the psychic aspect of reality alone.

Jung argues that even if we accept the reality of the physical world, everything we know about it is mediated to our consciousness in the form of impressions and images that are psychic phenomena. It is these images of which we are directly conscious. We infer the existence of the physical world as what must have given rise to the images, but we do not experience that physical world directly. "Even physical pain," he writes, "is a psychic image which I experience . . . my sense impressions—for all that they force upon me a world of impenetrable objects occupying space—

are psychic images, and these alone constitute my immediate experience, for they alone are the immediate objects of my consciousness."[88] Again:

> We are in truth so wrapped about by psychic images that we cannot penetrate at all to the essence of things external to ourselves. All our knowledge consists of the stuff of the psyche which, because it alone is immediate, is superlatively real.[89]

The same is true in the case of the spiritual aspect of reality. Even if we accept that this exists and that it is responsible for certain experiences we may have—of illumination, creativity, beauty, senses of presence—Jung would argue that it is actually the psychic effects that we experience directly. The hypothetical source of these effects—spirit itself—can only be known indirectly as an inference. Jung gives the example of being "beset by the fear that a ghost will appear." In such an experience, he says, "my fear of the ghost is a psychic image from a spiritual source. . . . As for the spiritual process that underlies my fear of the ghost, it is as unknown to me as the ultimate nature of matter."[90]

When this epistemological emphasis is applied to the more specifically religious and sacred areas of experience, it can easily appear, as Edward Whitmont observes, that Jung is attempting "to substitute 'psyche', 'soul', or 'contents of the psyche' for the divine or spiritual reality 'out there' . . . to substitute the subjectively human for the objectively transcendent, or at least to treat the latter as if it were a mere epiphenomenon of the former."[91] Nevertheless, as Whitmont goes on to note, "this was decidedly not Jung's belief or intent"—the impression Jung misleadingly creates being due to "ambiguities of terminology, and even attitude."[92]

Whitmont suggests a number of possible reasons for this ambiguity concerning the reality of the spiritual. One is Jung's "suspicions about theology, colored by the problematic relationship to his father, a theologian."[93] Compounding this would have been "the need to be accepted by fellow scientists of the late nineteenth century with its Cartesian and positivistic bias."[94] Another reason may have been the "introverted bias" that was a feature both of Jung's personality and of the psychological system he developed. This bias "expresses itself in . . . an ambiguous terminology in respect to psyche and projection" that "fails to make a clear distinction between the psyche as a vehicle of experience and the non-psychic object 'out there' even though that object be endowed with formal qualities, intentionality, and spirit of its own."[95]

However, the most significant reason for Jung's ambiguities of terminology and attitude regarding spirit was his self-professed adherence to

Kantian epistemology. Put briefly, Kant argued that we are only able to experience things as they appear to us (as "phenomena") and that these appearances are inevitably preorganized by the inherent structuring dispositions of our mind (a priori categories of understanding). What things are like in themselves (as "noumena") Kant claimed we have no way of knowing. Of particular significance within this view is the implication that we cannot have direct knowledge of God or the soul or of any other alleged spiritual realities.[96]

Throughout his life Jung repeatedly and consistently stated his adherence to this epistemological viewpoint of Kant's. Indeed, as Stephanie de Voogd points out, he always implicitly and sometimes explicitly referred to it as *"the* theory of knowledge"—as though there could be no alternative theories.[97] For Jung, believing himself to be following Kant, all that we can experience and know directly are psychic images, things as they appear to consciousness, "phenomena." What gives rise to those psychic images—matter in itself, spirit in itself—these cannot be directly experienced or known; they are "noumena." In particular, Jung thought that his distinction between the archetypal ideas or images that we actually experience and the irrepresentable archetype as such that hypothetically gives rise to those ideas and images was a straightforward mirroring of Kant's distinction between the phenomenal and the noumenal.

If this mirroring were as straightforward as Jung supposed, it would in fact play into the hands of his critics. For, as de Voogd observes, "so long as the distinction is maintained between a noumenal X and a psychic X, the noumenal X is going to sound like the real thing and the psychic X like its poor copy."[98] However, it has been argued that Jung's epistemological formulations are not as close to Kant's as he believed and may even have implications that could help to dissolve Kant's worldview. De Voogd, for example, suggests that "Jung's archetypal psychology implies an epistemological stance which renders the noumena–phenomena distinction wholly unnecessary."[99] This distinction, she argues, could be dissolved by undertaking "an evaluation of Kant's epistemology in terms of *esse in anima* [psychological existence], an exercise aimed at seeing through to the fantasies at work in the *Critique of Pure Reason*."[100] To do this would provide a perspective on and understanding of Kant's epistemology that would be an alternative to Kant's own rational understanding—not necessarily dispensing with or invalidating Kant's view, but compensating for its one-sidedness.[101]

Jung's claim to be adhering to a Kantian epistemology has also been challenged, from a different angle, by Wolfgang Giegerich.[102] According to Giegerich, Jung believed that it would suffice to pay his toll to Kant simply by constantly assuring us that all his theoretical statements (about archetypes, synchronicity, the autonomous psyche, the psychoid, etc.) were not intended as metaphysical statements, but only as hypotheses, models or the like and that he was, e.g., not speaking about God himself, but only about the God image in the psyche.[103]

However, Jung himself clearly saw through "the illusion that by calling, e.g., psychological powers 'moods,' 'nervousness,' 'delusional ideas'—in short 'symptoms' instead of 'Gods' or 'daimones'—anything would be changed as to the reality of these powers."[104] In other words, Jung's quasi-empirical terminology is something of a mask: "it does not make any real difference whether we assert that we are speaking 'only' about the God image in the soul or whether we believe we are speaking about God himself. In either way we speak about God."[105] Within Kant's epistemology, by contrast, Jung's "hypotheses" and "models" would still carry the logical status of metaphysical statements, and so would be refused the "empirical" status Jung repeatedly claimed for them: "As long as Jung clings to his label 'empiricist first and last,' Kant would show him that he has no right to posit, for example, a psychoid archetypal level in which the subject-object dichotomy would be overcome."[106]

Giegerich's further argument is that Jung effectively "paid Kant only a token toll";[107] his repeated tributes are a defense "to shield the precious contents of his inner life against the full impact of Kant's insights."[108] The reason for this defensiveness is that "Jung, not having gone all the way through Kant, could not imagine that there might be land beyond Kant."[109]

Giegerich agrees with de Voogd that Jung's insights are profounder and more far-reaching in their implications than Jung's own conscious formulations of them usually allow. "Whenever [Jung] exercized conscious control over his theorizing," Giegerich suggests, "and intended to be critical, he wanted to freeze his amazing psychological insights on the logically lowest level, the ontic level of 'empirical findings.'"[110]

Whitmont likewise takes exception to this unnecessary distorting and obscuring by Jung of his own insights. He argues that Jung clearly did believe in the perception by the psyche of nonpsychic events. "Parapsychological research into the *psi* factor," he notes, appealing, by way of example, to evidence that Jung himself would accept, "has demonstrated conclusively that we do perceive by means of extra-sensory psychic perception both subjective states of others as well as objective, non-psychic events (space-time, distant events and actions)."[111]

However, rather than treating these nonpsychic events as nonpsychic, Jung is forced by his "inadequate definitions and epistemology concerning 'soul' and 'psyche'" to consider them too as psychic.[112] The result of this is that "the meaning of these terms ['soul' and 'psyche'] becomes easily over-extended."[113] Thus, in particular, "the term 'reality of the psyche', which Jung uses for the 'objective' or 'transpersonal' psyche, extends the accustomed meaning of psychic reality toward transpersonal events."[114] Whitmont concedes that "the transpersonal objects of experience might better be called powers, energies, archetypes, dynamics, or psychoid factors—if we must avoid speaking of Gods and daimons," but he adds emphatically that "at any rate, they are to be regarded as experiences *sui generis*."[115]

What emerges from this is that there is a category of experiences, distinguishable in its own right, that has traditionally been called spiritual and that one can indeed call psychic but only at the cost of expanding the meaning of this latter term until it is able to assimilate what has traditionally been meant by the spiritual. Thus, when Jung claims that "the sole immediate reality is the psychic reality of conscious contents" he is in effect making a semantic point only, based on an arbitrary decision to designate as psychic what used to be called spiritual.[116] Inasmuch as "psychic" appears simply to be the word he has chosen to refer to anything immediately experienced, his claim ultimately seems to be tautological.

However, it is clear that, no matter how misguided, Jung's Kantianism and his epistemological efforts in general were attempting to articulate something of importance. This would seem to be that our perceptions of the physical and spiritual aspects of reality inescapably involve a psychic component that renders those perceptions to some extent subjective. Our inherent psychological limitations cause us to subjectivize and anthropomorphize our experiences, so that purely objective experience of reality is not possible. However, as Whitmont again points out, admitting the "psychological limitation of our subjective perception" is not necessarily incompatible with acknowledging that what one is perceiving is objective being. "Our anthropomorphizing experiences of the transpersonal and its qualities" could, he suggests, "more appropriately be called *symbolic perceptions*": "*Symbolic perception* acknowledges objective being as perceived in subjective terms."[117] Thus, it makes perfect sense to speak of spiritual reality as being directly experienced, so long as one recognizes that such spiritual experience is likely to be colored by the psyche. Being colored by the psyche, however, is something very different from being only psyche.[118]

Self-Revelation of Spirit

Before concluding this discussion of spirit one further important point needs to be made. The preceding has offered a conscious characterization of spirit. As was pointed out earlier, this is not entirely satisfactory, since spirit eludes definition in conscious conceptual terms: hence, the paradoxical, metaphorical, and apophatic language of the mystics.[119] Jung in particular is aware of this problem: "how can we bring within the orbit of our thought those limitless complexes of facts which we call 'spirit' and 'life' unless we clothe them in verbal concepts, themselves mere counters of the intellect?"[120] He suggests that

> when the idea or principle involved is inscrutable, when its intentions are obscure in origin and in aim and yet enforce themselves, then the spirit is necessarily felt as an independent being, as a kind of higher consciousness, and its inscrutable, superior nature can no longer be expressed in the concepts of human reason. Our powers of expression then have recourse to other means; they create a *symbol*.[121]

The symbol "points beyond itself to a meaning that is darkly divined" and thereby "describes in the best possible way the dimly discerned nature of the spirit."[122] But in what manner is this symbol created? The way Jung frames his answer to this implicit question is particularly interesting: "because of its original autonomy, about which there can be no doubt in the psychological sense, *the spirit is quite capable of staging its own manifestations spontaneously.*"[123] Jung considers two kinds of this, as he calls it, "self-revelation of spirit":[124] dreams and fairytales.[125] In each case, spontaneously arisen symbols are considered to reveal aspects of the nature of spirit that in important ways supplement and modify one's conscious conception of it. In later chapters of this study (especially chapter 6) I explore the possibility that synchronicities—the content of which, as we shall see, is also often symbolic—may be another form of such "self-revelation of spirit."

CHAPTER 3

THE SPIRITUAL DIMENSION OF SPONTANEOUS SYNCHRONICITIES

In this chapter I aim to establish in greater detail the main points of relationship between spirit and synchronicity by looking more closely at a number of spiritual concepts that can be readily extrapolated from my definition and characterization of spirit—concepts that represent, as it were, specific facets of or perspectives onto spirit. The spiritual concepts whose relationships to synchronicity I shall discuss are numinosity, miraculousness, transformation, unity, transcendence and immanence, providence, and revelation. Naturally, my treatment of each of these major concepts, as well as of their many interrelationships, can only be partial. There are also many concepts that could have been explored but, because of limited space and my own limited knowledge, they have had to be omitted—for instance, such Eastern concepts as Tao, karma, or dependent origination. However, my intention is for the following selection and discussion to be illustrative rather than exhaustive or fully representative. It will be sufficient if by the end of the chapter this selection has served to show the mutually illuminating congruence of synchronicity and spirit.

NUMINOSITY: *MYSTERIUM TREMENDUM ET FASCINANS*

Numinosity was mentioned in the previous chapter as one of the specific attributes by which spirit can be differentiated from psyche and matter. We also saw that numinosity is one of the characteristic features of synchronicity for Jung.[1] However, given that the term "numinous" has come to be used often in a rather loose way to refer simply to any kind of powerful emotional charge or affect, it is worth showing that, as originally understood by Rudolf Otto, it can be related to synchronicity very closely. To demonstrate this, I shall bypass the considerable secondary literature that has accumulated on the topic of the numinous and focus simply on Otto's writings.

Otto introduced the term "numinous" in his book *Das Heilige* (1917; translated into English as *The Idea of the Holy*, 1923) to refer to the irreducible nonrational and nonethical aspect in the idea of God or "the holy."[2] In his own words, the numinous is "a special term to stand for 'the holy' *minus* its moral factor or 'moment,' and . . . minus its 'rational' aspect altogether."[3] A numinous experience, therefore, is one in which or through which this nonrational, nonmoral aspect of the holy is directly apprehended. According to Otto, "the nature of the numinous can only be suggested by means of the special way in which it is reflected in the mind in terms of feeling."[4] However, the numinous object, that is, the *numen* itself, the nonrational aspect of the holy, should not be mistaken for the numinous experience. The latter is an effect of the former, its manifest expression. The numinous is not something merely subjective but is "felt as objective and outside the self."[5]

According to Otto, in discussing the numinous "we are dealing with something for which there is only one appropriate expression, *mysterium tremendum*."[6] He elucidates the idea of the numinous by analyzing the component words in this expression. Implicit in *tremendum* he finds the qualities of "awefulness," "overpoweringness," and "urgency."[7] The term *"mysterium"* he considers to refer to a reality that is "wholly other,"[8] that is, "quite beyond the sphere of the usual, the intelligible, and the familiar."[9] The adjective *"tremendum"* emphasizes the more daunting qualities of the *mysterium*. In addition to these, Otto draws attention also to the more attractive quality of "fascination."[10] "These two qualities," he remarks, "the daunting and the fascinating, now combine in a strange harmony of contrasts" resulting in a "dual character of the numinous consciousness."[11] Because of this additional quality of fascination, Otto's key expression is sometimes expanded to *mysterium tremendum et fascinans*.

If we consider these component elements of numinosity in more detail, we can see that Otto's characterization of each of them brings out qualities that are also readily discernible within synchronistic experiences. Departing from the sequence of Otto's analysis, let us consider first the *mysterium*, that which is experienced as being "wholly other." Otto mentions two ways in which "this feeling or consciousness of the 'wholly other'" can be evoked by an object or experience.[12] One way is if the object or experience, while being perfectly natural, is nonetheless "puzzling" or "of a surprising or astounding character; such as extraordinary phenomena or astonishing occurrences."[13] Otto suggests that, in this kind of case, consciousness of the wholly other is not intrinsic to the natural objects or experiences themselves but is only evoked by them indirectly through association with other kinds of feeling and consciousness which are intrinsic to natural experiences, these latter kinds of feeling and consciousness being similar to but nonetheless *qualitatively different from* consciousness of the wholly other.[14] In other words, natural experiences are not in themselves capable of evoking genuine consciousness of the wholly other; when they appear to do so, it is simply through association. However, it is also possible for consciousness of the wholly other to be evoked in a second way, namely, directly. This happens through an experience or object that "has no place in our scheme of reality but belongs to an absolutely different one, and which at the same time arouses an irrepressible interest in the mind"; in other words, an experience or object that is "supernatural."[15] Otto illustrates this by referring to the effect on us of stories about ghosts, which are such "supernatural" objects.[16]

Synchronicities are clearly capable of evoking consciousness of the wholly other in the first of these ways: they involve contingent events none of which in itself need be impossible, hence they can be considered natural occurrences; and the qualities of being to some degree "extraordinary" and "astonishing" are implied in their inherent notability. However, synchronicities may also be able to evoke consciousness of the wholly other in the second of the ways mentioned—that is, directly— inasmuch as it is also possible to view synchronicities as supernatural occurrences. Considering not the individual events composing the synchronicity but the composite event of the synchronicity itself, we perceive the existence of a kind of relationship—a relationship of meaningful acausal paralleling—that, according to our usual understanding of the natural course of things, should not exist, and that is, therefore, arguably "supernatural." This characteristic of synchronicities is most conspicuous in cases that take the form of apparently paranormal events: clairvoyant, telepathic, psychokinetic, or precognitive synchronicities. However, it is also implicit in all other synchronicities simply by virtue of the fact that they involve meaningful acausal paralleling. It appears, then, that the feeling or consciousness evoked by synchronicity may not just be similar to the feeling or consciousness of the wholly other but may have fulfilled Otto's conditions for actually being that feeling or consciousness.

Turning next to the components of the adjective "*tremendum*," we have to consider whether synchronistic experiences can exhibit the qualities of awefulness, overpoweringness, and urgency. At first sight these three terms seem too strong to be applied to the majority of synchronicities. Certainly such experiences can have their daunting aspect, but this normally takes the form of a fairly mild disturbance rather than the sort of extreme disturbance suggested by the three terms. However, as Otto makes clear, what is most important in the ascription of these three terms is the *quality* of the experience in question, not its degree of intensity. Awefulness, for example, has not so much to do with natural fear, however intense, as with a sense of "uncanniness":

> The awe or "dread" *may* indeed be so overwhelmingly great that it seems to penetrate to the very marrow, making the man's hair bristle and his limbs quake. But it may also steal upon him almost unobserved as the gentlest of agitations, a mere fleeting shadow passing across his mood. It has therefore nothing to do with intensity, and no natural fear passes over into it merely by being intensified. I may be beyond all measure afraid and terrified without there being even a trace of the feeling of uncanniness in my emotion.[17]

Uncanniness is a quality that certainly can attach to synchronicities—even the skeptical mathematicians Persi Diaconis and Frederick Mosteller refer to "that spooky feeling" that coincidences can evoke.[18] This uncanniness may be less or more intense, but its mere presence in any degree is enough to establish the awefulness of the synchronistic experience.

By a similar line of reasoning, synchronicities can also be seen to have the quality of overpoweringness. The feeling of this "starts from a consciousness of the absolute superiority or supremacy of a power other than myself."[19] It is not just a question of being overpowered by something greater than but commensurable with oneself, as one could be perhaps by another person or by the authority of an institution or even by a natural force such as a hurricane. What is important again is the quality of what is conveying the feeling of overpoweringness. This must be something "other than myself," having in relation to me not just relative but "absolute superiority or supremacy." Its nature must be such that I cannot conceivably challenge it. Another person, an institution, even a force of nature such as a hurricane I can potentially resist and pit my own power against. But I cannot challenge or resist the genuinely numinous. I have not, and cannot have, any control over it. One is reminded here of William James's identification of one of the essential features of mystical experiences as being that they are experiences that typically the mystics suffer, rather than something they do or control.[20] There is a similar situation with synchronicities. These happenings are notoriously unpredictable. They can happen at any time to any person, and they can involve any content of consciousness and the world. One is helpless to control them, and in this sense they have over one "absolute superiority or supremacy."

Third, there is the quality of urgency, that is, "the sense of a power that knows not stint nor stay, which is urgent, active, compelling, and alive."[21] This can also be evident in synchronicities, especially in the way such experiences often irresistibly excite and stimulate one—urging one sometimes into even quite specific activities and trains of thought, or at least into a general state of inquiry as to the possible meaning of one's experience.

So much for the daunting aspect of the *mysterium*. There remains, finally, the more attractive aspect of its also being *fascinans*, that is, "something that allures with potent charm, . . . something that entrances."[22] The interest and attention that synchronicities can arouse is alone witness enough to the fact that they can share this charm and power of entrancing. Indeed, this quality of fascination, along with that of urgency, is precisely what often draws experiencers of synchronicity into attempting a more fully articulated exploration of the phenomenon.[23] Thus, all the component elements of numinosity—otherness, awefulness, overpoweringness, urgency, and, finally, fascination—can be found to be present, admittedly often in subtle forms, within synchronistic experiences.

It was appropriate to consider numinosity as the first spiritual concept to which to relate synchronicity since, the numinous being essentially nonrational, it is the aspect of an experience likely to impact on one most immediately. Furthermore, as I have just indicated, it is often precisely the numinous charge of an experience—in particular its elements of urgency and fascination—that stimulates one to subsequent rational analysis of that experience and its possible significance.[24] It should not be thought, however, that the numinous is nonrational only in the sense of being prerational and a stimulant to reasoning. It is also, as it were, "postrational" or "transrational" in the sense that it refers to an aspect of experience that cannot be exhausted by any amount of rational analysis and that remains vivid and intact even after all such analysis.

MIRACULOUSNESS

The critical moment in the breakup of the friendship of Friedrich Nietzsche and Richard Wagner was, according to Nietzsche's version of events, when the two men sent each other copies of their latest works: Wagner sending a score of his opera *Parsifal* and Nietzsche sending a copy of his book *Human, All Too Human*. Each work was deeply antithetical to the spirit of the other artist. Nietzsche, no great friend of theological concepts, nonetheless marvels at how the two works, each destined to alienate its recipient, must have crossed in the post through, as he puts it, "a miracle of meaningful chance."[25] Though Nietzsche's choice of expression here was undoubtedly influenced by his predilection for hyperbole, the incident does nevertheless serve to illustrate how synchronicities can strike a person—even the most unlikely of persons—as impossible happenings and therefore as being akin to the miraculous.

Miracles are commonly understood as violations of natural law. They are thus conspicuous expressions of spirit's ability to transgress the usual limitations of psyche and matter. The spontaneous transformation of water into wine, for example, is something that, according to the laws of nature, should not happen. The notion of violating natural law can be refined by pointing out that it refers to the laws of nature only as we currently know them. In the future, our understanding of nature may allow for events that are currently inexplicable and apparently miraculous. Or, under a slightly different understanding of what is implied by "nature," we may hold that apparently miraculous events are in fact natural, whether we ever understand their mechanism, simply because they occur. Miracles, then, let us say cautiously, are usually taken to be violations of natural law as this is currently understood by us.

In his essay "The Miraculous" (1965), R. F. Holland gives what he considers to be two necessary conditions for an event being accounted a miracle in the sense of being a violation of natural law. These conditions are that the event must be (1) empirically certain and (2) conceptually impossible:

> If it were less than conceptually impossible it would reduce merely to a very unusual occurrence such as could be treated (because of the empirical certainty) in the manner of a decisive experiment and result in the modification of the prevailing conception of natural law; while if it were less than empirically certain nothing more would be called for in regard to it than a suspension of judgement.[26]

Certain difficulties with these conditions have been pointed out by Colin Brown, in particular the fact that the conditions seem to be "disqualifying from consideration all alleged miracles in the more remote past" (specifically the miracles of Christ), since the testimony for these remote events can never result in empirical certainty.[27] However, at different periods and among different communities the criteria needing to be met for an event to be considered definitely to have happened (that is, empirically certain) will by no means always have been as rigorous as they are in the present scientific climate. To many people throughout

The Spiritual Dimension of Spontaneous Synchronicities 45

past centuries and still to certain people today, historical testimony, especially if reinforced by claims to grace and revelation, may well be sufficient to create a sense of certainty that something actually happened. As for the notion of conceptual impossibility, this could be relativized in much the same way as I have attempted to relativize Jung's conception of acausality. With these qualifications in mind, Holland's two conditions do indeed seem to have articulated the underlying reasoning in the ascription of the term "miracle"; and certainly they could be valuably applied to the assessment of more recent events for which the status of miracle is claimed.

Interestingly, however, Holland does not restrict the category of the miraculous to what he calls the "violation concept."[28] In addition to this he introduces what he calls "the contingency concept of the miraculous."[29] He sees no reason why certain types of coincidence should not also be accounted miracles.[30] He gives the example of a child standing on a railway track along which a train is approaching; the train stops just before reaching the child. The reason for its stopping had nothing to do with the child being on the track; it so happened that, for reasons that had their own perfectly intelligible causal history, the driver fainted and released pressure on the automatic control lever. The child's mother, who witnessed the incident from a position of helplessness, accounted the saving of her child a miracle. Yet, no natural law was violated either in the child being on the track or in the train stopping when it did: both events can readily be accounted for in terms of natural causes.

Holland's example appears to be hypothetical. An actual incident that illustrates his argument is the following. The fifteen members of the choir of a church in Beatrice, Nebraska, used to gather in the church building for practice on certain evenings at 7:20 P.M. On the evening of March 1, 1950, all fifteen members were late:

> The minister and his wife and daughter had one reason (his wife delayed to iron the daughter's dress); one girl waited to finish her geometry problem; one couldn't start her car; two lingered to hear the end of an especially exciting radio program; one mother and daughter were late because the mother had to call the daughter twice to wake her from a nap; and so on. The reasons seemed rather ordinary. But there were ten separate and quite unconnected reasons for the lateness of the fifteen persons.
>
> It was rather fortunate that none of the fifteen arrived on time at 7:20 P.M., for at 7:25 P.M. the church building was destroyed in an explosion [when the boiler blew up].[31]

What makes a coincidence a miracle, according to Holland, is principally that it evokes the same kind of religious response as would a miracle of the violation kind:

> [W]hatever happens by God's grace or by a miracle is something for which God is thanked or thankable, something which has been or could have been prayed for, something which can be regarded with awe and be taken as a sign or made the subject of a vow.[32]

In the case of the choir practice incident we are in fact told that "the members of the choir . . . wondered if their delay was 'an act of God.'"[33] Holland maintains, therefore, that

> to establish the contingency concept of the miraculous as a possible concept it seems to me enough to point out (1) that . . . there are genuine contingencies in the world, and (2) that certain of these contingencies can be, and are in fact, regarded religiously in the manner I have indicated.[34]

It is even possible that people reluctant to accept the existence of miracles involving violations of natural law may nonetheless be able to accept the existence of miracles that fit the contingency concept—and be just as powerfully affected by them. Consider, for example, the following synchronistic experience reported by Guy Lyon Playfair. In 1981 he was doing research for an American television company into the events that took place at Fatima, Portugal, in 1917, where three children claimed to have seen visions of the Virgin Mary. Huge crowds used to go to the spot and on one occasion, in the sight of as many as one hundred thousand people, the sun apparently burst through the clouds, went round in zigzag circles, bathed the landscape in all the colors of the rainbow, and finally fell to earth. Playfair, who was himself skeptical of such tales, had been examining the relevant Portuguese papers on microfilm at the British Library's Colindale branch, and then went down to the cafeteria where he "thought about what a Jesuit scientist named Pio Sciatizzi called the most obvious and colossal miracle in history." Playfair's account continues:

> I stared at the clouds over Colindale. As I was below ground level I could see nothing else. It was a windy and overcast day and thick layers of low-lying cumulo-nimbus swirled past. I watched the peaceful and relaxing display for a few minutes.
> Then came the miracle.

> The clouds parted, and the sun appeared briefly through an alignment of gaps in at least three layers of cloud, its rays reflected in sudden bright spots on their edges, and the solar disc itself visible through a protective shield of mist. The lower cloud layer was moving faster than the upper ones, and for one or two seconds the bright spots moved from one edge of the gap above to the other, giving a striking impression of a zigzag motion of the sun—a feature common to many of the eye-witness accounts from Fatima. Seen through moving clouds, I found, it is indeed the sun and not the clouds that can appear to move, as it reappears after each brief occultation. The whole effect was uncannily similar to what I had only just finished reading about; the sighting took place slap in the middle of my field of vision and the timing was exactly right. A few minutes earlier, and my attention might have been on my food and drink. A minute later I would have been on my way home.

On the one hand, this experience gave Playfair insight into how the incident at Fatima may not have been such a "colossal miracle" after all; but on the other hand, the insight was conveyed to him in a way which, although "a wholly natural phenomenon in itself," seemed miraculous in its own right. He acknowledges that he would no doubt have interpreted his experience differently had he been a believer in the events at Fatima, but adds that in either case "its effect would probably have been very similar."[35]

TRANSFORMATION

A capacity to effect significant transformations in consciousness is another of the attributes of spirit as I characterized it in the previous chapter.[36] Indeed, transformation of consciousness plays a particularly important role within many meditative and mystical systems, both Eastern and Western, where it is understood to be a concomitant of certain levels of spiritual insight or attainment.[37] It is also clearly implied in the concept of religious conversion, whether this occurs in an individual suddenly or gradually.

Regarding the possible transformative effect of synchronicity in these kinds of spiritual sense, something of this has already been seen in the case of Jung's patient whose fundamental orientation toward reality was radically changed by the synchronicity involving the scarab beetle. The specific details of the transformation brought about by this or any other synchronicity can only be seen with close reference to the actual case histories. Nevertheless, it is also possible to point out on a more general level some of the factors that contribute to this transformative potential of synchronicity. Each of these factors is intrinsic to every synchronistic experience, though they may not always all be equally appreciated, since some require more sophisticated interpretative abilities on the part of the experiencer if they are to have their full impact.

The first and most basic transformative effect of synchronicities derives from the sheer enigma they present, the fact that they appear to relate events together in a way that defies our normal understanding of what kinds of relationships are possible. On an intellectual level, we can be stimulated by this enigma to think outside our normal patterns and conceptual frameworks, or at the very least to think more resourcefully within our old patterns. On an emotional level, we have to accommodate the disturbance to our complacency, a disturbance that could be experienced negatively as a crisis and threat to our psychological stability or positively as a release of energy and an awakening to wider potentialities. Coming out of the blue, the synchronicity stimulates us suddenly into a higher level of intellectual and emotional activity, a level that, as well as being more intense, is also—insofar as it jolts us beyond the limits of our old patterns of thought and feeling—more liberated.

A second form of transformation that can be effected by synchronicity is personality extension through reordering of the experiencer's memory and interests. Of course, there are many kinds of experience, not just synchronicities, that can have this effect, but in the case of synchronicities, largely because of their enigmatic nature, it can be especially powerful. When a striking synchronicity emphasizes a particular content, one becomes much more likely to pay attention to this content. At the very least it becomes more prominent in one's memory, and often, further than this, one can be stimulated to think about and research into its possible deeper meaning. Sometimes this can result in a far-reaching reorientation of one's whole personality. If, for example, one has not been spiritually inclined but then finds synchronicities repeatedly directing one's attention to this area of experience, one's attitude toward it may be significantly transformed.

However, extension of personality through being opened up to wider ranges of experience is not the final or most radical transformative effect intrinsic to the nature of synchronicity. More fundamentally transformative is the shift that implicitly takes place in synchronicities from an observer-centered orientation to the world to a more centerless or holistic state. In this latter state the observer comes to be viewed as continuous with the observed world and as equally objective to it, while, correspondingly, the observed world comes to be experienced with the kind of subjective intimacy that usually attaches only to the observer.[38]

In a typical synchronicity, one sees manifesting in the external world the parallel of some inner idea or image with which one is identified. Because of the paralleling, this identification transfers somewhat to the external expression, with the result that one comes to experience oneself as being partly externalized in the world. That which one formerly took to be separate from oneself, objective, turns out to be the same as that which one took to be oneself, one's subjectivity. Thus, from a state in which one is centered inwardly in one's psychic processes one is shifted into a state in which one's sense of identity extends beyond the psyche into the physical world. In this way one's identity is decentered—the observer becoming objectified while the observed is rendered subjective. The resultant holistic state of perception, however briefly it lasts, marks a profound transformation that can have far-reaching implications.

Of course, this transformative effect is not necessarily experienced explicitly in all synchronicities, and even when it is explicitly experienced it may be so in various degrees. The main factor determining the extent to which it is experienced is how integral to one's sense of identity is the image, idea, or interest that forms the psychic component of the synchronicity. The more integral it is, the more fully one is likely to feel one's identity center shifted when the synchronicity occurs. Thus, the transformative effect is likely to be experienced less radically when the synchronicity involves a psychic content that is not particularly important to one than when the psychic content consists of one's current most dominant interest.

UNITY

A further concept implicit in the notion of spirit is unity. I noted in the previous chapter how from the perspective of spirit the division that is usually experienced in consciousness between observer and observed can be perceived to break down and be replaced momentarily by a more unitive form of consciousness. There is plenty of testimony to support the possibility of unitive states of consciousness. The possiblity is enshrined in the *tat tvam asi* ("thou art that") of Advaita ("nondual") Vedanta. Expressed in one way or another observer–observed unity is also a theme that arises in the writings of a number of Christian mystics. Meister Eckhart, for example, could write that in certain mystical states "the knower and the known are one."[39] Within the twentieth century the idea received emphatic expression in, for instance, the teachings of Jiddu Krishnamurti, who would frequently remind those listening to his talks: "You are the world and the world is you."[40] "[W]e know at present," he remarked on one occasion, "there are the thinker and the thought, the observer and the observed, the experiencer and the experienced; there are two different states. Our effort is to bridge the two."[41] Nor are experiences of the unity of observer and observed exclusive to those specially involved with mystical and spiritual teachings. They can also happen spontaneously to ordinary people in the course of their everyday life. Such a class of people is represented by the initial 3,000 respondents to a questionnaire by the Religious Experience Research Unit in Oxford (now the Alister Hardy Research Centre), of whom 171 reported having experiences that involved a "feeling of unity with surroundings and/or with others."[42]

With regard to synchronicities, we shall see that these are able to facilitate the realization of unity on several levels: within oneself, between oneself and the world, and as an intrinsic feature of reality generally. The key to each level of realization is the simple fact that the component events of a synchronicity share the same content.

On the most basic level, the sharing of content can link together—and so unite—diverse contexts and areas of experience that, in the absence of the synchronistically shared content, would probably remain separate. From the perspective of Jungian psychology, this uniting could help further the processes of integration and individuation. Integration is the process of reconciling apparently disparate and conflicting elements within the psyche and the external world. Thus, one may need to reconcile one's conscious ego with suppressed or neglected aspects of one's psyche (what Jung terms the "shadow"), or with collective psychic contents that have never before been conscious, or with some aspect of society, or with culture, or with nature, or even in some sense with the cosmos as a whole.[43] All of this is the work of integration on different levels. Clearly, any kind of experience such as a synchronicity that establishes a strong relationship between one's consciousness and one of these other levels could potentially have an integrative effect. More specifically, the unification effected as integration is a function of the process of individuation as understood in Jungian psychology.

Besides being unitary in the sense of joining different informational contexts and of furthering the processes of integration and individuation, synchronicities can also effect, or point toward, a more fundamental union between qualitatively different areas of reality—most notably between the psychic and the physical and, often bound up with this, between the observer and the observed. The dynamics of this have already been explained in the preceding section while discussing the transformative effects of being shifted by synchronicity into a more holistic state of perception. We saw that, experientially, this can result in a sense of one's subjectivity being united with the objective outer world. In effect, this can be an experience of the apparent unity of psyche and matter. That is, in terms of the synchronistic content, there seems to be no difference between one's psyche (in the form of the inner state) and the external physical world (in the form of an actual outer event); through sharing the same content they in a sense momentarily cease to be differentiated.

In addition to being experienced directly, unity may also be rationally inferred from synchronicities. The rational inference might follow on the immediate experience as a means of accounting for it. Alternatively, the inference could be made without necessarily having actually been conscious of experiencing unity through a synchronicity. Again, having once made the inference and thus having come to appreciate the unitive implications of synchronicity, one could then, when one next has a synchronicity, actually experience it as unitive. Whatever the relationship between experience and inference, both kinds of realization are possible.

The inference is quite straightforward and takes the following form. One has observed the same content manifesting in two or more independent contexts that are not only independent but involve different fields of reality—one manifestation usually being psychic and the other physical. A possible way of accounting for this is to accept that the content that appears to be one and the same in both contexts is indeed one and the same. In the synchronicity we are seeing two different facets of one thing. It appears in two contexts because it is being viewed at a level of reality in which differentiation prevails, the level of ego-consciousness in Jung's terminology. However, at a deeper level of reality, the unconscious in Jung's model, such differentiation does not exist. At this deeper level psychic and physical qualities are fused in a unitary psychophysical continuum. A content might exist at this level as a kind of archetypal form capable, when it crosses the threshold into the world of ego-consciousness, of being diffracted into a number of diverse spatiotemporal contexts and into the seemingly so different fields of psyche and matter. These differentiated aspects are what we observe in a synchronicity, but they retain enough clues—in the form of their uncanny paralleling of one another—to enable us to discern that originally they were united. Thus, we can infer the content's essential unity and along with it the fundamental unity of the fields of reality—most usually, psyche and matter—in which it has manifested.

The essence of the above line of reasoning was followed by Jung. Referring to the parapsychological work carried out by J. B. Rhine and his co-workers, Jung stated that

> we now know that a factor exists which mediates between the apparent incommensurability of body and psyche, giving matter a kind of "psychic" faculty and the psyche a kind of "materiality," by means of which the one can work on the other.[44]

From this he argued that "all reality would be grounded on an as yet unknown substrate possessing material and at the same time psychic qualities."[45] This unknown substrate Jung referred to as the "psychoid unconscious," and for the unitary worldview that it entails he adopted the medieval alchemical term *"unus mundus"* (one world). Referring more specifically to synchronicity, he considered that this principle "suggests that there is an interconnection or unity of causally unrelated events, and thus postulates a unitary aspect of being."[46]

Marie-Louise von Franz, one of Jung's principal collaborators, puts the point even more forthrightly:

> [S]ynchronicity requires two essentially heterogeneous world systems, whose sporadic interlocking causes certain aspects of wholeness to manifest themselves.... The coincidence of the two realms in synchronistic phenomena is our only *empirical* indication of unified existence to date.[47]

The remark that synchronistic phenomena provide our "only empirical indication of unified existence" requires some qualification. We have already seen that mystical experiences, whether cultivated or spontaneous, constitute another form of such "empirical indication." Even if von Franz excludes such experiences because, though empirical in the the sense of being experiential, they are not empirical in the sense of being susceptible to external observation, nonetheless there still exists another category of phenomena that do, in the more scientific sense of the the word, empirically indicate a unitary stratum to reality. In fact, this is a category of events of which von Franz is herself evidently very much aware, namely, those enigmatic quantum physical phenomena wherein matter displays a number of curiously "psyche-like" qualities: nonlocality, discontinuity, indeterminacy, and the fact of being affected by observation. Wolfgang Pauli, on the basis of his profound involvement in the development of quantum mechanics, remarked that

> modern science may have brought us closer to a more satisfying conception of this relationship [of mind and body], by setting up, within the field of physics, the concept of *complementarity.* It would be most satisfactory of all if physis and psyche could be seen as complementary aspects of the same reality.[48]

Niels Bohr, who first formulated the principle of complementarity as a resolution of the paradoxes of quantum physics, also considered that "materialism and spiritualism [that is, the physical and the psychic], which are only defined by concepts taken from each other, are two aspects of the same thing."[49] And more recently, David Bohm's Implicate Order theory—that has its roots in an attempt to reconcile the seemingly incompatible implications of relativity theory and quantum theory—offers a model of reality in which "the mental and the material are two sides of one overall process that are (like form and content) separated only in thought and not in actuality. Rather, there is one energy that is the basis of all reality."[50] Not only synchronistic phenomena and mystical experiences, therefore, but "the latest conclusions of science"—to quote Jung again—"are coming nearer and nearer to a unitary idea of being."[51]

However, among the phenomena that indicate a unitary level of reality, synchronistic experiences occupy a special place. Mystical experiences of union are almost exclusively subjective in the sense that when someone is having such an experience nothing happens in or to the outer world that would be noticed by an independent observer (apart, perhaps, from electroencephalograph and similar readings and certain behavioral traits of the experiencer). Conversely, in the case of quantum physics, the phenomena are almost exclusively objective in the sense that, while they may exhibit "psyche-like" behavioral properties, no one actually experiences the inner psychic workings of the anomalously behaving particles in the way, for example, that we all experience the activity of our own psyches. In contrast to both of these, what is interesting about synchronistic experiences is that they are equally both subjective and objective. The inner psychic aspect of a synchronicity, unlike that supposed to attach to quantum events, most definitely is experienced directly; and the outer physical aspect of a synchronicity, unlike that said to pertain to mystical experiences of unity, most definitely is susceptible to being registered by independent observers. Thus, if von Franz is not quite accurate in asserting that synchronistic phenomena are our "*only* empirical indication of unified existence to date,"[52] she may be right to draw attention to them as being our *best* such indication.

TRANSCENDENCE AND IMMANENCE

Two further concepts that can be explicated from the characterization of spirit offered in the previous chapter are transcendence and immanence. Transcendence is implied in the very fact that spirit can be differentiated from the psychic and physical at all; it cannot be reduced to but "rises above" or "transcends" them. According to the *Macmillan Dictionary of Religion*, for example, transcendence means "going beyond or surpassing." Although it is "most commonly used of the way God is believed to exist beyond and independent of the world," it is also the case that "in other contexts transcendence is understood as the surpassing of ordinary experience from within the world."[53]

Such a concept can readily be applied to synchronicity. When Arthur Koestler published a selection of "Anecdotal Cases" of synchronicity, many of which had been sent to him in response to newspaper appeals, he arranged them in a number of loose classificatory categories.[54] The first four of these—"The Library Angel," "Deus Ex Machina," "Poltergeists," and "The Practical Joker"—while perhaps not intended as serious scientific categories, nonetheless testify to a very common response to synchronicities, namely, seeing them as the expressions of some agency outside of our normal psychic and physical spheres of experience. The coincidences have been brought about by (in Koestler's cases) an angel, a god (*deus*), a spirit (*Geist*), or an archetypal figure (the practical joker or trickster). More explicitly, Stephen Jenkins, whose synchronicity involving the four horses was used as an illustration in the previous chapter, responds to some of his observations of synchronistic phenomena by asking: "Is some intelligence (or more than one) manipulating things—in the widest sense—in order to influence us for some mysterious purpose?"[55]

It appears, therefore, that one can be led to make an inference from the occurrence of synchronicity to the existence of a transcendent intelligence. However, it can also happen that belief in a transcendent intelligence already exists and, rather than being inferred from synchronicity, is invoked as an already intellectually satisfying principle capable of adequately explaining synchronistic occurrences. Thus, for example, St. Thomas Aquinas, in a discussion of providence, says the following:

> When a master sends two servants to the same place, their meeting may seem to them a chance encounter. So a happening may seem haphazard or casual with respect to lower causes when it appears unintentional, but there is nothing fortuitous about such events with respect to a higher cause.[56]

If by "lower causes" we understand all normally recognized ways of psychophysical interaction and by "higher cause" we understand some transcendent ordering intelligence, then Aquinas is giving precisely the kind of explanation of synchronicity we have just indicated.

Whether one starts, as Jenkins appears to do, from the experience of synchronicity and from that infers the existence of the transcendent, or, like Aquinas, reasons back from an acceptance of the transcendent to an understanding of synchronicity, in both cases the same implicit reasoning is present: that if there are two or more psychophysical events that are manifestly connected through their meaning yet not by any normal causal means, this can be accounted for by assuming the events to have been coordinated from a level transcendent to the field of normal psychophysical causality.[57]

The specific nature of the inferred transcendent reality can be referred to in a wide range of ways reflecting different outlooks and beliefs. One might conceive of it as a single Divinity, whether a personal Being or an impersonal Absolute. It could be an abstract principle of order and meaning such as Tao. Again, one might think of it as a spiritual dimension inhabited by a plurality of higher beings: gods, demons, angels, ancestors, and so on; or as an extension of inner reality whose expressions originate from a higher self or from a constellation of archetypal factors. The fact that we can conceive of such a wide range of possible forms the transcendent might take undoubtedly reflects diverse features of our psychological makeup. Just as our psychology shows tendencies sometimes toward personality and sometimes toward impersonality, sometimes toward unification and at other times toward pluralization, so our conceptions of the transcendent unknown reflect this. Of course, it could also be the case that reality at a transcendent level is paradoxically both personal and impersonal, both unitary and plural, and that we conceive it as such not because we are projecting our own psychology onto reality but because our psychology accurately reflects reality, as microcosm to macrocosm.

Theologically, it is often considered important to balance the concept of transcendence with that of immanence, understood as "God's indwelling and omnipresence in the world"[58]—a quality indicated in my characterization as spirit's interpenetration or interfusing of the psychophysical. Indeed, problems are thought to arise if either of these concepts receives undue prominence:

> If transcendence is emphasized at the expense of immanence, God [or however spiritual reality is conceived] is in danger of becoming so distant from his creation that he ceases to be of any relevance to humankind. Similarly, if immanence is too heavily emphasized, there is a danger of degenerating into pantheism.[59]

Synchronistic experiences can as readily be related to immanence as to transcendence. Although the anomalous paralleling involved in synchronicities can suggest the operation of some transcendent factor, it is always the case that the anomalous event itself takes place within the psychophysical domain of ordinary experience. It cannot be simply reduced to the psychic and physical, and is therefore arguably spiritual, but neither, by definition, can it occur in the absence of the psychic and physical. Thus, from a spiritual perspective, one can view synchronicity as maintaining "an equilibrium between the two poles of transcendence and immanence."[60]

PROVIDENCE

The understanding of spirit as something that both transcends the normal psychophysical world and operates immanently within it helps evoke the further spiritual concept of providence. Succinctly, providence is "the belief that all things are ultimately ordered and governed by God towards a purpose."[61] In my characterization of spirit in the previous chapter, I drew attention to the properties of spontaneity and autonomy, which suggests that spirit is not simply limited by the unfolding of psychic and physical patterns of activity but can initiate something from beyond the psychophysical. I also drew attention to the properties of intelligence and purposiveness, which suggests that the patterns of activity that spirit initiates can be ordered and meaningful. If one assumes that this ordered and meaningful patterning of the psychophysical by spirit operates on a significant enough scale, one begins to approach certain traditional understandings of providence.

Synchronistic experiences, as likewise involving the properties of spontaneity, autonomy, intelligence, and purposiveness, can easily suggest the operation of providence in the above sense.[62] In fact, the notion of purposive ordering has already entered the picture several times in the discussion of transcendence. Koestler's classificatory categories of "The Library Angel" and the "Deus Ex Machina," for instance, imply the idea of an intelligence ordering events to some benevolent purpose. Jenkins, too, was quoted as wondering whether "some intelligence (or more than one) [might be] manipulating things . . . in order to influence us for some mysterious purpose."[63] And the passage quoted from Aquinas to illustrate the possible relation between higher and lower causes was taken from a discussion specifically of the concept of providence.

One is perhaps most likely to view synchronicities as providential when their consequences are conspicuously momentous. Thus, for example, Ira Progoff relates the following story about Abraham Lincoln.[64] In his early years Lincoln had intimations that he had an important destiny to fulfill but realized that he could only do so if he developed his intellect and acquired some professional skills. Unfortunately, since he lived in a frontier environment where the necessary tools for professional study were very difficult to find, it looked as though his aspirations would not be fulfilled. Then one day a stranger came to Lincoln with a barrel full of odds and ends. The stranger openly admitted that nothing in the barrel was of any value but, being desperate for the money, he urged Lincoln to buy it for a dollar. Out of kindness Lincoln agreed. Later, when he came to clear out the barrel, he found among the other contents an almost complete edition of Blackstone's *Commentaries*. As Progoff notes, "It was the chance, or synchronistic, acquisition of these books that enabled Lincoln to become a lawyer and eventually to embark on his career in politics."[65] The consequences of this fortunate coincidence were significant not just for Abraham Lincoln but for the history of a whole people.

However, even when the consequences of a synchronicity are not as momentous as this on the collective level, they may still be felt to be so on a more personal level—if, for example, the synchronicity directly helps an individual to find his or her vocation or partner or place to live.[66] Even if it is only a question of the synchronicity seeming to further some short-term and relatively unimportant interest—turning up a needed object or piece of information, for instance[67]—the experiencer may nonetheless be led by this to infer that a similar kind of benevolent ordering could also be operating more widely and in more important matters. Indeed, one could make this kind of inference even if one's own latest synchronistic experiences were not conspicuously beneficial at all. If synchronicity can reasonably be regarded as the operation of a transcendent intelligence, sometimes producing obviously beneficial effects, it is reasonable to suppose that such a transcendent intelligence could be operating beneficially quite generally, even if the benefit is not always readily discernible by us or conforming to our expectations as to what constitutes benefit.

REVELATION

The same combination of attributes—spontaneity and autonomy along with intelligence and purposiveness—are involved in the spiritual concept of revelation. This term is generally used to refer to "disclosures offered by God or from the divine as distinguished from those attained by human processes of observation, experiment and reason."[68] However, I would prefer to articulate it as "communications to human consciousness from a level transcendent to our normal psychic and physical functioning." I should also make clear that I am concerned primarily with personal revelations rather than with the kind of collective revelations represented, for instance, by the scriptures of many of the major world religions.[69]

To appreciate how synchronicity might be related to revelation we need to introduce a further distinction regarding the sources from which the meaning of synchronicities can be derived. This is the distinction between the meaning that can derive from the essential form of synchronicities and that which can derive from their specific content. The *essential form* of a synchronicity is those features that define a happening as a synchronicity: namely, that there should be at least two events that parallel one another acausally, notably, and meaningfully. Clearly, since all synchronicities, in order to qualify as such, must possess the same essential form, any kinds of meaning derivable from this essential form will apply to every synchronicity.[70] The *content* of a synchronicity, by contrast, consists of the specific point or points of paralleling between the coinciding events and so varies from one synchronicity to another. The meaning derivable from such content will therefore also vary from one synchronicity to another.

The relationship of synchronicity to each of the spiritual concepts I have considered so far, and, hence, the case for synchronicity being accounted spiritually meaningful, primarily depends for its appreciation on essential form. For example, it was the intrinsic anomalousness of the notable acausal paralleling in synchronicity that justified relating synchronicity to the concepts of miraculousness and (at a general level) transformation. It was also this that provided the grounds for the inference by which synchronicity was related to the concepts of a transcendent or unitary aspect of reality. The connection of synchronicity with these spiritual concepts could therefore be made on the basis of any synchronicity, since they all necessarily involve this essential form.

However, in the case of the concepts of transformation (at a more specific level), of providence to a certain extent, and of revelation very clearly, much often depends on the content of the synchronicity as well as on its essential form. The appreciation of a transformative effect, an act of providence, or a revealed communication depends on what the specific effect, act, or communication is, and this is something that, while it may have its generalized aspect, usually differs significantly from case to case.

The contents that emerge through synchronicity are, or can readily be resolved into, images or ideas. In our attempt to discern the possible meaning in synchronicities we need to make it one of our strategies to examine the specific meaning of each such content. Doing this, the first thing we notice is that, if indeed the contents do have some specific meaning, that meaning is rarely explicit. To get some hold on this meaning often requires a detailed analysis and amplification of both the content and its contexts, and above all an appreciation of the fact that the images and ideas involved are generally symbolic in character.

The sense in which I understand the term "symbol" follows Jung, for whom symbolic expression is "the best possible formulation of a relatively *unknown* thing."[71] A symbol is thus to be distinguished from "a conventional sign" that consists of "associations that are more completely and better known elsewhere" and from allegory that involves "an intentional paraphrase or transmogrification of a known thing."[72] Elaborating on his own understanding, which may be influenced by Jung, the Jesuit theologian Avery Dulles describes a symbol as "a sign pregnant with a plenitude of meaning which is evoked rather than explicitly stated."[73] Any attempt to achieve a "propositional explication" of a symbol, he argues, "to the extent that it achieves literalness, leaves out things tacitly perceived through the symbol; it is incomplete, and by fragmenting the density of the symbol, blunts its power."[74]

Dulles highlights four further properties of symbols as I too wish to understand them. These are, first of all, *participation*:

> [S]ymbolism gives not speculative but participatory knowledge—knowledge, that is to say, of a self-involving type. A symbol is never a sheer object. It speaks to us only insofar as it lures us to situate ourselves mentally within the universe of meaning and value which it opens up to us.[75]

Second, we have *transformation*: "Symbol, insofar as it involves the knower as a person, has a transforming effect."[76] The third property is the effect on *commitments and behavior*: "symbolism has a powerful influence on commitments and behaviour. . . . It stirs the imagination, releases hidden energies in the soul, gives strength and stability to the personality, and arouses the will to consistent and committed action."[77] The fourth property is an ability to generate *new awareness*: "symbol introduces us into realms of awareness not normally accessible to discursive thought. . . . By putting us in touch with deeper aspects of reality symbolism can generate an indefinite series of particular insights."[78]

Dulles draws attention to these four properties in the course of an attempt to show "the parallelism between the properties of symbolic communication and of revelation,[79] and his discussion of revelation provides a useful framework for the more detailed exploration of the possible relationships between this concept and synchronicity.

Dulles identifies five principal ways in which the concept of revelation has been understood. He evaluates each of these "models of revelation," pointing out their respective strengths and weaknesses.[80] Then he introduces the concept of "symbolic mediation,"[81] suggesting that revelation is essentially a form of "symbolic disclosure" and that a symbolic approach to revelation "can incorporate what is valid in the five models and at the same time correct what is misleading in them."[82] This emphasis on symbolism facilitates the connection of revelation to synchronicity, which, as I understand it, is also through its content a form of "symbolic disclosure."

Dulles calls his first model the "doctrinal" or "propositional" model. In this, "revelation is understood on the analogy of authoritative teaching. God is seen as an infallible teacher who communicates knowledge by speech and writing."[83] The adherents of this model generally claim that the statements in their accepted text of revelation are to be taken as literal expressions of the truth about whatever they describe (hence, the model is called "propositional"). Dulles argues that this model can be made more acceptable and cogent by considering that the "speech and writing" through which the "teaching" is revealed should (at least in a large number of cases) be viewed symbolically rather than literally.[84]

The parallel between this and synchronicity should be clear from what has already been said. In certain cases, the synchronistic content either itself consists of speech and writing or is easily resolvable into these. The resulting statements can then be considered a form of "teaching": informing, directing, exhorting, and so on.

Dulles's second model is the "historical." In this

> revelation is depicted as a series of historical events which have given the community of faith its corporate identity. God is represented as the transcendent agent who brings about the revelatory events and by means of them makes signs to his people.[85]

Again Dulles uses the concept of symbolic mediation to increase the plausibility of this model of revelation, showing how certain revelatory events, without denying their historical factualness, only take on their full meaning when viewed symbolically. For example, many of the events in the life of Christ can be more richly understood when viewed symbolically—as built "on certain cosmic archetypes"[86]—but this is by no means incompatible with the possibility that those events really occurred.

Relating this to the present subject, it seems possible that certain synchronicities could be viewed as historical sign-events. A synchronicity is an event, it occurs at a specific moment in time, and it can be seen as a sign. The material that has come to my attention does not seem likely to give any "community of faith its corporate identity"—it seems too ambiguous and multifaceted for that, as well as too free in drawing on any and every religious and cultural tradition for its content. However, if one allows for this eclecticism, the synchronistic event can certainly be viewed as a sign for some party, even if this party comprises only the one person who experiences the synchronicity. A series of such synchronistic events might then make up a form of "revelation history," again even if only for their individual experiencer.[87]

The third of Dulles's models is what he calls the "experiential" model, in which "revelation is interpreted on the basis of an immediate interior experience. God is viewed as the divine visitor, the guest of the soul. He communicates by his presence."[88] The principal improvement made to this model by the concept of symbolic mediation is that it removes the problem of conceiving how an experience of God could be totally "immediate." As Dulles remarks, "Even the highest mystical experience, which dispenses with normal mediations through concepts and images, still rests upon inner effects of grace that in some way mediate the encounter itself."[89] Further, "[T]he symbol itself, in its full dimensions, includes the experience of grace."[90]

The parallels between synchronicity and this experiential model of revelation do not depend so much on an appreciation of the nature of synchronistic content. Revelation conceived as God visiting the soul and communicating by his presence is more akin to the experience of numinosity that we considered earlier. The qualities implicit in the experience of numinosity—otherness, awefulness, overpoweringness, urgency, and fascination—are, like the experience of grace, subtle inner effects mediating the encounter with the divine. In a sense, synchronicity itself could be considered a symbol that includes these qualities.

The fourth of the models in Dulles's survey is the "dialectical": "In the dialectical model revelation occurs through a powerful, transforming word, such as the proclamation of the Cross and Resurrection."[91] Representatives of this way of viewing revelation (Dulles specifically mentions Karl Barth and Rudolf Bultmann)

> denied that God's presence and activity could ever be discovered within the realms of historical fact, doctrinal statement, or religious experience. And yet they were convinced, in faith, that God was present and active in human history, language, and experience. To express the paradoxical reality of God's presence and absence they had recourse to a succession of affirmations and denials, statements and counterstatements, which seemed to them to respect the mystery of God.[92]

Dialectical theologians themselves have been wary of attempts to view the divine "word" as in any sense symbolic, fearing that it might thereby come to be considered just one symbol among many and so lose its special status as originating from the divinely transcendent rather than from human consciousness. But as Dulles points out, it would still be possible to consider that "of all symbols it [the word] is the most spiritual and the most akin to the divine."[93] There are strong similarities between the nature of symbols and the kind of dialectic involved in the above conception of revelation:

> [S]ymbol, as we have noted, is capable of transcending differences which, to discursive reason, appear insurmountable. The symbolic approach, like the dialectical, is at home with inscrutable mystery. It refuses to reduce meaning and intelligibility to the narrow confines of conceptual logic.[94]

Relating this to synchronicity, it is necessary again to emphasize that I do not consider such synchronistic experiences as have come to my attention to give, in their totality, direct support to any specific traditional revelation, hence, not to such a "word" as "the proclamation of the Cross and Resurrection." However, abstracting the concept of "dialectical revelation" from its specifically Christian context, there are again striking similarities between this conception and the nature of synchronicity. As we have seen particularly in relation to the concepts of miraculousness and transformation, synchronicity is also intrinsically paradoxical in nature. If the dialectical theologians are indeed identifying something important about revelation—its fundamentally paradoxical nature—then synchronicity, as itself a profoundly paradoxical form of apparent communication, may not be unrelated to this.

Dulles's fifth and final model of revelation is what he calls the "awareness model." In this, "revelation takes the form of a breakthrough in the advance of human consciousness. God reveals by luring the imagination to construe the world in a new way."[95] This model is highly compatible with the concept of symbolic mediation. As Dulles points out, "Partisans of the 'consciousness' model commonly regard symbolic communication in one form or another (image, metaphor, parable, story, and the like) as the prime bearer of revelation."[96]

Again, synchronicity can be related to this model of revelation both through its essential form and through its content. A synchronistic content, being symbolic, can clearly qualify as a potential "bearer of revelation" along the lines of the last quoted statement. As for the essential form of synchronicity, we have already seen that this can have a profound transformative effect on consciousness—such transformation being, in effect, the emergence of a new awareness.

Synchronicity, then, can be related to a basic conception of revelation primarily because synchronistic content can be seen as a form of higher-level communication to human consciousness.[97] In addition to this, there are several further ways in which it can be related to some of the more sophisticated conceptions of revelation. Of particular significance is that the content of synchronicities can be viewed symbolically, while the concept of revelation is also enriched by being so viewed.

CHAPTER 4

SYMBOL, MYTH, AND SYNCHRONICITY
THE BIRTH OF ATHENA

To give greater substance to the whole of the preceding discussion, it is necessary now to begin a detailed examination of some synchronistic case material. Such material as has been described so far in this work has consisted mostly of the one-off experiences of a variety of separate individuals, and indeed this is the kind of material that has usually received attention in published collections.[1] In what follows, I shall instead consider an extended series of closely interrelated incidents that were almost all experienced by a single individual. This will be followed in the next chapter by an even more extensive series of such incidents. In general, a series of synchronicities has the advantage over a collection of one-off experiences of enabling patterns of meaning to emerge that are considerably more complex and articulated—and, hence, usually also both more impressive in terms of their unlikeliness and more conducive to the discernment of possible levels of spiritual significance. In my commentary on the incidents, there will be occasion to mention each of the spiritual concepts examined in the previous chapter. When any specific concept is invoked, the full details of its possible relationship to synchronicity will not be repeated but can be considered to be present implicitly and to form the background out of which specific implications come sharply into focus.

"THE BIRTH OF ATHENA": A SYNCHRONISTIC NARRATIVE

The material to be considered in this chapter consists of the synchronistic experiences of Edward Thornton, which have been recounted by him in his autobiographical book *The Diary of a Mystic* (1967).[2] Thornton, a self-made wool merchant in Bradford, England, showed an early propensity toward various kinds of mystical experience, which he developed through a lifelong practical interest in both Eastern and Western religions. Shortly after the Second World War he was introduced by the Dominican Fr. Victor White to Jung and his associates in Zürich. There Thornton underwent analysis and trained to become a Jungian therapist himself, though he afterward came to feel that this was not his true vocation. Nonetheless, he became imbued with the Jungian way of thinking and framework of concepts, including the synchronicity concept, and this must have prepared him to observe and appreciate (and, let it be said, interpret after a particular fashion) the following series of events that occurred to him in the mid- to late 1940s.

We should note at the outset that Thornton presents his synchronicities within a work specifically dealing with his "mystical" experiences. It is no surprise, therefore, that he should continually emphasize precisely the spiritual aspect of synchronicity. He states that he is going to describe his synchronicities within the context of a consideration of how, as he puts it, "it often happens that the highly sensitive type of mind that we call mystical, causes unusual modifications in the physical organism with which it is linked."[3] In other words, his concern is with the psychophysical implications of spiritual transformation. Primarily, this involves apparently psychosomatic symptoms, but significantly it appears in his case also to involve synchronistic occurrences. The account is presented as much as possible in the experiencer's own words, though with commentary interspersed. The individual incidents are tagged with numbers in order to help clarify their parameters within my text and also to facilitate subsequent reference to them.

(1) Thornton relates that the following occurred on October 20, 1944:

> During a period when I was particularly devoted to our Blessed Lord . . . I saw in clear daylight [he was in his living room] a vision of what, to me, was the interior of a Greek Temple. . . . In front of me stood what I took to be an altar upon which was the image of a white owl.[4]

(2) He was, he says, "all the more moved by this scene when I began to return to ordinary consciousness, as during meditation the previous day, I had had the vivid impression of a live owl."[5]

(3) Further, "some days before that [I] had experienced a dream in which a flock of owls came swooping down over my head as I walked through a wooded glade."[6]

Thornton soon learned one of the main symbolical meanings of the owl and found that this gave profound personal significance to his experiences:

> [T]he owl was the bird sacred to Athena the Virgin-goddess and Protectress of Athens. Her supreme attribute was said to be that of Divine Wisdom. Later, when I started to offer particular devotion to the Blessed Virgin, I found that one of Her aspects, contained in the Lorettan Litany is *Sedes Sapientiae* (Seat of Wisdom); consequently I found that I had a special affinity with the Eternal Mother in her aspect of Divine Wisdom.[7]

The word "consequently" in this statement is suggestive. Thornton implies that his inner experiences, symbolically interpreted, actually made him aware of, "revealed" to him, his affinity with the Virgin Mary. This is the first indication that he is effectively viewing his experiences as a form of personal revelation, that is, as a transcendentally originating communication to his conscious mind of information having personal spiritual relevance. The specific content of this revelation is that a divine being, the Eternal Mother, has a special interest in him, an interest that he will later come to see as virtually providential.

(4) The above events occurred before Thornton's meetings with Jung and involvement with analytical psychology. When, a few years later, he started going out to Zürich, "the owl," he says, "again began to appear in my dreams and visions."[8]

(5) And:

> I also found that a couple of owls had come to nest quite near to my garden in Yorkshire, reminding me continually of their presence by hooting at night. Although this may seem to be a perfectly natural phenomenon, we had never before had owls in our garden as far as anyone could remember.[9]

This appearance of the owls in the garden was the first physical event in the series. As such it also marks the occurrence of the first conspicuous synchronicity (that is, it involves a meaningful acausal paralleling of inner psychic and outer physical events). One would like more detail than Thornton provides regarding the temporal relationship between the appearance of the real owls and the further "dreams and visions" of owls, since the nightly hooting suggests itself as an obvious possible cause of at least some of these dreams and visions. However, even if a normal causal factor of this kind cannot be excluded from having played *some* part in the events, it is inadequate on its own to account for the overall pattern of meaning that was soon to emerge, some of which only linked in to the owl incidents obliquely and could not be appreciated by Thornton until later when he was in possession of knowledge concerning a certain myth.

(6) Thornton reports the following dream for March 17, 1948: "I was examining the back of my brother's head. At the top of the spinal column there was a wound which reminded me of a vagina."

(7) This caused him to recall that "About a month earlier I dreamt that my head was to be shaved after the manner of a monk in the oriental tradition.[11]

(8) Then, May 10, 1948,[12] he dreamed he

> was in a room where an operation was to take place, before a class of medical students. Professor Jung was in the vicinity. Before the operation began, all stood up and sang a hymn. When we came to the end I continued with: *Gloria Patri, et Filio, et Spiritui Sancto*, but soon realized that this was not part of the hymn, and felt somewhat embarassed. A surgeon standing by me, however, smiled and assured me that I need not worry as many make the mistake of continuing as I did. It appeared to be the school song.[13]

With these dreams we have three further inner experiences. At this stage they seemed thematically unrelated to the earlier owl incidents, though Thornton recognized that they too required to be interpreted symbolically. He suggests:

> The dream where the stress is laid on the vagina-like wound contains the first intimation of symbolic copulation and a consequent birth, but in a spiritual sense, as the next head-shaving dream implies. The so-called school-hymn in the latter has close association with a hymn to Aesculapius, the God of Healing.[14]

Again, the experiences appear to be revealing (through symbolism and allusion to an ancient healing ritual) a specific meaning to Thornton: namely, that something may be going to happen that has to do with a spiritual rebirth effected through sickness and recovery. As yet, however, there was no indication as to what, exactly, all this might mean in relation to his life. Indeed, the whole series of incidents we are considering is remarkable for the amount of relevant associative and prefigurative detail that emerges before its full significance is brought into focus by the critical events. Two more prefigurative inner experiences were the following.

(9) Thornton had an "interior vision" during meditation on June 7, 1948, in which he saw "[t]he luminous form of two owls sitting upon the branch of a tree with the full moon behind them. As I gaze upon them they merge into one."[15]

(10) Then, on September 23, 1948, he had a dream in which

> I was going the round of solitary cells in a prison with my brother, whose job it was to awaken the various inmates by chopping their foreheads with an axe. Each occupant was found kneeling in the classical Christian way at a prayer desk, with his head resting on a block. As we entered the last cell my brother gave one chop at the slumberer's forehead and immediately awakened him. I felt that I was the one to whom this had happened and became fully conscious.[16]

(11) It was not until the following year, 1949, that Thornton felt he began properly to understand these dreams and other experiences. The key was provided when he heard Karl Kerényi lecturing in Zürich on Pallas Athena and expounding the main myth concerning the goddess's birth. Kerényi (quoting the Homeric Hymn to Athena) related how

> "Hephaistos . . . assisted at the birth and smote Zeus's skull with a double-edged axe or [a] hammer. Pallas Athene sprang forth. . . . All the [im]mortals were afraid [and astonished at] the sight of her, as she sprang out [in] front of aegis-bearing Zeus, from his immortal head, brandishing her sharp javelin. Mightily quaked great Mount Olympus beneath the weight of the owl-eyed maiden."[17]

Through this episode from myth Thornton was able to appreciate the interconnection of his two series of inner experiences, those concerning the owl and those concerning some kind of wound or operation to the head. Both related to the myth of Athena's birth: the first because she is symbolized by the owl and the second because her birth was effected by an axe blow to Zeus's head. The timeliness of Thornton's learning about this myth can itself be considered a synchronicity.

Knowledge of the myth enabled Thornton to crystallize his own interpretation of the meaning of the events so far. He considered the overall pattern to represent "the prefiguration of a dynamic experience which is related to the feminine principle in that attribute of its validity which is expressed in masculine psychology, namely, the birth of Divine Wisdom in man."[18] This interpretation again illustrates how Thornton was viewing his experiences within a spiritual framework. The actual content of "the feminine principle . . . expressed in masculine psychology" clearly derives from his involvement in Jungian psychology. This itself reaches into spiritual concerns: the balancing of the feminine and masculine components of the personality was, at certain levels of its accomplishment, equated by Jung with mystical union, the *mysterium coniunctionis*.[19] Beyond this, we can again see how Thornton is implicitly presenting his interpretation or understanding as something that the events themselves have revealed to him. What they have revealed is the fact that some "dynamic experience" is impending—an experience that he anticipates will be spiritually transforming inasmuch as it will result in the emergence (within himself, the implication is) of divine wisdom. More specifically, it will be an experience or realization of the immanence of the divine, since, as he understands it, "Pallas Athena was a terrestrial, not a celestial Goddess."[20]

(12) The next and final episode before the full synchronistic status of the series of incidents began to reveal itself occurred on April 2, 1949. Thornton was visiting a local osteopath, having dislocated the little toe of his left foot. While the osteopath was massaging and strapping up his foot, she "quite unexpectedly" began telling Thornton some of her own experiences. She claimed to be "mediumistic," "a born healer," and she mentioned "an experience which impressed her profoundly." Thornton relates:

> She felt a crack open suddenly at the top of her head while lying in bed, and blood was running down from it all over her body. Upon touching herself she discovered that there was no blood and that she was quite well, but felt that the end had come and that she was quite ready.

The osteopath came to believe that this experience related to her need to accept unconditionally her vocation as a healer: "she realized," Thornton tells us, "that a power was working through her, and that she must submit to it absolutely." She told Thornton as he was taking his leave of her that "she had never before spoken so intimately to anyone."[21]

This incident paralleled to a remarkable extent the inner experiences that Thornton had been having so far, as well as his interpretation of them. Just as he had been dreaming about wounds to the head and had considered these dreams to constitute some kind of revelation concerning a providentially ordered spiritual transformation (the birth of

Divine Wisdom, as he articulated it), so the osteopath hallucinated having a wound on her head, took the experience as a kind of revelation concerning her vocation, and was profoundly transformed by it. Even more striking, however, as we shall now see, was the prefigurative nature both of this encounter with the osteopath and of Thornton's other dreams and visions.

(13) On April 20, 1949, eighteen days after the visit to the osteopath, Thornton "experienced a terrible spasm beginning, as it seemed, in the left foot, and working up to the heart."[22] The left side of his body became paralyzed and his speech was impaired. He was taken to the Duke of York's Hospital in Bradford where initial diagnoses suggested the problem lay in the upper region of the cerebral hemisphere behind the right forehead. Later he was moved to Leeds Infirmary where it was confirmed that he had a tumor over the right hemisphere, on which it would be necessary to operate.

Thus, Thornton's dreams regarding wounds to the head and an operation taking place (6, 7, 8, 10) proved to be synchronistic with his actual life. It is also interesting to note that the osteopath felt moved to relate her head-wound vision while massaging Thornton's left foot (12)—the part of his body where the symptoms of his illness first manifested.

(14) Once diagnosed and admitted to the hospital, Thornton remembered two other relevant dreams. First, on December 24, 1948, "I was looking in a glass and I or someone was drawing a silver wire from my right temple."[23]

(15) The second dream had never been written down but Thornton says he "remembered it quite vividly": "I was looking in a glass and found that the skin on my right temple was like parchment, as if it had dried up after a wound."[24] Thornton had his analyst Dr. C. A. Meier, one of Jung's associates in Zürich, informed of these dreams by telephone. Meier assured him that they gave "a perfect prognosis concerning the illness and operation."[25]

(16) It was not only Thornton's series of head-wound dreams that proved synchronistic. His dreams and visions involving owls proved to be so as well—and in a way that, at the time, impressed him even more powerfully. Having been moved to Leeds Infirmary, he was composing himself for the night when

> I happened to look out of the window, and to my great amazement saw a colossal bronze owl looking down on me from the top of one of the spires of Leeds City Hall which was situated directly opposite . . . the image of the owl seemed to be just outside of my window.[26]

This appears to have been the most critical experience in the whole series and the one that moved Thornton most deeply:

> I experienced a shudder, both of dread and holy awe, and the synchronicity of the happening struck me as soon as the first shock seemed to subside, and I realized its implication. I was under the special patronage of the Eternal Mother in her aspect of *Sedes Sapientiae*.[27]

His interpretation seemed to be further confirmed for him when, "casting my eyes further over to the right, across the tops of the buildings beyond the City Hall, I saw the figure of Athena with helmet, shield and lance, standing out above the tops of the surrounding buildings."[28] (This statue, he later learned, stood on a public hall known as the Coliseum.)

The outstanding feature in Thornton's descriptions of this critical synchronicity is the sense he conveys of its numinosity. A fairly strong emotional charge had accompanied some of his earlier inner experiences, making them especially "vivid" or giving them the quality of "visions" that he was "moved by."[29] But there was nothing to equal the "great amazement," the "shudder, both of dread and holy awe," the "shock" of this present "breathtaking experience" that conveyed "the overwhelming reality of the protecting grace of the Divine Mother."[30] This additional emotiveness in Thornton's responses undoubtedly owes something to the perilous physical condition he was in at the time. Its main cause, however, appears to be that he was encountering here not just a somewhat unusual inner experience but a radically anomalous synchronicity: quite miraculously the external world seemed to be participating in his inner spiritual drama. As we have seen, Rudolf Otto, in his characterization of the factors that contribute to the sense of numinosity, specifies that the "feeling of uncanniness" is of paramount importance—more so even than sheer intensity, which may or may not accompany the uncanniness.[31]

Once more Thornton considered his experience to be revealing to him the same basic message—that he was "under the special patronage of the Eternal Mother in her aspect of *Sedes Sapientiae*." However, whereas before he spoke of having a "special affinity"[32] with her, now he speaks of "special patronage" and, a little further on, of "special protection"[33] and "the protecting grace.[34] Within his more perilous situation, and under the influence of his extraordinary synchronistic experiences, he seems to have felt that Providence was operating for him more directly and intimately. Thus, for example, the presence of the bronze owl and the statue of Athena caused him to find "great significance in the fact that I had been removed to Leeds."[35]

It is probably in the light of this sense of Providence that we should view the next episode in Thornton's narrative. That same night, while under the influence of his "breathtaking experience," he "suddenly became aware that I had to prepare to die."[36] He reflected on his life and faith and eventually reconciled himself to the fact of dying, to the point where he says he "actually welcomed the experience." However, "no sooner had I accepted the situation thus, than I knew in full clarity that I was not yet required to die." As soon as he realized this, he "fell into an undisturbed sleep of peace and never had the slightest qualm or doubt as to the outcome of the operation."[37]

What Thornton went through here was a particularly powerful form of symbolic death, in the course of which he felt he made a "full and perfect renunciation" of all his worldly attachments. In other words, his attitude toward life was significantly transformed. Some of his realizations—for example, that he "had to prepare to die" and then that he "was not yet required to die"—again suggest strongly that he felt himself to be in communication somehow with an intelligence that was conveying to him, that is, revealing, these imperatives and certainties. As he narrates it, the whole experience is given the sense of having been providentially ordered for the sake of its transformative effect.

(17) The operation was performed on May 10, 1949. In several details it paralleled particularly closely Thornton's earlier dreams. The dream about his head being shaved (7) was fulfilled when, as he relates, "at 8 A.M. a male nurse arrived and shaved off my hair."[38]

(18) After the operation, when the bandage was eventually removed from his head, "I discovered that my skull had been cut right down the middle, thus fulfilling in the outer world the head-chopping dream [10] which I had experienced on September 24th of the previous year."[39]

(19) And third, "I was also later to establish that I had experienced foreknowledge of the operation accompanied by the Hymn to Aesculapius in the early morning exactly one year before."[40] That is, the operation was on May 10, 1949, while his dream of attending an operation had taken place on the morning of May 10, 1948 (8). Moreover, just as the operation commenced, a religious community with which Thornton had been associated began saying a High Mass on his behalf—thus reflecting the ritual and hymn of the dream.[41]

(20) One final incident closes the series. The following year, 1950, was pronounced Holy Year by the Vatican, and Thornton decided to visit Rome on a pilgrimage. There, he recounts:

> I was taken to see the small temple of Athena, and shown a photograph of two figures of the Goddess. This seemed to

confirm the interior vision in which I had seen two owls which merged and became one [9]. It was pointed out to me that the two figures which stand side by side are identical, except for the engraved image on the front of each shield.[42]

Though Thornton is not explicit about it, this motif of two becoming one, especially as it occurs in a spiritual context, again suggests the idea of mystical union. One might even relate it to the phenomenon of synchronicity itself inasmuch as synchronicity involves the paradoxical uniting of ostensibly separate aspects of reality (usually, as we have seen, an inner psychic event and an outer physical event having no normal causal connection). Indeed, Marie-Louise von Franz, developing certain suggestions of Jung's, has commented on the remarkable incidence of doubling and twinning motifs in imagery related to synchronicities.[43] That Thornton too may have had in mind the union of apparently separate aspects of reality, specifically of the spiritual with the material, is suggested by the comment with which he concludes his narrative: "One of the most profound experiences which I gained through this illness and the operation was an increased awareness of the Divine Immanence in the material universe."[44]

SYMBOLIC, MYTHIC, AND RITUAL MOTIFS

Altogether here I have isolated twenty incidents within Thornton's narrative. These vary in nature from visions, impressions during meditation, and dreams to physical events either observed by the experiencer but independent of him (for example, hearing the owls that had nested in his garden) or else actually happening to him (for example, his symptoms and operation). According to the definition offered earlier—that a synchronicity involves the meaningful acausal paralleling of events, usually of an inner psychic and an outer physical event—there are nine incidents within Thornton's series that have a strong claim to being synchronistic (5, 11–13, 16–20), or eleven if one includes the implied fulfillment of the two dreams reported to Meier (14 and 15).[45]

Two principal motifs run through the incidents: the owl motif and the head-wound/operation motif. On first appearance, these two motifs seemed totally unconnected. However, as the series of events unfolded it came to seem increasingly likely that they were connected. The key to appreciating this was an understanding of the motifs symbolically and in relation to a particular myth.

To recapitulate: The main symbolic resonance of the owl motif stemmed for Thornton from its association with the Greek goddess

Athena. Among Athena's principal attributes are virginity, protectiveness, and divine wisdom. These seemed to Thornton to parallel sufficiently strongly certain attributes of the Virgin Mary for him to make the further move of considering her—the Virgin Mary—also to be symbolized by the owl. Consequently, he was able to view his initial owl experiences as indicating that he had "a special affinity with the Eternal Mother in her aspect of Divine Wisdom."[46]

The head-wound/operation motif in its various appearances involved details that, on a symbolic level, particularly associated it with the ideas of spiritual rebirth and the awakening of consciousness, as Thornton himself appreciated.[47] Again, the dream in which the prisoners were awakened by being struck on the forehead with an axe—and which resulted in Thornton himself suddenly becoming "fully conscious,"[48] that is, literally awake—received spiritual coloration from the fact that each prisoner "was found kneeling in the classical Christian way at a prayer desk."[49]

In the light of these symbolic interpretations Thornton was in a position to appreciate at once the relevance to his experiences of the ancient Greek myth of the Birth of Athena. The owl incidents were related to the myth because the owl can symbolize Athena; and the head-wound/operation incidents were also related to the myth because Athena's birth was supposed to have been effected by an axe blow to Zeus's head. Thus, knowledge of the myth revealed to Thornton a hitherto unsuspected connection between his two seemingly independent clusters of experiences. Both, it appeared, were aspects of a single emergent pattern of meaning. Furthermore, Thornton was in a position to make a symbolic interpretation of the myth as a whole. He had already related Athena (and the Virgin Mary) to the quality of divine wisdom, the vagina-like wound to a spiritual birth, and the head-chopping to awakening consciousness. When his new knowledge of the myth encouraged him to bring these associations together, it was understandable that he should interpret the Birth of Athena symbolically as the spiritual experience of "the birth of Divine Wisdom in man."[50] The specifically spiritual emphasis in this interpretation was reinforced by the dream references to rituals: the ritual of shaving the head (7) expressed renunciation of one's baser nature in favor of devotion to spiritual principles; and the ritual hymn to Aesculapius (8) conveyed the idea of there sometimes being a spiritual dimension involved in the process of physical sickness and recovery.

THE SPIRITUAL DIMENSION

It is abundantly clear from the manner in which Thornton responded to his synchronistic experiences that he himself was viewing them in a spiritual light. In summary, he appears to have believed that the transcendent or Divine, in the form of the Eternal Mother, was working directly in his life, revealing specific meanings to him and providentially arranging his experiences in order to bring about his spiritual transformation.

It is important to note that many of the experiences Thornton relates are dreams, visions, meditational realizations, and critical life events that are powerful in their own right. This might lead one to suspect that the core of Thornton's beliefs regarding his relationship to the Divine, as well as regarding the content of his specific "revelations," could have been sustained even if these experiences had entirely lacked their eventual synchronistic status. However, I think it can be shown that in the actual event, synchronicity contributed to the spiritual character of Thornton's experiences much that would otherwise have been absent or present only to a lesser degree.

First, synchronicity enhanced the sense of numinosity about the experiences. It is true that a fairly strong emotional charge had accompanied some of Thornton's earlier inner experiences, making them especially "vivid" or giving them the quality of "visions" that he was "moved by."[51] But there was nothing to equal the "great amazement," the "shudder, both of dread and holy awe," or the "shock" that he says attended his "breathtaking" synchronicity of seeing the bronze owl from his hospital bedroom.[52]

Second, synchronicity made available an inference that strengthened Thornton's sense of the transcendent. If two or more events are ordered but not from within the psychophysical, in the sense that the psychic events do not cause the correlated physical events or vice versa, then it may be that these events are ordered from a level that transcends the psychophysical. Thornton made this inference continually and quite naturally, most conspicuously when he inferred from his synchronicity of seeing the bronze owl that he was "under the special patronage of the Eternal Mother."[53]

Third, synchronicity gave to Thornton's series of experiences the character of a minor miracle. His various dreams and visions and encounter with the osteopath all related significantly to his subsequent illness and accompanying experiences, yet there seemed to be no plausible causal connection between the two sets of events. Their meaningful coordination seemed to transgress the usual limitations of what is considered psychophysically possible.

Fourth, synchronicity justified Thornton in considering the content of many of his experiences to be revelatory. For once one has inferred the operation within one's experiences of something transcendent, it is a simple step to viewing the specific content of those experiences as communications from the transcendent, especially when that content, as in Thornton's case, is highly intelligible. This step was taken by Thornton throughout. The owl visions revealed to him his "special affinity with the Eternal Mother";[54] the head-wound/operation dreams revealed to him a "first intimation of symbolic copulation and a consequent birth";[55] when synchronistically coordinated, the two series of inner events revealed to him "the prefiguration of a dynamic experience . . . the birth of Divine Wisdom in man";[56] and seeing the bronze owl from his hospital bedroom revealed to him that he "was under the special patronage of the Eternal Mother in her aspect of *Sedes Sapientiae*."[57] Whereas earlier Thornton spoke of a "special affinity" with the Eternal Mother, now, under the impact of his synchronicity, he speaks in more direct and intimate terms of the "special patronage," the "special protection,"[58] and "the overwhelming reality of the protecting grace of the Divine Mother."[59]

Fifth, synchronicity had a profound unifying effect on the whole field of Thornton's experiences. The very fact that an intimate noncausal connection can be experienced between the outer physical world and one's inner subjectivity implies that the separateness usually experienced between inner and outer, psychic and physical, or self and world can to a significant degree be dissolved. This is symbolically expressed, as well as perhaps actualized, in Thornton's dreaming of two owls merged into one, then subsequently seeing the photograph of the two near-identical figures of Athena.[60] More generally, one could say that through revealing a profound paralleling between the psychic and physical events, synchronicity as it were adds a missing half to each, making the psychic events more embodied and the physical events more ensouled.[61] Thus, Thornton's appreciation of the myth of the birth of Athena deepened immensely when he found it being symbolically enacted in his own life. Conversely, his appreciation of the significance of his physical illness owed much of its depth to his ability to relate it to a psychic background of intimately acquired symbolic and mythic knowledge. Even further, the sense of unity was recognized by Thornton as existing not just between the psychic and the physical but between the psychophysical as a whole and a transcendent, spiritual, or divine aspect of reality.[62] Hence, he concluded his narrative by stating, "One of the most profound things which I gained through this illness and the operation was an increased awareness of the Divine Immanence in the material universe."[63]

Sixth, and finally, synchronicity contributed substantially to the transformative impact of Thornton's experiences. Through establishing new relationships among psychic and physical events, synchronicity can effectively reorder both the general field of the psychophysical and the individual consciousness of the experiencer. Thus, Thornton's inner dreams and visions about owls and about a wound or operation to the head were brought into a new and more ordered relationship by his timely synchronistic encountering of the myth of the birth of Athena. This in itself deepened his understanding of the process of transformation in which he felt himself to be involved. Later, the synchronistic paralleling between his inner experiences and illness precipitated even deeper transformations, such as his experience of symbolic death and rebirth.[64]

A SKEPTICAL UNDERTOW

Thornton's account of his experiences is presented in such a way as to maximize the sense of their spiritual significance, and we have seen that they clearly exhibit most of the characteristics of spirit that have been highlighted in this study. However, having dwelled at length on these spiritual implications, it is as well to recall that alternative kinds of interpretation are also possible, including interpretations aimed at reducing the whole episode to normally understood physical and psychological dynamics. Thornton does not engage with such reductive possibilities—an omission that makes his narrative one-sided and in danger of evoking an equally immoderate skepticism in uncommitted readers. I shall conclude my discussion of Thornton's experiences by articulating what a strongly reductive explanation might look like. In doing this, however, I shall attempt to maintain a balance both by showing some of the limitations of such attempts at reduction and by drawing closer attention to a number of detailed features that support a spiritual interpretation.

There are several general reductive strategies that could be invoked. As many commentators have noted,[65] it is always possible that events that seem highly improbable may not be so; that those which really are improbable can be accounted for by considering that remarkable things do sometimes happen purely by chance; and that the apparent meaningfulness of such events could stem from the projection of meaning onto them, rather than the discovery of meaning in them. Potentially more damaging, however, are a number of more focused criticisms such as the following.

Thornton tells us that there are three owls on the Leeds coat of arms.[66] One can therefore assume that the image would appear on many public buildings around the city as well as on civic publications. Thornton, born and brought up in nearby Bradford, would almost certainly have been exposed to this imagery and have absorbed some of it, albeit subliminally. This could at least partly account for the notable incidence of owl imagery in his dreams and visions. More specifically, his first-mentioned dream of owls (3) could explain causally why the owl appeared over the next few days in his impression during meditation and in his daylight vision (2, 1). As for the actual owls appearing near his garden (5), this is, in spite of Thornton's assurance that it had never happened before, not, after all, something that could not occur in the normal course of things, especially since we are considering a period of over five years between the first and last of the owl incidents related in the narrative (1944–50). Furthermore, once these real owls were in the garden, surely, as suggested earlier, their noisy presence would be a likely cause of any subsequent inner experiences involving owls (4, 9).

The various head-wound/operation incidents are a little more difficult to explain away on the basis of the information provided. However, one could suppose that the tumor that eventually led to Thornton's paralysis (13) and need for an operation (17–19) was already incipient when each of his apparently prefigurative dreams occurred (6–8, 10, 14–15)—the first of them a little over a year before the illness manifested. Thornton could have intimated the problem unconsciously and this intimation could have caused the projection in dream imagery of hints as to what would need to be done about it: namely, the carrying out of an operation (8, 14–15) that would involve shaving the head and splitting open the skull (6–7, 10).

The seemingly impressive interconnection of the two series of incidents, as we have seen, can only be appreciated in the light of the myth of the Birth of Athena (11)—a myth of which Thornton claims he was unaware until after both series were well under way. However, it is not impossible that he had been casually exposed to this myth at some earlier time and that knowledge of it (albeit unconscious knowledge) then played a part in constructing and ordering his subsequent experiences involving the owl and head-wound motifs. This is all the more likely when we consider that he spent a good deal of time in Zürich moving within Jungian circles where myth in its many varieties was one of the major topics of interest.

Turning to the remaining physical events, the osteopath may have subliminally picked up on Thornton's emergent symptoms, since she was treating him for a problem to the left foot, and it was the left foot in which Thornton's paralyzing spasm first appeared. Unconscious awareness of this immanent problem could have moved her to relate the most nearly parallel event in her own experience (12). As for the incident that seemed to make the profoundest impression on Thornton, seeing the bronze owl and the statue of Athena from his hospital window (16), the strikingness of this would be lessened if it were indeed the case that objects such as this very owl and statue and other similar representations elsewhere in Leeds themselves partly caused the appearance of owl imagery in Thornton's inner experiences in the first place. Finally, as for seeing the photograph in

Rome of the two nearly identical statues of Athena (20) and finding in this a parallel to the interior vision in which two images of owls seemed to merge into one (9), this could be a straightforward case of overinterpretation. At least eighteen months separate the two incidents; the parallel only works if one makes the symbolic equation owl = Athena; and the relationship between twoness and oneness is different in each incident (the two owls merged visually into one, but the two figurines of Athena remained separate and could only be considered "one" insofar as they were identical except for the detail on their shields).

These kinds of skeptical argument seem actually to be invited by Thornton's own failure to engage, even implicitly, with a more critical perspective on his experiences. However, though many of the arguments contain legitimate points, they do not ultimately undermine either the synchronistic or the spiritual status of Thornton's narrative as a whole.

In response to the skeptical interpretation, it can be emphasized that all of the specific points made in support of it represent possibilities only. For example, Thornton's state of knowledge or ignorance regarding the myth of the Birth of Athena was most probably just as he stated. Similarly, we should probably credit him with having the sense to realize that real owls hooting in his garden might cause him to dream of owls. If he omits to specify that his dreams occurred prior to the nesting of the owls, this may well be because he considers the point too obvious to need mentioning.

If we accept—as there is every reason to—that Thornton did not initially know either that Athena could be symbolized by an owl or that she was supposedly born through an axe blow to Zeus's head, then the convergence of motifs and happenings within the episode he relates is indeed impressive. Two initially very different images—the owl and the head wound—turn out to be aspects of a single pattern of meaning and are thereby mutually enriched and completed. One associative pathway leads from the image of the owl to the Greek goddess Athena, from there to the attributes of virginity, protectiveness, and divine wisdom, and thence to the Virgin Mary—a key devotional figure in Thornton's life. Another pathway leads from the image of a head wound or operation, tinged with an aura of spirituality, to the myth of the Birth of Athena, and therefore also to the concept of the birth of divine wisdom in man. Finally, these two already convergent clusters of images and associations further converge with actual events in Thornton's life, reflecting what happens to him both on an outward physical level (to his body and in his environment) and on an inward spiritual level (in regard to his death-and-rebirth experience and the awakening in him of new insights into Divine Immanence).

With regard to the paralleling between inner and outer events (that is, the synchronicities themselves), many of these are remarkable for the specificity and unlikeliness of their detail. Images such as shaving the head and cutting open the skull are hardly common; yet, the latter in particular occurs first in a dream, then in an outwardly encountered myth, and finally in Thornton's actual life. Similarly striking is the parallel between a dream of a vagina-like wound and encountering a myth about a birth from a wound. Again, the dream about attending an operation not only occurs exactly a year before Thornton's actual operation but also conspicuously involves a ritual hymn. Thornton, whether conscious of the parallel at the time or not, had a mass said on his behalf while he was being operated on. Finally, even if some of the dreams and other apparently prefigurative experiences could have been caused by unconscious awareness of the incipient illness, this still could not explain the circumstance of going to see the osteopath who herself just happened to have had an experience closely paralleling Thornton's, in spite of the very unusual content of the experience.

In general, then, the reductive interpretation depends on arguments that are ad hoc and establish only possibilities rather than strong probabilities. It implies ungenerously that the experiencer has a poor memory, poor critical faculties, and may also be downright deceptive, while at the same time possessing a remarkable ability to intuit future states of his organism. It also requires forcibly isolating his experiences from one another and thereby occluding such telling features of his account as the sheer quantity of incidents involved, the repetition and remarkable interconnection of themes expressed by their content, and in general their mutually supported intelligibility. In conclusion, while there may be a case for wanting to temper some of Thornton's own interpretative excesses, one can explain away his experiences in their entirety only by being even more excessive and heavy-handed oneself in the direction of skepticism.

CHAPTER 5

MULTIPLE SYNCHRONICITIES OF A CHESS GRANDMASTER

We come now, in this and the following chapter, to the exploration of a body of spontaneous synchronistic case material that in certain respects is even more remarkable than Thornton's. It too concerns the experiences primarily of a single individual for whom the spiritual aspect of reality is of great importance. In this case, however, the material had not been published at the time of my study of it and had therefore been spared much of the selectivity and polishing that have undoubtedly helped shape Thornton's narrative.[1] The present collection is, in fact, considerably more extensive and complex than Thornton's and seems to have been approached by the experiencer in a much more inquiring manner. Unlike Thornton, the present experiencer was, at the time of these experiences, not specifically oriented either toward any traditional religious system or toward the framework of Jungian psychology (though he was certainly aware of and somewhat informed by both). Accordingly, while the present material may not offer as neat and satisfying a story as does Thornton's, it compensates by revealing a richer array of features of synchronicity.

In this chapter I present the coincidences in a predominantly descriptive manner. I have three aims in view. First, I wish simply to exhibit the material, in however partial a form, in order to draw attention to the fact that such complex and extended series of synchronicities do indeed occur and on occasion get recorded. Second, I wish to show something of how the experiencer himself responded to and understood his coincidences.[2] Third, I wish to prepare the ground for reporting, in the next chapter, on my attempt at evaluating and interpreting the coincidences.

I begin by giving a brief account of the experiencer, based primarily on what he reveals about himself in his narrative (mainly details about his intellectual and spiritual preoccupations). Then I proceed to a discussion of the coincidences themselves. After a general description of the material—

indicating its quantity, the manner of its occurrence and recording, and a number of its salient features—I offer a condensed retelling of five of the principal (interconnected) themes running through it. This is followed by an account of how the experiencer himself responded to and interpreted these events, emphasizing in particular the ways in which his beliefs and attitudes appear to have been modified by them. Finally, in further illustration of both the material itself and the experiencer's responses to it, I present a more detailed account of one small group of coincidences by which the experiencer himself was particularly impressed.

THE EXPERIENCER

The material under consideration was made available for me to study by James Plaskett and consists almost entirely of his personal experiences.[3] Plaskett was born on March 18, 1960. During the period of my main contact with him (August 1991 to late 1993) he lived either in or within commuting distance of London, which was the principal base for his various occupations as advertising executive, columnist for the *New Statesman*, part owner of two shops, and semiprofessional chess player. Regarding the last of these occupations, he is a world-ranking chess grandmaster and former British Chess Champion (in 1990). Attending chess events has involved him in a considerable amount of traveling both in this country and abroad (mostly in Europe).

I remained in communication with Plaskett by letter and telephone, and had an opportunity to discuss his material with him in some depth when he visited me in Lancaster, England, on March 28, 1992. He struck me all along as being intellectually very sharp and particularly intense and enthusiastic when it comes to examining his coincidence experiences. In July 1993 he completed a questionnaire designed to measure the relative prominence within his personality of introversion and extraversion, and of the four functions of thinking, feeling, intuition, and sensation. The results suggested that he was predominantly introversive, having thinking as his strongest function but with intuition a close second (such that on other occasions intuition could easily take precedence).[4]

The specific areas of Plaskett's interest that emerged during personal contact were essentially the same as those evident from his written material. Of central importance to him appeared to be the question of the scientific status of purported paranormal events.[5] This was one of the major factors informing his conscientious recording of his coincidences.[6] It also led him to take an interest (in spite of initial skepticism) in astrology[7] and to be concerned with the question of whether the results claimed for meditative yoga could in any way be demonstrated to others.[8]

Underlying, or at least related to, the issue of the status of paranormal events was a long-standing preoccupation with "questions of meaning, purpose, philosophy, religion, etc."[9] He also manifested in his written material an interest in problems of moral judgement.[10]

Regarding the paranormal and related anomalies, he is far from being uncritical: as I noted, he was initially skeptical toward the claims of astrology, and he bluntly dismisses "the infamous Bermuda triangle" as "a concept which I personally regard as nonsense."[11] The kind of coincidences that he himself experienced, however, he quickly came to believe were significant, specifically as "an indicator of something glimpsed but yet to be clearly seen or understood."[12] Nevertheless, he cautiously admits that on occasion certain connections he makes "are, perhaps, stretching things a bit";[13] that some of his experiences involve the possibility of cryptomnesia;[14] and that having "encountered a lot of coincidences involving certain themes . . . may have made me on the lookout for them."[15]

At the level of metaphysical speculation, Plaskett states that "I have never been able to believe that the universe is an accident or that human life is meaningless."[16] He considers that "immortality is the pivot of the human condition"[17] and writes that "the concept of a Higher Self was one I had long accepted."[18] He mentions that he developed an early belief in "the superiority of yoga to Religion, for here an act of *investigation* into the questions which are of most interest to human minds was possible."[19]

This interest in questions of meaning and spiritual development was apparently first awakened through a book called *Teach Yourself Yoga* that he found in his family home when he was eleven.[20] By the time of his main coincidence experiences, the range of intellectual and spiritual influences to which he had exposed himself can be assumed to have been fairly broad: "my search for answers," he says, "has been eclectic."[21] He mentions reading Dante's *Divine Comedy* "as part of a programme of classical literature I had compiled to read."[22] Elsewhere in his material he refers to a notebook in which he began listing "all the books I could remember ever reading."[23] A photocopied page from this, which he has occasion to reproduce, lists under the heading "Psychology" some thirty-two titles including *The Primal Scream*; *Lateral Thinking*; *Access to Inner Worlds*; *The Undiscovered Self*; *What Do Women Want?*; *The Inner Eye of Love*; *Man and His Symbols*; *Synchronicity: An Acausal Connecting Principle*; and *New Pathways in Psychology: Maslow and the Post-Freudian Revolution*.[24] Elsewhere again, Plaskett refers to being impressed on reading a book by the transpersonal psychotherapist Roberto Assagioli, and he also mentions having read Arthur C. Clarke's works on paranormal and related subjects and Ian Wilson's *The After Death Experience*.[25] In addition, he must have acquired a fair amount of knowledge from friends and acquaintances with whom he discussed his ideas and experiences. He mentions a friend who could interpret one of his dreams in terms of motifs from Arthurian legend, and other friends among whom was one who was interested in Sufism and another who "spoke enthusiastically of the philosophies of e.g. Krishnamurti and The Bhagwan."[26]

Aside from his synchronicities, Plaskett mentions having had some "alterations in my consciousness," specifically "a handful of experiences, always whilst sleeping, of glorious compassion and sensitivity." He adds, however, that he appreciates that "I have no right to expect accounts of such experiences to be accepted by others, because there is zero evidence for them.[27] He had set himself early on the goal of achieving *samadhi* (the final consummation of the act of union between personality and Soul) but, he says, "after so many years I felt that, sadly, I was going to have to reconcile myself to never achieving my target." Nevertheless, his altered-state experiences "clinched for me that the full potential range of human consciousness is way beyond the estimations of mainstream psychology and also supported the idea that attempts to know more about the Soul may bear fruit."[28]

The overall picture that emerges from these scattered biographical details is of someone who lives exposed to a high degree of complexity and diversity, both in the circumstances of his outward life and inwardly in terms of his engagement with cultural and spiritual ideas. He has a lively, sharp, and interested mind that seems to gravitate toward areas of inquiry (notably parapsychology and spirituality) that, as he envisions them, could potentially challenge accepted standards of scientific knowledge. In regard to these areas he is, in general, open and exploratory, retaining a healthy edge of criticism while at the same time candidly admitting his own provisional beliefs.

It might be argued that if there is a sort of mind that could be particularly apt to discern meaningful connections between events where others might not perceive them, Plaskett has such a mind: richly informed, intuitive, hungry for meaning in the first place, and with a natural chess player's ability to pursue complex and subtle avenues of thought. This raises the question of whether the connections so perceived genuinely are anomalous, as the theory of synchronicity would have it, or can be adequately accounted for in existing causal terms, for instance, as the projections of an oversubtle mind or the perceptions of a normally constituted but usually unnoticed level of interconnection in reality. As I have noted, this question is one of the preoccupations, sometimes explicit and sometimes implicit, of the experiencer himself.

THE MATERIAL
Recording and Presentation by the Experiencer

Plaskett reports that in the early months of 1988 he became the focus of an extraordinary number of complexly and intricately interrelating series and clusters of coincidences. Being in the habit of recording interesting events that happened to him, he immediately began to record these coincidences and by August 8, 1991 (when I received my first communication from him), his total collection of incidents ran into the hundreds. However, I shall base my comments in this study on a group of some ninety or so of these (most of them among the earliest) that Plaskett has ordered into a form of loose narrative.[29]

Plaskett's coincidence material, as initially made available to me, consisted of a "Main Text" (of 82 mostly typed pages) plus four "Appendices" (of 38 mostly typed pages). It included photocopies of photographs and of extracts from books, newspapers, personal journals, and the like, which illustrate the coincidences he describes. Later, in July 1992, Plaskett sent me a revised presentation of his narrative. The material was somewhat better organized but substantially the same. The principal differences were that a few minor incidents from the initial version had been excised and a considerable amount of reflection and speculation on matters arising from his experiences, as well as accounts of a number of pertinent recent coincidences, had been added (some of it in a fifth appendix). The material now consisted of 133 pages (87 pages of narrative and 46 pages of appendices).

My comments in this chapter will be based on Plaskett's revised presentation. A factor that therefore needs to be borne in mind is that by the time he prepared this and sent it to me, he and I had already communicated several times by letter and telephone and we had met and discussed his material in some depth when he visited Lancaster on March 28, 1992. Some of the new emphases that appear in the revised presentation may well have been influenced by his exposure to my specific interests in synchronicity. At one point, for example, he quotes (with acknowledgment) the results of some of my research into his earlier presentation,[30] and there is also a notable increase of references to themes such as meaning and spirituality and the problem of observation and participation, with which I was particularly concerned. I do not mean to suggest that these were not also genuine preoccupations of Plaskett's, but it may be that he decided to accentuate these implications of his material partly because he knew them to be of interest to his new audience.

However, for the purposes of the present study, this should not cause any problems. My primary aim is to explore spiritually oriented understandings of and responses to synchronicity, which both are possible and have in fact been found satisfying to some experiencers or to others who have considered their reports. I do not suppose that any such understanding or response does or should arise in total isolation from the more general climate of beliefs and ideas within which a person moves. If Plaskett's revised presentation of his material has in fact been influenced by his conversations with me, this was probably no more so than his initial presentation was influenced by the real or hypothetical audience (of parapsychologists or friends of varying degrees of intelligence and skepticism) for which that version was written.[31] Furthermore, any influence I may have had presumably affected things in ways that accorded with what he believed and was happy to express anyway. Such, at any rate, is the implication of the words with which he closes his revised presentation: "I [now] knew," he says, "that I had told the story as well as I could."[32]

Quantity and Thematic Recurrence

The most obvious feature of Plaskett's coincidences is their sheer quantity. Shortly I shall be retelling some forty or so of the events involved in his narrative. It seemed necessary to relate this many incidents in order to create an adequate impression of the bulk and momentum of the collection as a whole, as well as to provide sufficient material for illustrating the various points I wish to make in the next chapter. In fact, these forty plus incidents represent less than half of the entire narrative; and the narrative itself represents only a small portion (perhaps less than one-sixth) of Plaskett's entire coincidence material at the time of my working on it.

A second outstanding characteristic of the material to which attention needs to be drawn here is that the contents of the coincidences seem to express certain recurrent themes. This was noted by Plaskett himself and given as the reason for his chosen mode of presentation: "because particular *THEMES* seemed to be recurring," he wrote in a letter to me accompanying the first version of his material, "and because the events did not seem unconnected I chose a Narrative rather than a simple listing."[33] He proposed the following list of "recurrent motifs" for me to note in particular:

1. *STAR.*
2. *UNICORN.*
3. *GIANT OCTOPUS.*
4. *(RED) EAGLE.*

5. *PERCEVAL, AND THE MYTHOLOGY OF THE HOLY GRAIL.*
6. *COMING UP FOR AIR.*
7. *DANTE'S PARADISO.*
8. *SYMBOLS OF THE SOUL i.e. (STAR, UNICORN), FATHER (+ Son Co-operation), UPRIGHT TRIANGLE, SWAN.*
9. *CHESS.*
10. *METEORITES.*[34]

When I came to analyze the material myself, I found that this division into motifs reflected Plaskett's evaluation of their symbolic significance at least as much as the frequency of their occurrence (the motif of the unicorn, for example, to which Plaskett seems to attach a great deal of importance, occurs only twice). Also, Plaskett's list overlooks certain motifs that are significant both in terms of their quantity and in terms of their symbolism (for instance, the motif of eyes and vision). It seemed to me more helpful to identify the following five principal themes (each incorporating several subthemes); they are listed here in the order of appearance of their first main clustering:[35]

1. Celestial phenomena (including moon, stars, meteorites).
2. Arthurian legend (including Parsifal, the Holy Grail, the Round Table).
3. Dante's *Paradiso* (including principally the eagle but also Beatrice, threefoldness, the rose).
4. Sea monsters (including octopus, Leviathan, coming up for air).
5. Eyes and vision (including blindness, one-eyedness, the third eye, new ways of looking).

Additional, less frequently recurring, themes that can be identified include the unicorn (two incidents), identity (six incidents), chess (five incidents), the union of opposites (six incidents), and the date December 22 (four incidents).

FIVE THEMES

Over the following pages I present a condensed retelling of a substantial selection of incidents relating to the five principal themes mentioned above. In doing so I have partly disentangled each of the thematic strands from the more complexly interwoven texture of Plaskett's narrative. The selection is intended to be fairly representative of the narrative as a whole and includes less conspicuously impressive incidents as well as the more conspicuously impressive ones. In fact, disembedding some of the incidents from their full contexts has sometimes resulted in them losing a certain amount of their impact; but this seemed an unavoidable loss, hopefully affordable and at any rate compensated for by some gain in clarity. As with the Thornton material in the previous chapter, I have tagged the individual coincidences with numbers in order to help clarify their parameters and to facilitate subsequent reference to them.

Celestial Phenomena

There are in all about twenty coincidences referring to this general theme, which includes the subthemes of moon, stars, and meteorites.[36] Nine of these incidents are related below, three in the present section (1–3) and a further six in subsequent sections (10, 11, 18, 19, 28, 29). The first main cluster occurred in late-January/early-February 1988.

(1) Plaskett had learned by chance on December 22, 1984, that one of the craters on *the far side of the moon* is called "Plaskett's Crater."[37] Now, in January 1988, he discovered that the first map of *the far side of the moon* was published on the day he was born (March 18, 1960).[38] He was naturally intrigued that a crater should have been given the same name as him on the very day on which he was born.[39]

(2) In early February 1988, Plaskett discovered serendipitously (while searching for information on Plaskett's Crater) that in the constellation *Monoceros* there is an astronomically significant binary star called Plaskett's Star. This became particularly meaningful for him when, a few days later, he was looking in an encyclopedia for references to Percival and the Arthurian legends (the content of some of his other recent coincidences) and chanced to notice on the inside cover of one volume of the encyclopedia a star map and in particular the constellation *Monoceros*, together with its translation, "*The Unicorn*," which until then he did not know. It happened that only a few days earlier he had given to a short sequence of coincidences he had written up the title "*The Unicorn* Spoor."[40] Plaskett had used the image of the unicorn to convey the idea that just as an animal that has never been seen (for example, a unicorn) could be inferred to exist if it left behind adequate traces (its "spoor" in the form of tracks and droppings), so the existence of "something" can be inferred from the "traces" that are what we experience as coincidences.[41]

(3) The issue raised here of proving the reality of phenomena that are not readily amenable to scientific testing was further awakened for Plaskett by another of his coincidences involving celestial phenomena. Craters, such as those on the moon, result from the impact of large mete-

orites. The fall of meteorites is an event that, like alleged miracles and paranormal phenomena (including coincidences), neither is susceptible of being produced to order in a scientifically controlled environment nor, historically, has it been so common in its spontaneous occurrence as always to have been considered indisputably real. Nonetheless, showers of meteorites were eventually observed to occur that were sufficient to persuade the scientific community of the reality of the phenomenon. On this point Plaskett reproduces the account of Arthur C. Clarke:

> Towards the end of the eighteenth century a commission of the French Academy of Science formally endorsed the Jeffersonian viewpoint that stones couldn't possibly fall from the sky. Unfortunately for the distinguished members of the commission, the matter was settled rather decisively when many *thousand* descended at the town of L'Aigle, not far from Paris itself.[42]

Plaskett considers that it may be possible for a similar thing to happen in the case of coincidences (that is, the decisive occurrence of an overwhelming quantity of well-observed incidents). He thus came to make *a symbolic association between meteorites and coincidences*. He was therefore intrigued to notice the following when, in May 1988, he read one of Arthur Koestler's books on coincidence:

> In 1970, while I was working on the biography of Paul Kammerer, the Austrian biologist who wrote *The Law of the Series*, dealing with coincidences, *a whole series of coincidences seemed to descend on me—like a meteor shower on a summer night.*[43]

He came upon the simile again (he does not specify exactly when) in some writing of Laurens van der Post who describes how it can happen under certain circumstances that *"coincidences crowd in on one like the salvoes of stars shooting out of the night* in Southern Africa towards the close of the year."[44]

Arthurian Legend

Altogether, about twenty-one coincidences can be seen to refer to this general theme, whose subthemes include Parsifal, the Holy Grail, and the Round Table. Eight of these incidents are recounted here, seven in the present section (4–10) and one in a later section (29). The first main cluster was on February, 14–15, 1988.

(4) On November 5, 1986, Plaskett had a dream that involved the actor *Lance Percival*. A friend suggested that this might be directing his attention to Arthurian legend, since two of the prominent Arthurian knights are *Lance*lot and *Percival* (or *Parsifal*). Plaskett knew next to nothing about these legends, though he was now intrigued to find out. However, he did not get around to it until early in 1988 (over fourteen months later) when his curiosity was reawakened by media references to a production of Wagner's opera *Parsifal*. An article on the opera in *The Sunday Times* for January 31, 1988, included a picture of the singer who was performing the part of *Parsifal*. Plaskett noted *a striking resemblance between the singer as he appeared in the photograph and himself*.[45]

(5) A fortnight later, on February 14, Plaskett happened to notice a brief appearance of the actor *Lance Percival* on the television in a clip from a 1962 satire program. He remarks that this was almost certainly the first time the actor had appeared in his life since his dream of 1986.[46]

(6) These two coincidences were enough to move Plaskett to begin looking up references to Arthurian legend in the encyclopedias and other works that he had at his disposal. While doing so, whole clusters of Arthurian coincidences occurred.[47] For example, he had noticed on the television program *Antiques Roadshow* (broadcast earlier on February 14) that one of the items evaluated was a *round table*. The following morning he was, as he says, "pondering intently on whether this antique had a legitimate right to be included as part of the Arthurian confluence." Over the radio, no more than three seconds later, came mention of a proposed "*round table* meeting" of international politicians.[48]

(7) Shortly after this, the same morning, he saw on a television news program that the composer of the musical *Camelot* had just died.[49]

(8) The following day he went to his local library to check in *The Radio Times* for the name of the presenter of the radio program that had mentioned the phrase "round table meeting." Turning through the pages he happened to see on the Film Guide page that at 3:00 P.M. on Sunday, February 14 (that is, the same day as he had seen both the antique round table and the actor Lance Percival), BBC 1 had shown the film *Knights of the Round Table*.[50]

(9) On the way into the library he had been thinking of his friend Ray *Ferrer* whom he had once persuaded to sponsor financially another man called *Baker*. The actor playing King Arthur in the film was Mel *Ferrer*, while his treacherous nephew Mordred was played by Stanley *Baker*.[51]

(10) In pursuing associations to the Arthurian legend, Plaskett inevitably came across references to the Holy Grail. The grail is, in perhaps the commonest version of the legend, the dish that was used by Jesus at the Last Supper and in which later the blood dripping from his wounds

on the cross was caught by Joseph of Arimathea. The latter brought this sacred dish to England where, having mysteriously disappeared, it later came to be quested after by the knights of King Arthur's court as a source of great spiritual renewal. Plaskett was particularly interested in the derivation of the word "grail" as he found it in the encyclopaedia he consulted on February 14–15, 1988: "The word may be derived through old French from the Latin *crater* ("bowl")."[52] Thus, through the word "*crater*," two major clusters of coincidences that had begun happening to him more or less simultaneously—those to do with celestial phenomena and those to do with Arthurian legend—proved to be intimately linked.

Dante's *Paradiso*

Referring to this general theme (which includes the subthemes of the eagle, Beatrice, threefoldness, and the rose) there are again about twenty coincidences in all. Twelve are related here, nine in the present section (11–19) and three in the next section (20, 29, 30). The first main cluster was on March 6–9, 1988.

(11) On February 15, 1988, just when the Arthurian legend and celestial phenomena coincidence clusters were at their densest, Plaskett borrowed from his local library two books he had long been meaning to read: Dante's *Purgatory* and *Paradise*. *Purgatory* he had already previously read in part, so he soon finished it and moved on to *Paradise*. He had not been aware of the exact structure of this book and was surprised to find that Dante's ascent through Paradise, under the guidance of his beloved Beatrice, took the form of a cosmic journey first to the *moon*, then through the planets to the fixed *stars*, and finally to the Empyrean and the Celestial *Rose*. Plaskett could not help noticing that his own coincidental "journey" had also begun with the *moon* (Plaskett's Crater) and progressed on to the *stars* (Plaskett's Star in the constellation Monoceros). Interestingly, Plaskett's journey also ended up within a rose of sorts, for Monoceros and Plaskett's Star exist within the region of the *Rosette* Nebula.[53]

(12) As with the two previous themes, whole clusters of minor coincidences began to occur that seemed to reinforce the relevance of the Dante theme. The majority occurred while Plaskett was reading Cantos XVIII and XIX. In these cantos Dante is in Jupiter, the Heaven of the Just, and observes the souls of *the Just* who form themselves as lights into a giant *ruby eagle*. It was on March 7 when Plaskett first read about this connection between justice and the eagle. Later that night, in an episode of *Kojak* on television, he watched how a *coin thief* was trying to make vast sums of money selling stolen coins, which he referred to as "*Eagles*,"

but was eventually caught and *brought to justice*. One of the groups of sinners the souls of the Just denounce in Canto XIX (while in their form as an eagle) is *coin counterfeiters*.[54]

(13) While reading this and later watching the television program, Plaskett happened to be wearing a sweater he had been given that had on it the outline, as he describes it, "of a bird of prey, it could be a hawk, a falcon or *an Eagle, etched in red* over the left breast."[55]

(14) The image of the red eagle already had well-established associations for Plaskett, since it was the emblem of the main school he had attended.[56] He narrates further that he had been *unjustly* forced to be withdrawn from this school just a few months before his "A" levels. The principal reason for this was his alleged lethargy. What the school failed either to know or to take into consideration was that this lethargy was a symptom of incipient diabetes. Years later (in December 1984) Plaskett revisited the school and vented his accumulated rage at the headmaster. The best the latter could come up with was: "Well thank goodness you've got that off your chest," to which Plaskett had bellowed back: "It's not a question of getting something off my chest! It's a question of *justice!*"[57]

(15) Plaskett stayed up all night on March 7–8, 1988, as he says "reading and re-reading all the coincidences which Cantos 18–20 contained for me." In the morning, while standing talking to his mother in the hallway, he noticed a letter addressed to his aged grandmother, who had recently been moved to a new rest home: the new place (Plaskett now learned for the first time) was called *Eagle Home* in a town called *Eagle*.[58]

(16) Strangely, Plaskett did not know what Christian and second names were indicated by his grandmother's initials "B. C." Under the impact of the preceding coincidences, however, "a suspicion," he says, "began to form in my mind." When his father came downstairs he asked him. The answer: *Beatrice* Constance.[59]

(17) In the *Divina Commedia* and *Vita Nuova*, Dante's Beatrice is associated with the number *nine*, to which special symbolic significance is attached as the one number whose only root is three, that is, the Holy Trinity. In the light of this, Plaskett found it "noteworthy" that the day of his coincidence now, March 8, 1988, was his grandmother Beatrice's *90th* birthday.[60]

18) Plaskett noted some suggestive connections between the Dante/eagle motif and the motifs of meteorites and the moon. On May 15, 1988, while reflecting on some of his coincidence experiences and their possible significance, he suddenly had a realization. This was, in Plaskett's own words, that

the meteorite shower which forced the French Academy of Science to concede that there were such things as meteorites, a shower which proved that the authoritative statement of U.S. President Thomas Jefferson that "There are no rocks in the sky, therefore rocks cannot fall from the sky" was false, landed on a town called L'AIGLE—THE EAGLE![61]

(19) This in turn stimulated what he judged to be another possibly relevant association. It is widely considered that one of the technologically as well as symbolically most significant achievements of mankind during the twentieth century was the first manned landing on the moon. The significance of the moon within Plaskett's coincidences has already been illustrated. Now, following on from his previous realization, he recalled the first words spoken after the Apollo 11 module touched down on the moon: "*The Eagle* has landed."[62]

Sea Monsters

Altogether, about fourteen coincidences refer to this theme, which includes the subthemes octopus, Leviathan, and coming up for air. Eleven are recounted here, ten in the present section (20–28, 30) and one in the next section (35). The first main cluster was on March 9, 1988.

(20) On March 9, 1988, the day after his main cluster of Dante coincidences, a note arrived from the public library informing Plaskett that a book he had ordered (five months previously) had now arrived. This was Arthur C. Clarke's *Chronicles of the Strange and Mysterious*. The chapter he turned to and read first was chapter 5, "Of Monsters and Mermaids." In this the story is told of a shrimp and crab fisherman operating from Bermuda whose boat (a reasonably large vessel at fifty feet) was pulled along by some creature tugging on one of his laid traps. Chromascope sonar showed the creature to be pyramid-shaped and all of fifty feet high. This as well as other indications suggested that the creature was a *giant octopus*.[63] There were several curious things about this for Plaskett. In the first place, the man's boat was called *Trilogy*. Obviously such a name has an abundance of significance in relation to Dante, whose preoccupation with the numbers three and nine was noted above (17) and the last book of whose *three*-part poem Plaskett was also reading at this time. Furthermore, the specific section he was reading by now—Cantos XXIV to XXVI—also contains the *third of three* discourses (*logoi*) on faith, hope, and love.[64]

(21) Then there was an odd incident that had occurred two days previously. Plaskett took down from his bookshelf what he thought was a

volume of sixty-five short stories by W. Somerset Maugham in order to look up a quote about how there must be an underlying purpose behind the evolution of such an unlikely thing as human life. By mistake he took down instead a similarly jacketed volume containing six novels by George Orwell. One of these books was copublished by Heinemann/*Octopus*, while the other was copublished by Secker and Warberg/*Octopus*. Both books were *very large*.[65]

(22) The Orwell book that he had mistakenly taken down happened to fall open in the middle of the novel *A Clergyman's Daughter*. This description, "*a clergyman's daughter*," made Plaskett think of an acquaintance of his to whom it applied, and since there happened to be some *parallels between events in the novel and what he knew of her situation*, he tentatively mentioned this to her when he next saw her during a chess tournament between March 28 and April 6, 1988. The novel in the Orwell book immediately following *A Clergyman's Daughter* was *Coming Up for Air*. The *parallels with his friend's situation* extended to this novel also, and Plaskett mentioned this too when he saw her. She was shocked, as she had recently chanced to come upon a copy of this latter novel when she was going through her old things in the attic on a visit to her mother's. She had actually reread the novel and *herself had registered some of the parallels*.[66]

(23) The period of her visit to her mother's had been highly emotive for her for various reasons, and she had even been moved to write down a dream—something she normally never did. The dream (dated February 14, 1988—the date, incidentally, of several of Plaskett's Arthurian legend coincidences) involved *synchronized swimming*. In view of the other coincidences, she asked had Plaskett recorded any dream on that day. He consulted his dream diary and discovered that he too had dreamed about *synchronized swimming*. On checking, Plaskett could find no television program broadcast the evening before the dreams that might account for the appearance of the same image in both their dreams.[67]

(24) Plaskett's dream account also mentioned some birds, *great-crested grebes*. It turned out that during her visit to her mother's his friend had bought a card on the front of which were some birds—*great-crested grebes*.[68]

(25) Two days after reading about the giant octopus (one *sea monster*) Plaskett received a letter from Greenpeace showing on the front a large whale (another *sea monster*). The whale was shown *coming up for air*.[69]

(26) Furthering the monster association, the whale was referred to in the letter as "*Leviathan*." Then references to *Leviathan* began to appear in the press (for example, *The Sunday Times*, February 14, 1988) as it was approaching the 400th anniversary, on April 5, of the birth of the philosopher Thomas Hobbes, author of *Leviathan*.[70]

(27) In the Greenpeace letter that Plaskett received, it was recommended to boycott all *Icelandic fish*. On April 5, 1988, about three weeks after reading this and on the actual anniversary of Hobbes's birth, while Plaskett was participating at the chess tournament referred to previously, one of the other competitors offered him some of the snack he was eating: a packet of dried *Icelandic fish*.[71]

(28) These coincidences surrounding the theme of *sea monsters* and the attendant theme of *coming up for air* led Plaskett to experiment in making a prediction (or "extrapolation" as he preferred to call it) to the effect that "*in the next few days* there would be *a major news story* about *something coming out of the sea . . . something very large, very strange and which had been submerged for a very long time*." He predicted this to four reliable and basically skeptical friends. Two days later, on March 15, 1988, *The Times* and *The Guardian* ran the story about how maritime archaeologists from Oxford University had discovered a huge cargo of ancient Greek pottery in a wreck off the northern coast of Sicily. The find was heralded as "one of the most important this century." Plaskett's prediction thus turned out to be accurate on the following six points: it was a *major news story*, it happened *within the next few days* of the prediction being made, it was *something very large* and *very strange*, *it came from the sea*, and it had been *submerged there for a very long time*. Interestingly, the event tied in with Plaskett's coincidences even more intimately than he managed to predict: the wreck was found in the *crater* of a live volcano (this largely accounting for the treasure's excellent state of preservation).[72]

(29) The next coincidence draws together several of the themes that have been mentioned so far. In early November 1988, Plaskett borrowed from the public library Roberto Assagioli's book *Psychosynthesis*. As Plaskett explains, "'Psychosynthesis' was a term coined by Assagioli to describe a system of psychology and psychoanalysis which incorporated the idea of 'a spiritual reality.'"[73] Plaskett found that Assagioli gives the following "Exercises for Spiritual Psychosynthesis":

> We outline here three exercises—each of which combines various techniques—that have been found in practice to be particularly effective, both in therapy and in self-realisation. These are:
> 1. Exercise on the *legend of the Grail*
> 2. Exercise based on *Dante's* Divine Comedy
> 3. Exercise of the blossoming of the *rose*.[74]

(30) The parallels here between Assagioli's devised exercises and Plaskett's spontaneous experiences are striking enough in themselves, but

what truly astounded Plaskett was a particular case history mentioned by Assagioli in the course of his discussion of Dante. Another psychotherapist, using a technique analogous to Assagioli's Dante exercise, that is, getting the patient to visualize first of all making a descent (as into the Inferno) and then making an ascent (as through Purgatory and Paradise), reported that one patient, during the descent stage of the exercise, "encountered an *octopus* in the depths of the ocean which threatened to engulf him."[75]

Eyes and Vision

This general theme has in all about twelve coincidences referring to it and includes the subthemes of blindness, one-eyedness, and the idea of a new way of looking (including the concept of the "third eye"). Ten incidents are related here (31–34, 36–41). The first main cluster was in early May 1988.

(31) Plaskett records that on March 7, 1988, he found himself "chuckling over the memory of a story" he had told to some chess-playing acquaintances in December 1984. The story was *an episode from the American television sit-com "Taxi"* in which the taxi driver unsuccessfully tries to overcharge a *blind* passenger. At 4 A.M. in the morning of March 8—the night Plaskett stayed up rereading Cantos XVIII to XX of Dante's *Paradiso*—he saw that *"Taxi" was on the television* and quickly realized that he was watching *the very episode he had thought about the previous day.*[76]

(32) A week later, on March 15, 1988, he experienced an unusual optical illusion while walking alongside the river that runs through the center of Bedford, the Great Ouse: he seemed to see a single cloud in the sky in the form of a sharply defined upright *triangle*. It seemed so strange that he called two students over to witness it as well and they were equally astounded. When Plaskett walked on further, however, it soon became apparent that the "cloud" was in fact the dark triangular top of a white building that was otherwise indistinguishable against the cloudless sky. About a month later he returned with a camera to try to capture the effect on film. He did this successfully and the photographs are reproduced among his material. What his photographs also captured, however, quite unintentionally, was the front of the adjacent Swan Hotel: the pedimented top of this building, with a single half-circular window at its center, bore a remarkable resemblance, he later discovered, to certain representations of the *"third eye."*[77]

(33) The main cluster of eye incidents occurred in May 1988. On May 2, Plaskett was watching on television a live discussion about people who had been on *blind dates*. He thought how his brother had met his wife on a blind date "but how the idea of such an introduction did not

appeal" *to him personally*. Two days later an issue of a lighthearted chess magazine called *Kingpin* arrived in the post with a humorous article describing how the magazine's charlady was "inconsolable since *Jim Plaskett* turned down her offer of a *blind date*." Plaskett adds promptly after quoting this that "in fact no such offer had been made (although I would have turned her down)."[78]

(34) Another incident occurred on May 8. Plaskett was having breakfast in a hotel in the village of Bendern in Switzerland (he was in the country for a chess event) and was annoyed by the large number of flies around. As he swatted at one, he recalled an unpleasant experience in 1985 when he had similarly swatted at a fly and had *knocked one of its eyes out* blood from it staining a page in one of his notebooks.[79] With him in the hotel now he had Laurens van der Post's book *The Heart of the Hunter*. Later that morning he continued reading from it and on page 182 came upon a story of how a group of baboons "fall upon young Mantis and kill him. They batter his head so that *the eye falls out*, and they can pick up the eye and play ball with it."[80]

(35) Interestingly, when Plaskett consulted his old diary to look up the incident of swatting the fly's eye out, he discovered that on the same day the following coincidence had occurred: he had been thinking of Orwell's novel *Coming Up For Air*, then three hours later read in another of Laurens van der Post's books, *Yet Being Someone Other*, the following words: "only when that answer ended the primordial dialogue did the men gasp, as if *coming up for air* out of an unfathomed deep themselves, and start to talk again."[81]

(36) In the afternoon of the same day, May 8, 1988, Plaskett's opponent in the day's chess game, a diabetic like himself, revealed when they were talking afterward that "in 1985 he had gone totally *blind in his right eye* through diabetic complications, and he retained only 80% vision in the other one. There was," Plaskett adds, "nothing in his demeanour to suggest that he was *partially sighted*."[82]

(37) The following day *the left lens from Plaskett's glasses fell out*.[83]

(38) On his way to Switzerland Plaskett had bought (for the first time ever, he says) a copy of *The New Scientist*. He was attracted by the cover article on near-death experiences. The issue of the magazine impressed him sufficiently to make him think of taking out a *subscription*, but he considered it *a bit pricey*. When he arrived home from Switzerland, however, he found among his mail an unsolicited but personally addressed invitation "to take an introductory offer of *a discount subscription* to *The New Scientist*."[84] He recalled that during a conversation with a friend in 1987 he had said he thought "the phenomenon of coincidence meant that what we really needed was '*a new science*' to deal with it."[85]

(39) Also shortly after his return from Switzerland, on May 16, 1988, the following occurred. Plaskett turned to *The Observer Magazine* of the previous day to look at Michael Stean's chess column on the games page. However, on this occasion the chess column was not there; it had been replaced by another column that Plaskett had never seen before, called "Collecting." The column (which Plaskett reproduces) shows a photograph of a jewel followed by its description beginning: "Most arresting of all miniatures is *the single eye*, like this *right eye* of a lady set in a gold brooch with pearls and rubies."[86]

(40) A couple of years later, in May 1990, Plaskett experienced a further coincidence involving *the theme of eyes in relation to a book by Laurens van der Post*. He was reading page 96 of *The Dark* Eye *in Africa* in which the author considers, in Plaskett's words, "the problems [particularly in regard to *colonialism*] which ensue from European man's tendency to concentrate on the merely visible, physical aspect of reality whilst tending to neglect the unseen but equally vital spiritual dimension of the universe."[87] Van der Post referred to William Blake's appreciation of this problem and to the fact that the poet had actually used the phrase "the *one-eyed vision* of science." Plaskett's television was on in the background showing a program about the Cannes Film Festival. He reports that Barry Norman concluded a review of Ken Loach's film *Hidden Agenda*, which is about the behavior of the security forces in Northern Ireland, with the words: "At least it brings passion and commitment, albeit *one-eyed*, to a serious problem."[88] Plaskett adds that "many people also view the situation in Northern Ireland as a *colonial* one."[89]

(41) One final incident can be mentioned. On March 28, 1992, Plaskett visited me in Lancaster in order to discuss his coincidence material. When he arrived he realized that he had been in Lancaster before but could not remember when or why. Then it occurred to him: he had been traveling from Barrow-in-Furness to Bedford and had had to change coaches at Lancaster bus station. In the short time he was there he had done one notable thing: "I had been suffering severe problems with my right *contact lens* and my *eye* was smarting so badly that I *removed the lens* and purchased an *eyepatch* in the center of Lancaster and immediately donned it."[90]

RESPONSE AND INTERPRETATIONS OF THE EXPERIENCER

In writing up his coincidences, Plaskett's aim appears to have been primarily just to record "as simply and clearly as possible" the events that happened to him.[91] He makes no comparable attempt to provide a full account either of their effect on him or of his interpretation of what they might mean. Nevertheless, when occasion arises, he does make a number of informative comments, and he also offers at various points, if not exactly a systematic interpretation, then at least some fairly extensive reflections. I shall now present some of these, beginning with the emotional and practical effects and then moving on to the ideas that the experiences seem directly or indirectly to have stimulated.

Numinosity and Practical Effects

First, we can notice a certain general *emotional impact*, ranging in strength from the mildly intriguing to the powerfully numinous. At the outset of his account he characterizes his coincidences as a whole in fairly low-key fashion simply as "events which struck me as improbable and noteworthy."[92] Later on he describes one particular coincidence (not included in my selection) as "to my mind a very powerful one."[93] Again, he narrates that while reading chapter 5 of Arthur C. Clarke's *Chronicles of the Strange and Mysterious*—a book that he reckoned contained "most interesting material"—certain coincidences occurred (for example, 20 and 21) that "were even more intriguing than the content of the chapter itself."[94] Then, speaking toward the end of his account, he states that for him his experiences as a whole "have mysteriously combined to form a numinous and enduring source of wonder."[95]

Frequently, these kinds of numinous effects had *practical consequences*. Often this took the form of stimulating Plaskett to pursue a certain line of research. For instance, following the coincidence involving the actor Lance Percival (5) he was prompted to look up all the information immediately available to him on Arthurian legend.[96] Again, he "was so struck by the cluster of eagle-related coincidences [which happened in relation to his reading of Dante's *Paradiso* (for example, 12–14)] that I read and re-read through Cantos 18–20 throughout the night."[97]

Sometimes the practical effect took the form of *trying to get his coincidences witnessed and evaluated by others*. When one coincidence (again not related above) involving a magazine article occurred at a chess event, he "grabbed the attention of a passing player" and emphasized to him and the person reading the magazine "that they should not forget where precisely this magazine had been open as I went by. . . . I fear they were each rather bemused! But I felt I had to bring witnesses in."[98] More generally, Plaskett says he was "so struck by the clusterings involving The Unicorn, The Grail, The Eagle, The Giant Octopus, etc. that I felt I had to show it to some 'authority' on such matters to see what their reaction would be."[99]

The Nature of Coincidence

A more conspicuous effect of the coincidences was to reveal to Plaskett, or stimulate him to further reflection on, certain ideas or insights. Many of these concern *the nature and significance of coincidences* themselves. One incident, for example (involving the tracks and droppings of unknown animals), confirmed for him his understanding of coincidence as "an indicator of something glimpsed but yet to be clearly seen or understood."[100] Quite apart from this uncertainty regarding the significance of the phenomenon as a whole, he came to realize that, with some coincidences, even the meanings of their individual contents often "are not so immediately or clearly apparent and require a little more thought."[101] He also came to appreciate that some "were not isolated incidents but revealed a surprising interconnectedness."[102] Regarding the status of coincidence in terms of its possible scientific or rational acceptability, he refers approvingly to Koestler's point that "the stock argument against accepting meaningful coincidence in principle, that it breaks the laws of causality, no longer holds because . . . in modern physics the principle of causality is no longer [universally] applicable" (Plaskett's words).[103] More significantly still, Plaskett reflects on the ability of coincidence to transmute the seemingly meaningless in life into something truly meaningful (see especially the discussion of the Hartston Case below).[104]

Related to this transmutative power of coincidence is the fact that coincidences seem to occur more frequently in response to or in cooperation with intentionality on the part of the experiencer—a phenomenon that Plaskett several times refers to as *the "triggering" effect*. In his own words: "so many of the coincidences . . . happened when I was investigating or pondering a related matter";[105] "there was the sense of the act of investigation 'triggering' the coincidence";[106] "an act of enquiry into meaning (however casually undertaken) leads to a coincidence";[107] "I had the strong sense that my own acts of investigation were having a 'triggering' effect upon the coincidences."[108] In further comment on this phenomenon, he quotes with approval some words of Laurens van der Post:

> I have noticed that when one renounces an established order and the protection of prescribed patterns of behaviour and, out of a longing for new meaning, commits oneself to an uncertain future, like a fish to the sea, that [*sic* in Plaskett] coincidences crowd fast in on one like the salvoes of stars shooting out of the night in Southern Africa towards the close of the year.[109]

This Plaskett relates to his own experience in regard to his coincidences. In explanation for an act he describes of having wrenched himself free from a set of personally stifling circumstances, he says: "I only knew that I had to strike out on my own if my inquiries into meaning and purpose were to progress," adding: "So I did . . . and soon after many coincidences descended upon me."[110]

Finally, Plaskett expresses the belief that coincidences can also serve to communicate to their experiencer not just general ideas but very specific messages: "But when," he says, after the very last incident related in his narrative, "my hunch that there was truth in the ostensibly paradoxical assertion that 'The Journey Is The Goal' was confirmed through a coincidence that could not have been more perfectly timed, then I knew that I had told the story as well as I could."[111]

Meaning and Symbols

Plaskett was also stimulated by his experiences to reflect on *the nature of meaning*. We have noted his belief that an inquiry into meaning can generate coincidences, and also that within the coincidences themselves there exist levels of meaning beyond the mere fact of their improbability (see, further, the Hartston Case below).[112] In fact, it seems that the improbability could actually stimulate inquiries into meaning: "The improbability of this," he remarks, after one coincidence (30) that linked two of his main thematic clusters, "struck me so forcibly that I began to take the idea of the *meaning* underlying symbols even more seriously."[113] Further than this, certain meaningful coincidences centering on the seasonal turning point of the winter solstice led him to speculate that there might be "something profoundly Seasonal" about meaning: "Was it really so preposterous," he reports himself as musing, "to propose the Taoist concept that the Universe might contain other seasons; seasons of meaning?"[114] He does not elaborate too much on what this might entail, but it is clearly a further expression of his deep inability "to believe that the universe is an accident or that human life is meaningless."[115]

Plaskett's coincidence experiences alerted him in particular to *the meaning of symbols*: as he says, their conspicuously symbolic content "increased the attention I was giving to the significance of SYMBOLS."[116] An eleven-page appendix to his narrative reproduces extensive extracts from various writings either showing symbolism in action (for example, in the spiritually oriented psychotherapeutic context of psychosynthesis), or discussing the nature of symbolism generally, or, again, offering meanings of specific symbols.[117] One thought occurring to him was that "in the light of such coincidences it seemed reasonable to postulate that some symbols have a power and significance wholly independent of the human mind."[118]

The Nature of Reality

Also emerging out of Plaskett's response to his coincidence experiences were certain broader speculations concerning *the nature of reality or the universe*. He says he has "always thought that the universe is too organised to be just an accident," and although he claims to "subscribe to no faith," his coincidences have strengthened this belief:

> I found it very difficult to dismiss e.g. the coincidences with The Eagle, The Giant Octopus, or The Grail as just chance and hence I was naturally drawn towards theological speculations (for how much stronger do arguments for a Deity, stemming from "Good Design", become when such improbable clusters of coincidences are taken into consideration!?)[119]

He admits that "'the problem of pain' troubled me greatly," but relates how he found that reflections arising from one of his coincidences led him to a more "nonjudgmental attitude" in regard to this problem.[120] Elsewhere he expresses his sense of the importance of the qualitative aspect of reality in addition to its quantitative aspect, finding support for the assertion of the former in the developments of modern physics, where it is appreciated that even within a rigorous experimental situation the observer inevitably contributes in some way to what is observed.[121] Sometimes he is more specific about precisely what qualitative aspects there might be to reality. After one coincidence, for example, he comments: "Experiences like that, as well as many others that I have mentioned, left me in no doubt that Man does have a Soul or that he may, and probably should, seek to unify himself with it."[122] Then, toward the very end of his material, again with reference to his experiences as a whole, he states confidently that "it turns out that it is the things that I found by the wayside [that is, the seemingly trivial coincidences] that end up proving the reality of the spiritual dimension of the universe."[123]

Proof of the Paranormal/Toward a New Science

Plaskett is not concerned simply with asserting or believing in the existence of a spiritual dimension of reality. He wishes to see steps taken toward establishing its reality on a foundation as solid as that which supports the truths of science. This preoccupation comes to a focus for him in *the problem of proving the paranormal*. He sets out the problem in a series of lengthy quotes from authors evaluating the (more or less) current status of claims for the paranormal. Some, such as Martin Gardner, express extreme skepticism regarding the failure of parapsychology to produce a single paranormal result that can be repeated under controlled conditions. Others, such as Colin Wilson, point to the mountains of anecdotal evidence, much of it from totally creditable witnesses.[124] In the light of this division of viewpoint, Plaskett articulates the question for himself in the following way:

> Proving the anecdotal . . . attempting to provide PROOF for that which is not replicable, is beyond human control and is not amenable to laboratory investigation . . . HOW?[125]

At one point he expresses enthusiasm for a seemingly simple experiment that would involve checking the veridicality of observations allegedly made by patients while undergoing a near-death experience, when clinically they should not have been able to make those observations.[126] However, the strongest help in addressing the problem of proving the paranormal he considers to be the phenomenon of coincidence itself. He makes his case in the form of two analogies. One analogy is with the tracks and droppings of animals. If one finds animal tracks and droppings, that alone is good reason to suppose the existence of the animal, even if one has never actually seen the animal itself. Similarly with coincidences: even if we have not yet grasped what principle or mechanism (or indeed what being) may be responsible for them, nevertheless their very presence is an indication that something is going on that it may be worthwhile seeking to identify. In Plaskett's own words:

> Just as new droppings or tracks are not DIRECT PERCEPTION of a phenomenon but are intimations of something unknown, so meaningful coincidence is to me an indicator of something glimpsed but yet to be clearly seen or understood.[127]

A second analogous situation impressed Plaskett even more. It concerns the events at the beginning of the nineteenth century that led the French Academy of Science to accept the reality of meteorites. As we saw earlier (3, 18), the academy had "formally endorsed the Jeffersonian viewpoint that stones couldn't possibly fall from the sky," but had been forced to recant "when many *thousand* descended at the town of L'Aigle, not far from Paris itself."[128] The fall of these meteorites was unpredictable and nonrepeatable, yet it was an event sufficient to overturn dogmatic skepticism and establish a scientific fact. It was able to do this, we may suppose, for two principal reasons: because of the sheer quantity of meteorites that fell and because they left physical evidence in the form of many actual pieces of meteoric rock (as Plaskett emphasizes, "ROCK-SOLID EVIDENCE").[129] Similarly with coincidence experiences: they too represent a phenomenon of questionable status, whose occurrence is neither predictable nor repeatable to order; but—especially in the case of a collection like Plaskett's—they too can be persuasive by their sheer quantity and, if recorded and documented carefully as are Plaskett's experiences, can also leave forms of physical evidence.[130]

Impressive and suggestive though these analogies were to Plaskett, and may be to others, nonetheless they would not prove very easy to sustain in the face of reductionistic scientific attitudes. Accordingly, Plaskett turns his attention also to the question of whether *new approaches to science* might not be developed—or are in the process of being developed already. The impetus to reflect along these lines was given largely by the coincidences centering on the motif of "eyes" (31–34, 36–41)—with their various suggestions concerning the issues of limited vision and the need for new forms of perception. In particular, we can notice that the reproduced extract from Laurens van der Post's *The Heart of the Hunter*, which described the story of how Mantis was killed and battered until his eye fell out (34), continues immediately with the author remarking: "If there is any better image of what the over-critical faculty, the one-sided mind of pure reason, does to new creation, I have yet to meet it."[131] Also in this spirit, Plaskett quotes at length from Michael Shallis on a suggested distinction between "Descriptive Science and Instructional Science"—the latter more suited to understanding and manipulating the quantitative aspect of reality, the former to grasping its qualitative aspect.[132] Elsewhere, Plaskett reflects on the possibility of bridging the frequent divide between reason and belief through some such reconciling notion as "reason to believe."[133] He concludes by asking whether we ought not to recognize "A DIFFERENCE BETWEEN BEING SCIENTIFIC AND BEING RATIONAL."[134]

Precisely what kind of science Plaskett envisages by statements such as the preceding is not spelled out in any detail, but there are one or two hints in the observations and reflections we have encountered already. He notes, for example, that modern physics is no longer governed exclusively by the principle of causality but is a field replete with paradox as well as with a growing recognition of the participatory role of the experimenter in obtaining results.[135] The concept of participation strikes him as of particular relevance, since this gives some kind of scientific validation to his notion of "a person's experience of Meaning depending upon his attitudes and the manner of his living, that is to say the way in which he PARTICIPATES in life."[136]

A DETAILED EXAMPLE: THE HARTSTON CASE

I shall conclude this chapter by presenting in somewhat greater detail one further small group of interrelated coincidences. I do so largely because it would have seemed an omission not to show at least a few coincidences more or less in their full context. Another consideration, however, is that the selected small cluster illustrates particularly well many of the features and responses to which I have been drawing attention in the foregoing. Finally, it seemed important to present this cluster of coincidences because Plaskett himself expresses the view that it contains some of the most significant of his experiences.

Grandmasterly Castling

Around the end of March 1988 Plaskett began making attempts to have his coincidence material evaluated by a reputable person. Initial attempts to interest one of the major authorities in British parapsychology—Susan Blackmore or Brian Inglis—were not very productive, though the latter did encourage him to improve the presentation of his material. These improvements were carried out while Plaskett was present at an international chess tournament in Oakham, England, between March 28 and April 6, 1988. After completing them, he says, "I wondered who might serve as a rational and intelligent person to whom I could offer the material for consideration as soon as possible."[137] At the chess tournament there was someone present who seemed to meet Plaskett's requirements particularly well: William Hartston, a Cambridge-educated mathematician, industrial psychologist, prolific writer and television commentator on the subject of chess, and an international master of the game. He seemed appropriate for a number of reasons: he had a highly developed critical intelligence; he was already an acquaintance of Plaskett's; he happened to be in the same place as Plaskett just at the time when he had got his material into tidy form; and, as we have seen, Plaskett had been unable seriously to interest any of the authorities in parapsychology he had approached. Plaskett also recalled that, in a previous conversation, Hartston had mentioned having been asked to review a book about Michel and Françoise Gauquelins's controversial work on astrology; he had expressed disapproval of the unethical way some scientists had behaved when confronted with the Gauquelins's data, and had concluded with the sentiment that "more time should be spent on the investigation of such matters."[138] Memory of this conversation prompted Plaskett to think that Hartston, even though he was initially "utterly sceptical towards the idea of meaningful coincidence,"[139] nevertheless "might be somehow more receptive than most people."[140] After all, Plaskett says of himself that he "was not interested in 'preaching to the converted.'"[141]

Without even explaining what it was, Plaskett handed his material to Hartston and asked him for his comments. When he phoned to get these a few days later, Hartston had an incident of his own to report. He had been reading the coincidence numbered (18) in the collection Plaskett had given him. It was titled "FORGETTING ABOUT CASTLING IN A GAME WHERE A GM NORM WAS AT STAKE" and concerned a number of instances of chess games where the factor determining victory or defeat was the ability (or inability) of one of the players to make the move "*castles*" at a much later stage in the game than is usual.[142] In each case the result of the game was crucial to one of the players gaining (or failing to gain) the required number of points *to qualify for what is called a grandmaster norm.*[143]

While Hartston was reading this coincidence his television was on, showing an episode of a drama series called *A Very Peculiar Practice*, which concerns a medical practice in a Midlands university. The beginning of the episode in question was of a dream sequence based on Ingmar Bergman's film *The Seventh Seal*. In the film a knight plays a game of *chess* against Death and, in spite of having the advantage of the white pieces, loses. This would have been an impressive coincidence in itself, but it quickly became more so, since part of the twist given to the Bergman incident in its reworking for the television program was to have a character in the dream scenario say, "I'm not very good at chess: I don't even know how *to castle*."[144] According to Plaskett, "Hartston was so struck by the improbability of this that he asked 'How can that happen?'"[145]

The incident does indeed seem unlikely—that chess and castling should be mentioned on television just as Hartston (himself probably the best-known chess commentator on British television) was reading Plaskett's coincidence precisely about chess and castling. Initially, Plaskett too "thought only about the high improbability of the coincidence," but later, "very probably prompted by the discovery of something meaningful associated with so many of the coincidences that I had encountered, I looked for some discharge of meaning accompanying Hartston's experience."[146] Doing so, he found within the coincidence several further parallels to Hartston's situation.

The castling incidents that Hartston was reading about had all concerned critical moments where the result meant the difference between *achieving or not achieving a grandmaster norm*. It so happened that as a young man Hartston himself had narrowly missed becoming the first British player to gain the title of grandmaster. In fact, it was calculated in retrospect that he had *missed gaining one of his norms, and thereby the title, by the narrowest of margins possible*. Plaskett explains that "had the average rating of each of the competitors [in the critical event] been just one point higher, then the score that Hartston made would have been sufficient for a GM norm, i.e. IT WAS STATISTICALLY IMPOSSIBLE FOR HIM TO HAVE COME ANY CLOSER TO THE GM NORM."[147]

This alone made the coincidence singularly pertinent to Hartston. But Plaskett discerned further connections. He narrates how in 1976 Hartston was supplanted as England's top chess player by Tony Miles, who then also went on to become England's first grandmaster. Hartston's wife then left him for Miles, whom she subsequently married.[148] The particular connection Plaskett finds between these personal details and the present incident is that Hartston's wife "was and is a *medical doctor*"[149] who "is now *practising in the midlands*"[150] (the television program *A Very Peculiar Practice*, it will be remembered, concerned *a medical practice in the Midlands*). Plaskett also adds some further, rather more tenuous, associations: for example, he notes, presumably by way of comment on the above-mentioned "*home*-breaking," that "an Englishman's *home* is his *castle*";[151] also that to castle late in a game of chess, especially at high tournament level, is itself *a very peculiar practice;* and he suggests a possible relevance of the allusion to *The Seventh Seal* in the fact that in chess a pawn that advances *beyond the seventh* and onto the eighth rank "undergoes a stupendous increase in strength and status and becomes a queen."[152]

Plaskett suggested to Hartston that "in the light of this symbolic interpretation he was the only man in the world who could have had the coincidence"—a judgment with which Hartston apparently agreed.[153] Plaskett also reports that he himself "found Hartston's experience 'encouraging'; it was as if Life were providing a form of confirmation that in recording my coincidences in the first place I was 'on to something.'"[154]

Coincidentally Hartston

However, this was not the end of the matter. Five and a half months later, on August 15, 1988, Plaskett's friend, the woman who had been involved with him in the coincidences concerning Orwell's novel *Coming Up for Air* (22) and the dreams of synchronized swimming (23), bought in Cambridge a book she thought looked intriguing: *The Paranormal* by Stan Gooch. The book contains a twelve-page subsection entitled *"Synchronicity and Coincidence."* "After her own experiences," Plaskett relates, "it was naturally to that chapter that [she] turned first. When she started to read it she got a shock."[155] The section began as follows:

> In a recent pilot television programme designed to test the limits of intelligence, the names of the three contestants were *Hartston*, Burton and Walkington. All three end in -ton, and all three are names of towns—except for one letter (Harston *is* a town). The contestants were not of course chosen because of their names but because each of them had done extremely well in similar competitions on previous occasions.[156]

After giving two further similar examples, Gooch comments: "These items are three examples of what we call coincidence. They do not signify anything. In respect of such happenings we often prefix the word coincidence with the word 'meaningless'—we say 'a meaningless coincidence.'"[157]

When Plaskett showed the book to Hartston, the latter confirmed that he was indeed the person named. Plaskett observed that Hartston is actually "the man who happens to be named *first* in the *first* paragraph of the *first* example in the section [on *coincidence*]." This paralleled for Plaskett the fact that he himself had chosen Hartston (for the reasons mentioned above) "to be the *first* critic of my [*coincidence*] material."[158]

The impact on Plaskett of the whole Hartston episode was particularly profound:

> If I were made to choose one component of this whole business which demonstrated to me that there was something going on other than chance then it would have to be this.
>
> How could it "just happen" that I could have picked upon the person with whom Gooch begins the section on Synchronicity and Coincidence, a person who then went on to encounter a coincidence that astonished him whilst reading my material?[159]

The Limits of Intelligence

Again, however, this initial response was merely to the event's improbability. He says that "it was only after some time had elapsed that I began to think more about the possible *meaning* that it might contain" (Plaskett's emphasis).[160] He narrates that on the evening of October 19, 1991, it occurred to him that the fact that the program on which Hartston had appeared was "designed *to test the limits of intelligence*" may have been "somehow very pertinent indeed." *Hartston himself* is highly *intelligent* and, as an industrial psychologist, has published works dealing with "thought processes, calculation, psychology, etc."; while Plaskett, quite apart from his thinking ability as a chess player, says of himself that "in pondering the great questions of Philosophy and Theology I was aware of grappling with topics very much at *the limits of Human intelligence*."[161]

The morning after having these thoughts Plaskett bought a copy of *The Mail on Sunday* and turned to the chess column written by *Hartston*. The column contained a humorous sketch in which Hartston had to defend the thinking practices of chess players against the criticisms of a polar bear. At one point the polar bear pointed out that in the time it takes some players to make a single move, "you could read a short book, or watch a film, or attend a postgraduate lecture on some topic *at the limits of human knowledge*."[162]

The timeliness of coming upon this particular expression, and written by Hartston of all people, seemed, Plaskett says, "to support my hunch that straining the mind on matters at the limits of our intelligence had something to do with it [that is, the significance of coincidence]."[163] Though he expresses uncertainty as to "precisely what" this "something" might be, he nonetheless suggests that it may involve the way in which our lives can be made meaningful:

> Given that Gooch started his section with this incident in order to emphasise that it is meaningless, and that it was subsequently transmuted in my life into perhaps the most meaningful and staggering of coincidences, the question presents itself: Is there any such thing as a truly meaningless event?[164]

The initial meaninglessness of the event described by Gooch is made even greater when one considers that it only works as a coincidence at all if one overlooks the mismatch between Hartston's name and the name of the town Harston. In the light of this, Plaskett concludes his narration of the episode with the following reflection: "Perhaps the greatest significance of Gooch's choice of 'non-event' is how *anything* is meaningful in the sense that it has the potential to be transmogrified through our attempts to find meaning."[165]

Paralleling the transmutation of the meaningless into the meaningful, there was, according to Plaskett, a transformation within Hartston: initially, he was "utterly sceptical towards the idea of meaningful coincidence," but Plaskett quotes him as saying "'since I've had my experience I'm not so sure any more!'"[166] Persuading a highly intelligent skeptic that there may be important dimensions to reality not adequately covered by the mainstream scientific worldview is precisely what Plaskett hoped coincidence experiences such as his own might be able to do.[167]

Comments

This small series of experiences illustrates very clearly the so-called "triggering" effect that can happen in relation to coincidences. Hartston's act of examining Plaskett's material appeared to trigger the castling coincidence. Similarly, Plaskett's search for a suitable critic of his material seemed to trigger the coincidence involving Hartston and Gooch's book *The Paranormal*. Again, Plaskett's active reflection on the possible relationship between coincidence and the limits of intelligence seemed to trigger the incident involving Hartston's article in *The Mail on Sunday*.

With regard to probability, we can note that the castling coincidence seems to be rendered particularly improbable by the fine detail and specificity of the points of paralleling involved (not just chess but castling, not just castling but castling in a context with particularly meaningful associations for Hartston, and so on). This improbability is increased further by the fact that this first incident is followed and developed by two related coincidences.

The Hartston episode also illustrates the way one can move, as does Plaskett, from being impressed initially by the improbability of a coincidence to later appreciating its possible meaning. This move is explicit both in the castling coincidence and in the coincidence involving Gooch's book.

The particular meanings that Plaskett discerned in the Hartston coincidences reflect or epitomize some of those that preoccupied him in relation to his narrative as a whole. One meaning apparently being communicated was that coincidence has something to do with the limits of human intelligence. This relates to Plaskett's general concern with exploring ways of thinking and understanding (such as parapsychology, spirituality, and new science), which go beyond the limitations of the current consensus worldview. Again, the Hartston case seems to be making an important communication regarding the nature of meaning itself: that even the apparently most meaningless events can be transformed into something highly meaningful if one adopts an actively investigative attitude toward them. This reflects Plaskett's thoughts elsewhere in his material regarding the ultimate meaningfulness of the universe and the importance of actively participating in reality rather than just being an observer of it.

One final feature can be noted about this case that will come to be particularly relevant to the analysis I attempt in the next chapter. This is that the content and context of the first two of the Hartston incidents have to do specifically with the subject of coincidence itself. Hartston experienced the castling coincidence in relation to the coincidence material he was reading at the time; and the coincidence involving Gooch's book related specifically to a section of it on synchronicity and coincidence. These coincidences involving coincidence draw attention to a frequently occurring feature that might be called *the self-referring nature of coincidence*. There are two aspects to this: one is where (as we have just noted here) the content or context of a coincidence has to do with coincidence itself; the other is where the content, though not necessarily directly to do with coincidence, expresses meanings that are suggested also by the essential form of coincidence regardless of its specific content. This latter kind of self-referring is also exemplified by the Hartston incidents. For example, the essential form of any coincidence (regardless of its specific content) is such that it presents one with an experiential and conceptual enigma; it baffles one's feelings and thoughts and stimulates one to investigate beyond the normal range of one's understanding. This would appear to be reflected by the specific content of the Hartston coincidences, which express the idea of the limits of human intelligence. Again, it is intrinsic to the essential form of coincidence that it creates or reveals meaningful relationships between events that in themselves are either not meaningful or are not meaningful in that particular way. To appreciate this, one need only scan the contents of some of the incidents in Plaskett's narrative: in the absence of the coincidental relationship, there would be very little significance in, for example, the names Baker and Ferrer (9), the remark of a coin thief in an episode of *Kojak* (12), the image of great-crested grebes (24), or being offered a morsel of dried Icelandic fish (27). It is their role within the structure of a coincidence that renders these images and events meaningful (or more meaningful). This idea, of the meaningless being made meaningful, is, as we saw, reflected in the specific content of the coincidence involving Gooch's book.

CHAPTER 6

THE SELF-REVELATION OF SYNCHRONICITY AS SPIRIT
A MODERN GRAIL STORY

In the last chapter I introduced and presented a selection of incidents from the extended synchronistic narrative of James Plaskett. I then showed how he responded to these synchronicities. Doing all of this required a considerable amount of rearranging and sorting of his material in order to highlight the most frequently recurring themes and the experiencer's major conceptual preoccupations. My aim, however, was to allow the material and the experiencer's response to it to emerge predominantly on their own terms. In the present chapter, by contrast, I give myself much freer rein to engage in evaluations and interpretations of my own. For the most part these will not be incompatible with Plaskett's own responses, but neither will they be unduly limited by those responses. First, I briefly compare Plaskett's material with Thornton's (examined in chapter 4). I then assess the bearing of Plaskett's material as a whole on the question of the possible spiritual status of synchronicity. Finally, I report on my own attempt at a more sustained and systematic, but admittedly still highly speculative, symbolic interpretation of this material.

PLASKETT AND THORNTON: A BRIEF COMPARISON

In many ways Plaskett's material is similar to Thornton's and supports observations made with reference to the latter. Both sets of material consist of an extensive collection of synchronicities experienced and recorded by a single individual and found by that individual to be spiritually of great relevance. At the very least, this demonstrates the (not necessarily obvious) possibility of the occurrence of such bodies of coincidences and of their being responded to on a spiritual level.

Besides the sheer quantity of events involved, both collections also exhibit a remarkable recurrence and interconnection of motifs; in both cases the content proves to be richly symbolic; and both experiencers felt they could discern a high level of intelligibility within their experiences. The relevance of each of these shared features to the possible spiritual status of synchronicity will be discussed later in the chapter.

There are, however, equally significant differences between the two collections. As I have already noted, Plaskett's material, unlike Thornton's, was not originally intended for publication and can therefore be assumed to have been subjected to considerably less selectivity and polishing—a factor rendering it more difficult to study but also in many ways more rewarding.[1] I also noted that Plaskett, unlike Thornton, has no specific orientation either toward Jungian psychology or toward any traditional religion. He is much more critically engaged with his material and in particular is greatly concerned with problems of proving the reality of parapsychological and spiritual phenomena. Indeed, synchronicities seem much more central to Plaskett's spirituality than they do to Thornton's. Whereas Thornton already confidently assumes the existence of the spiritual dimension and its operation in his life, in Plaskett's case this is precisely one of the messages seemingly being conveyed to him by his synchronicities. Again, as was noted in chapter 4, almost all of the essential spiritual content of Thornton's experiences had already been conveyed to him by his purely inner experiences (dreams, visions, and so forth). The subsequent development of these into synchronicities served primarily to intensify them and render them more actual, gripping, and effective. With Plaskett's experiences, by contrast, it was usually within the synchronicities themselves that the spiritually relevant content first appeared.

Certain of the differences between the two collections derive from the fact that, while Thornton's is indeed extensive by comparison with the kind of one-off or small clusters of experiences that are usually reported, Plaskett's is vastly more extensive even than Thornton's, consisting as it does of some ninety-odd relevant incidents as opposed to twenty.[2] Thus, in Plaskett's material the thematic repetition is greater, both in terms of the number of themes and the number of occurrences of each theme, and correspondingly the interconnection of themes is also much more complex. This greater range and complexity of content may also render Plaskett's material open to a much greater variety of possible symbolic interpretations—a feature with which I shall have to contend when I hazard my own interpretation in a later section. The greater variety in Plaskett's synchronicities extends to their content, the contexts and mediums in which they are expressed, and the particular manner of their occurrence.

Regarding the content, whereas in Thornton's case there were basically just two motifs, with Plaskett's material there are, in my selection alone, five major themes each containing three or four subthemes. The material moves among and weaves together such diverse images as the moon, Parsifal, an eagle, a giant octopus, and blindness; or again, stars, the Holy Grail, Beatrice, Leviathan, and one-eyedness.

As for the contexts and mediums in which the images are expressed in the two collections, in Thornton's narrative all of the inner psychic events occur as dreams (except for three "visions"), while the outer physical events involve variously the behavior of live owls, hearing a lecture, being told a personal anecdote, suffering an illness and being operated on, and seeing statues on a building and in a photograph. The contexts and mediums in Plaskett's material include (on the more psychic level) dreams, memories, thoughts, and states of ongoing interest, and (on the more physical level) books, newspapers, mail, television and radio, past and present situations and events, personal communications, an item of clothing, and the facade of a building. Out of this variety in the Plaskett case a few kinds of context preponderate. On the psychic side, the commonest context is a state of ongoing interest, often evoked and sustained by previous physical incidents (for example, Plaskett's ongoing interest in the symbol of the eagle is evoked and sustained by his frequent encounters with this image in such physical contexts as a book, a television program, an item of clothing, and so on). This contrasts with Thornton's predominant psychic context of dreams. On the physical side, Plaskett's most frequent context is books, then to a lesser degree newspapers and magazines, and also television and radio. This also contrasts with Thornton, none of whose incidents involve these particular physical contexts. Probably not much more can be concluded from this than that coincidences can and do involve practically any kind of psychic and physical context.

Plaskett's collection also displays a greater variety of particular manners or forms in which the coincidences occur. Thornton's coincidences almost all follow the typical pattern of a conspicuously psychic event being followed by a conspicuously physical event. Many of Plaskett's coincidences likewise take this form (for example, 6, 9, 31, 34, 38).[3] The majority, however, as I have just indicated, have as their first event an ongoing state of interest that is in fact largely the result of previous physical events. In these cases one might want to consider the first event physical rather than psychic, this then being followed by a second event that is also physical (for example, 1, 8, 10, 12, 21). Most of Plaskett's coincidences have him as their sole experiencer, but there are a few that are interpersonal, involving the parallel experiences of two people (for example, 23, 24). Of these, one consists of two parallel psychic events (23), another of one psychic and one physical event (24). A further form of coincidence is where the decisive "second" event simultaneously parallels a number of previous events (for example, 10, 29). Again, there is one instance in which the coincidence is explicitly precognitive or predictive in form (28). Finally, we can notice certain coincidences involving the subject of coincidence itself (for example, 3, 23).[4] Some of these forms do occur within Thornton's narrative—in particular, I noted a strong, if unconscious, predictive element in his experiences. Generally speaking, however, Plaskett's is clearly the more varied collection on the count of manner and form of occurrence as on the other counts. On the one hand, this is no doubt primarily due to the fact that his collection is considerably more extensive than Thornton's. On the other hand, it may also partly stem from Thornton's having, under the Jungian influence, a more rigorous though at the same time narrower preconception of what kinds of conjunctions of events are to be allowed to qualify as synchronistic.[5]

THE SPIRITUAL STATUS OF SYNCHRONICITY

As seen in the previous chapter, Plaskett considered that his synchronistic experiences provided some kind of proof of—or at least "reason to believe in—the reality of the paranormal.[6] More specifically, they "proved the reality of the spiritual dimension of the universe."[7] While I do not believe synchronicities can, or should be expected to, prove anything in any strong sense about the ultimate nature of reality, I agree that they can indeed provide a body of suggestive evidence.

There are certain strategies that can be adopted to try to undercut any strong, or even moderate, claim for the evidential value of experiences such as Plaskett's. Individually each of the coincidences could undoubtedly be accounted for in terms of various reductive arguments from statistics and mainstream psychology.[8] More generally, the apparent high incidence of unlikely connections in Plaskett's material may be due to the fact that, on the one hand, he is exposed to an exceedingly large quantity of very diverse information anyway (most of his experiences involve high information sources such as books, newspapers, television, and so forth), while, on the other hand, the connections that he allows to count as significant are in many cases between fairly broad and sweeping themes rather than between specific details. Again, one could suggest that the nature of Plaskett's mind as characterized in chapter 5, its very strengths in fact, could dispose him to find connections where in reality there are none, or if there are, it is simply that they are usually unnoticed rather than that they are genuinely anomalous. Furthermore, Plaskett's long-standing beliefs and urgent desire to achieve something spiritually could have provided the psychological motives for misperceiving or misinterpreting his experiences. Compounding these difficulties is that Plaskett has then ordered his experiences into a narrative that, even if to a lesser degree than the Thornton material, is, one might argue, undoubtedly constructed so as to present his experiences (a choice selection of them) in the strongest light possible.

However, as I have noted several times already, criticisms such as these for the most part address themselves to possibilities only. In the case of each individual coincidence, and indeed of the collection as a whole, it remains equally possible that the events are, as they appear to be on the face of it, genuinely anomalous, suggesting the operation of some as yet inadequately appreciated feature of reality. This latter possibility gains additional support from some of the outstanding features of the Plaskett material to which attention has already briefly been drawn.

In the first place, many of Plaskett's incidents are indeed individually quite striking in terms of their improbability. He reports that he was particularly impressed by the coincidence involving his discovery that Plaskett's Star is in the constellation of The Unicorn (2); likewise by a couple of the coincidences involving his grandmother in relation to Dante's *Paradiso* (15–16); and above all by the small group of incidents involving William Hartston. Those I personally found most impressive include the two involving the dreams of synchronized swimming and great-crested grebes (23, 24), the successful prediction or "extrapolation" relating to the imminent emergence of something from the sea (28), and those involving Assagioli's "Exercises for Spiritual Psychosynthesis" (29, 30).[9]

Then there is the sheer quantity of incidents involved. If many of Plaskett's coincidences individually are improbable to a significant and suggestive degree, it is reasonable to suppose that the cumulative improbability of the collection as a whole must be considerably more so. That some coincidences might be expected to happen just in the normal course of things can readily be admitted, but it is another matter altogether when one is talking about tens and hundreds of such incidents.

Furthermore, this great volume of material has arisen, both as a whole and in its component clusters, within relatively short time spans. All except four (29, 30, 40, 41) of the incidents I have related occurred during the period from the end of January to the middle of May 1988, and a single day—February 14, 1988—provided the focus for no fewer than six of them (5, 6, 8, 10, 23, 26). This close temporal proximity of most of the incidents to one another constitutes a significant detail in their paralleling and, hence, contributes further to their overall improbability and impressiveness.

Again, not only is there a remarkable quantity and often quality of incidents, but their contents display an equally or even more remarkable recurrence of motifs. Within my limited selection there are eight conspicuous references to the theme of celestial phenomena (1–3, 10, 11, 18, 19, 28), eight to the theme of Arthurian legend (4–10, 29), twelve to that of Dante's *Paradiso* (11–20, 29, 30), ten to that of sea monsters (20–23, 25–28, 30, 35), and ten to that of eyes and vision (31–34, 36–41). It is true that once a theme was highlighted the experiencer would then very likely have been alert to any further occurrences of it, but this does not take away from the fact that in most cases the recurring appearances of the given theme are, so far as one can tell, causally independent of one another. Such spontaneous reiteration can only add to the unlikeliness and significance of the happening as a whole.

Finally, there is the often surprising and ingenious interconnection between the themes. It not infrequently happens that a coincidence occurs whose content seems simultaneously to express two (or more) hitherto apparently unrelated themes. Tracing the most conspicuous of these interconnections,[10] I found that the themes of Arthurian legend and of Dante's *Paradiso* are each related at various points to all of the other four principal themes, while the themes of celestial phenomena and sea monsters are each related to all themes except that of eyes and vision; the latter is therefore conspicuously related only to the themes of Arthurian legend and Dante's *Paradiso*. To give some specific examples: the theme of celestial phenomena is conspicuously linked to the themes of Arthurian legend (10), Dante's *Paradiso* (11, 18, 19), and sea monsters (28); while the coincidence involving Assagioli's "Exercises for Spiritual Psychosynthesis" (29) serves to interconnect the four themes of celestial phenomena, Arthurian legend, Dante's *Paradiso*, and sea monsters.[11] The unlikeliness of these interconnections contributes again to the improbability and, hence arguably, to the evidential status of the collection as a whole.

There is, however, another factor that can make a decisive contribution to one's evaluation of the possible evidential status of coincidences: their meaningfulness. That two events should fall together acausally and parallel each other in their content in a detailed way may be improbable and impressive. But it is considerably more improbable and impressive if, in addition to this detailed paralleling, the content of the coincidence or some aspect of the manner of its occurrence happens also to be highly meaningful (either just to the experiencer or more generally).

The issue of meaning is extremely broad and complex. In the previous chapter I presented an account of how Plaskett responded to his coincidences, the meanings that he considered them to be communicating to him more or less directly, and the further meanings to which they gave rise through stimulating or modifying certain processes of reflection. It will be remembered that he attached great importance in this respect to the conspicuously symbolic nature of the content of his coincidences. Many if not most of the contents of his narrative—the moon, the stars, the knight Parsifal, the Holy Grail, the eagle, the rose, the octopus, the third eye—are symbolically resonant. However, while registering this fact, Plaskett did not actually pursue the possibilities of symbolic analysis very far. It is, therefore, to my own attempt at such symbolic analysis that I now turn.

THE SELF-REVELATION OF SYNCHRONICITY: AN EXPERIMENT IN INTERPRETATION

Plaskett's own interpretation of his experiences is very restrained, not surprisingly considering that his primary stated aim was not interpretative but just "to present things as simply and clearly as possible."[12] In what follows I report on my own attempt at a fuller interpretation of Plaskett's material, both as a whole and with specific attention to the incidents comprising one of his major themes. In doing this I am hypothesizing that there is indeed further meaning to be discerned in the synchronicities. Of some of this possible meaning Plaskett was or could have been aware, but of much else he almost certainly was not aware. However, everything I suggest in the following is, I believe, broadly consonant with Plaskett's own interpretative statements, such as they are.

Method

My procedure in attempting to access further meaning in Plaskett's experiences was as follows. First, I identified all the individual synchronicities within his narrative and noted their interrelationships in terms of both chronology and content. Regarding the latter, it became apparent, as Plaskett had already suggested would be the case, that the content could be grouped according to a number of principal themes. Particular attention was given to the five largest of these thematic groupings (the five from which my selections in the previous chapter were made). Each coincidence was then analyzed individually, with specific attention being paid to its possible symbolic character. The first twenty-one incidents (reckoned chronologically) were analyzed in greatest depth;[13] these mostly concerned the themes of celestial phenomena and Arthurian legend. The remaining incidents were analyzed after the same pattern as the first twenty-one but in less depth.

The actual symbolic analysis of the synchronistic contents involved an imaginative and intuitive attempt to discern deeper, possibly archetypal, levels of meaning within the immediately presented images or ideas. Imagination and intuition were not, however, given entirely free rein. In general, I proceeded, by what seemed plausible stages, from the more explicit and uncontroversial levels of meaning to the progressively more embedded and tentative levels. Three principal checks were employed to minimize the element of arbitrariness in my interpretations. First, any relevant *subjective-level information* was taken into account. This included Plaskett's response to or beliefs about his experiences, as well as indications as to his immediate or long-term background preoccupations and circumstances. Effectively, then, I attempted to keep my interpretation as compatible as possible with Plaskett's own. Secondly, the meaning I felt able to elicit from any given synchronistic content was related to the meanings elicited from *other of Plaskett's synchronicities*. Bolder interpretations were only admitted if they could be substantiated by the prefiguration, repetition, or development of the same symbolic motif in other of his synchronicities. Third, comparison was made, where it seemed possible and appropriate, between my proposed symbolic interpretation of any content and *precedents* for this specific interpretation as they exist in previous studies of symbols whether within mythological, religious, literary, and other cultural contexts, or as they may have arisen within such more spontaneous contexts as dreams, visions, and indeed synchronicities themselves.

Finally, out of the whole body of symbolic meanings that I elicited from Plaskett's material I attempted to construct a more or less coherent overall interpretation, a summary of which is presented below. Insofar as it lends itself to articulation, it is principally this that might be considered the "revelation" communicated by this particular set of synchronicities.

Clearly, there are a number of limitations and potential problems with this procedure. First, the data that I am analyzing consist of verbal reports at several removes from any actual experiences. In each case there would be first the original experience, followed shortly by Plaskett's more or less immediate response to it. Some time afterward, perhaps on the same day but often upward of a week later, there was Plaskett's initial recording of the incident. Then there was his construction of his various records into a narrative; next, his revision of this narrative; and finally, my own interpretative engagement. In most cases, one can suppose that the basic shape of his original experience will have survived through all of this, but important nuances and details will undoubtedly sometimes have been lost, while others, not present in the original experience, may well have accrued.

Again, there is the problem presented by the very complexity and richness of material such as Plaskett's. Even granting its symbolical character—in fact, perhaps especially because of this—it may be open to too many varied possibilities of interpretation, with no guarantee that my own, or Plaskett's for that matter, is more valid than another that gives significantly different emphases. It is true that the material is far from being totally open, and the three checks mentioned above might save one from the worst kinds of interpretative excess, but nonetheless it has to be acknowledged that considerable latitude for divergence exists. The direction in which any particular person's interpretation goes probably depends to a significant extent on that person's own interests and preoccupations.

The whole issue is further complicated by the possibility that some of the incidents considered may not actually be synchronicities after all, while of those that almost certainly are, some may not in fact be related to the thematic groupings in which they have been included but may be related to a quite different pattern of meaning or even be of wholly independent significance. The mistaken attempt to accommodate these rogue incidents could cause an otherwise accurate interpretation to be deflected quite off the mark.

Symbolic analysis similar in most essentials to that which I attempted on Plaskett's synchronicity material is regularly undertaken within the context of Jungian psychotherapy with regard to the dreams and other fantasy products (including occasional synchronicities) of the analysand.[14] In fact, the Jungian practice has served as the inspiration and primary model for this present attempt at analysis. There is, however, a crucial difference between the two kinds of undertaking. In the psychotherapeutic context the analyst remains in close communication with the person whose experiences are being analyzed, and therefore has access to vastly greater amounts of subjective-level information. In particular, the analyst can receive continual feedback in the form of the experiencer's feeling-evaluation of any proposed interpretation of the experiences.[15] In the context of my analysis, by contrast, only very limited amounts of subjective-level information have been available and it has been impracticable to seek more; likewise, it has not been feasible to try to obtain much detailed feedback from the experiencer concerning my interpretations.

This point made, however, it is also possible that this lack of subjective-level information may not be as serious a limitation as it initially appears. It may, for instance, be the case that the primary focus of one's analysis of material such as we are dealing with here should be on the objective rather than the subjective level. Too much attention to the subjective level might obscure more important levels of collective and objective meaning—just as, for example, too much attention to the role of an author's personal life in the genesis of a novel might obscure rather than enhance one's appreciation of the work's more universal significance. Again, whatever particular orientation was guiding one's subjective-level interpretation would undoubtedly bring problems and limitations of its own. The context of a Jungian analysis, for instance, would be likely to involve certain deeply embedded theoretical and personal expectations in both the analysand and the analyst. These expectations would certainly color the resulting interpretations but not necessarily in ways that would optimally elucidate the material itself.

It can be noted, further, that Jung outlined a methodology for interpreting spontaneous fantasy products even in the absence of subjective-level information concerning the experiencer. With specific reference to dreams, he first cautions against any attempt to deduce their meaning from some supposed "general theory of dreams" or from other "preconceived opinions."[16] He then remarks:

> We are therefore obliged to adopt the method we would use in deciphering a fragmentary text or one containing unknown words: we examine the context. The meaning of the unknown word may become evident when we compare a series of passages in which it occurs.[17]

In the normal psychotherapeutic situation a large part of the "context" to which Jung here refers consists precisely of the subjective psychological background of the experiencer. However, when Jung was attempting to analyze the series of dreams and visualizations presented in Part II of *Psychology and Alchemy*, he was faced with a body of material that was not obtained under his direct observation and whose more subjective dimension therefore could not be explored in any great depth by him. He proceeded, accordingly, "as if I had had the dreams myself and were therefore in a position to supply the context."[18] He explains further:

> This procedure, if applied to *isolated* dreams of someone unknown to me personally, would indeed be a gross technical blunder. But here we are not dealing with isolated dreams; they form a coherent series in the course of which the meaning gradually unfolds more or less of its own accord. *The series is the context which the dreamer himself supplies*. It is as if not

one text but many lay before us, throwing light from all sides on the unknown terms, so that a reading of all the texts is sufficient to elucidate the difficult passages in each individual one.... Of course the interpretation of each individual passage is bound to be largely conjecture, but the series as a whole gives us all the clues we need to correct any possible errors in the preceding passages.[19]

Though with somewhat less confidence than is implied in Jung's concluding statement, this is essentially the method I endeavored to employ in regard to Plaskett's synchronistic experiences, which likewise seem to form a "coherent series" whose "meaning gradually unfolds more or less of its own accord."

Finally, I should make clear that I do not consider the interpretation offered below to be in any way conclusive. I wish to demonstrate only that some such interpretation is both possible and warranted. The material seems to me to exhibit sufficient intelligibility on the surface to suggest that there may be even greater intelligibility to be uncovered if one explores more deeply. I believe, therefore, that my own interpretation, even though nowhere near being conclusive, does have some plausibility and at the very least exemplifies the potential richness of such symbolic and spiritually oriented analyses.

Conceptual Themes

Applying the procedures outlined above, I discerned a number of conceptual themes running through the five content themes identified in the previous chapter. Initially, these conceptual themes included identity and participation; justice, correction, and integration; the existence of a transcendent or spiritual dimension, and journeying toward and connecting with this dimension; and proof of the paranormal, new perception, and the nature of synchronicity. Ultimately, however, they proved to be resolvable into the following four: identity, transformation, spirituality, and synchronicity.[20] Each of these was traced in its various aspects through the material as a whole and in particular through the selection of forty-one incidents related in the previous chapter.

Identity

The concept of identity is emphasized repeatedly throughout Plaskett's material. It emerges first through the highlighting of his surname in the two coincidences involving Plaskett's Crater and Plaskett's Star (1, 2).

The first of these also draws attention to his date of birth. Next, Plaskett's actual physical appearance was highlighted through the coincidence involving the remarkable resemblance between himself and the singer playing the part of Parsifal in Wagner's opera (4). Then there was an implicit identification with Dante established by means of the symbolic paralleling of Plaskett's "coincidental" journey with the cosmic journey of the Italian poet through paradise (11). Further incidents evoking the notion of identity might include the presence of the coincidentally significant symbol of the eagle on an article of clothing Plaskett was wearing (13), his behaving in a certain manner that paralleled that of the souls of the Just in Dante's poem (14), the mention of his actual person in a magazine item (33), and his learning of the effects on a chess opponent of an illness—diabetes—from which he also suffers (36). This repeated emphasizing of aspects of Plaskett's own identity—his surname, date of birth, appearance, experiences, clothing, behavior, actual person, and condition of health—can only serve to increase consciousness of the issue of identity generally.

More specifically, there are indications that Plaskett's experiences helped make him more sharply aware that there is a spiritual aspect to identity ("that Man does have a Soul"[21]). A number of coincidences, in addition to highlighting the concept of identity, also suggest the existence of and movement toward a higher or spiritual level of reality. Plaskett's Crater (1) and Plaskett's Star (2) are *celestial*, that is to say, *heavenly*, phenomena. Understand this symbolically, equating the heavenly with the spiritual, and Plaskett's surname and, hence, his identity appear themselves to be, or at least to be intimately attached to, spiritual phenomena. Again, the two figures with whom Plaskett has been implicitly identified, Parsifal (4) and Dante (11), are among the preeminent spiritual seekers in Western literature. Thus, attention is focused on that aspect of Plaskett's identity that is also spiritually seeking.

Another nuance to the identity theme—this one very clearly picked up on by the experiencer himself—is the emphasis on participation. This is suggested by the serendipitous manner in which certain coincidences involving the identity theme occurred: for example, it was while searching for information about Plaskett's Crater that the experiencer "accidentally" learned of the existence of Plaskett's Star in the constellation of Monoceros (2). Most clearly, however, the significance of participation is implicit in the coincidences identifying Plaskett with Parsifal (4, 5), as is explained in my amplification of those incidents below. In fact, the notion of identity will be seen to extend even further, to the point where the experiencer seemed virtually to be enacting aspects of the archetypal drama of Parsifal, inasmuch as he, like Parsifal, was seeking a form of

Grail (4, 10; also see below). Similarly, Plaskett seemed to be enacting aspects of Dante's spiritual drama, undergoing like him a symbolic journey through the cosmos (11).[22] This sense of enactment became more explicit through the coincidence involving Assagioli's psychosynthesis exercises (29). In these exercises, "symbols" (sometimes consisting of short episodes) from the legend of the Grail and from Dante's *Divine Comedy* are presented to a therapeutic group, each member of which is then asked "to introject the symbol, so to speak, *to identify himself with it.*"[23] There remains, however, the important difference that whereas with these exercises the symbolic identification and enactment is something undergone in a deliberate and controlled way, in Plaskett's coincidence experiences the identification and enactment came about spontaneously.

Transformation

The second conceptual theme that seemed to me to be particularly in evidence when I analyzed Plaskett's material was that of transformation. Again, this involved several aspects, many of them, naturally enough, relating to the preceding concept of identity.

First, there is the idea of a transformation from ignorance to knowledge, and from lesser consciousness to greater consciousness. This is implicit in the coincidence involving the first map of the far side of the moon (1): territory that had always been inaccessible to human consciousness now for the first time became known and charted. Interpret this symbolically, with the far side of the moon representing the unconscious, and we have allusion to a transformation from unconsciousness to consciousness. A similar idea is embedded in the story of Parsifal (evoked by coincidences 4, 5, and 10): as we shall see later in this chapter, Parsifal has to undergo a significant transformation in his understanding before he can realize his destiny of achieving the Grail. Again, the celestial journey of Dante, and analogously that of Plaskett (11), consists of a series of progressive transformations into ever higher and subtler states of consciousness and insight.

The idea of a transformation from normal psychophysical levels of experience to a spiritual level of experience, and vice versa, seems to be evoked quite often. Plaskett's Crater (1), being on the far side of earth's satellite the moon, lies at the extreme outer limit of connectedness to the terrestrial and faces into the heavenly or, symbolically understood, spiritual spaces beyond. Plaskett's Star (2), in turn, actually is situated out in these heavenly or spiritual spaces. Conversely, meteorites (3) are phenomena that come from out in the heavens and impact on the earth and moon—symbolically, a spiritual influence imprinting itself on the psychophysical. Again, within Arthurian legend (4–10) a crucial role is played by the quest for the Grail (10) as a spiritual object capable of effecting a profound regenerative transformation both of society and of nature itself (discussed later). Also, within many of the coincidences grouped under the theme of sea monsters (20–30) there is implied the notion of two levels of reality (water on the one hand, air or land on the other), with significant transitions and transformations taking place between them. Thus, there is the idea of "coming up for air" (22, 25; also 35) with the symbolic implication that sustenance needs to be drawn from a higher level. This, however, is balanced by the coincidence involving the great-crested grebes (24); these freshwater diving birds obtain *their* sustenance by penetrating from the higher dimension (air) into the lower (water). This suggests symbolically that not only is the psycho-physical dependent on the spiritual but that in some sense the reverse can also be the case.

Another aspect of the transformation theme is the idea of a movement toward greater completeness of being. In general, this takes the form of first recognizing some negativized or neglected feature of reality and then positivizing this through integrating it or discovering in it some unexpected value. This is the case with the motif of the giant octopus (20, 21, 30). One coincidence draws attention simply to the existence of this monstrous creature below the sea, it being detected largely through its negative power to interfere with the vessel *Trilogy* on the surface (20). Another coincidence then associates the image of the large octopus with a couple of books (21) that are subsequently found to contain information that proves positively valuable in relation to Plaskett's experiences (22). However, the transformation from an implicitly negative to an implicitly positive valuation of the octopus is clearest in the incident involving the report of the visualization exercise in which a patient imaginally "encountered an octopus in the depths of the ocean which threatened to engulf him" (30). The report reproduced by Plaskett continues: "the subject was asked to visualise himself going up towards the surface, taking the octopus with him. On reaching the surface, to the surprise of the subject, the octopus changed itself into the face of his mother."[24] Similarly, in the communication that Plaskett received from Greenpeace (25), there was an attempt to transform the image of the whale from that of something monstrous and unintelligent, and therefore to be exploited, into "a symbol of all that is vast and mysterious in the natural world . . . intelligent, intuitive, perhaps even thoughtful."[25] Finally, an even more explicit expression of the idea of something from below the sea being found to have great value when raised to the surface is the incident involving the discovery of the treasure of ancient Greek pottery (28).

In the case of each of these coincidences, it is a straightforward move to equate the sea with the unconscious. One can then interpret the octopus, whale, and pottery as contents of the unconscious. These, so long as they remain unconscious, are negative, misunderstood, or simply useless. However, when brought to the surface or at least related to more sympathetically, that is, when integrated more effectively into consciousness, they turn out to have unsuspected value. In terms of personal identity, the more successful one is at integrating the unconscious with consciousness, the more complete and balanced is one likely to be as a person.

Failure to achieve an adequate level of integration is likely to lead to dangerous imbalance, and it may be this that is alluded to in those coincidences that highlight the motif of justice and injustice. This motif is fairly explicit in some of the incidents involving the image of the eagle in relation to Dante's *Paradiso* (12, 13, and, especially, 14). It is perhaps also more subtly implied in other incidents in which either Dante's poem or the image of the eagle forms part of the background. Thus, the coincidences involving Plaskett's grandmother in relation to the "Eagle" rest home and the name "Beatrice" (15, 16) may be alluding to an injustice or imbalance in regard to the archetypal feminine (the "Grand Mother," Magna Mater). Similarly, the coincidence of the decisive meteorite shower landing on the French town of L'Aigle (Eagle) (18) may suggest the correction of a form of injustice in regard to the status of what we have found to be symbolized by the meteorites, namely, coincidences themselves and in particular coincidences viewed as celestially originating (that is, spiritual) phenomena. The latter suggestion is supported to some extent by the coincidence involving the two parallel dreams of synchronized swimming (23): here what is submerged—and therefore symbolically in need of being brought into consciousness—is a synchronized activity, which of course can readily be equated with the phenomenon of synchronicity itself.

There may also be an indication in Plaskett's coincidences as to what further state might be achieved as a result of these transformations toward greater consciousness and completeness: they may lead to a new kind of vision or perception. This is suggested generally by the whole content theme of "Eyes and vision" (31–41). More particularly we can note that the blind taxi passenger, in outwitting the driver who tries to cheat him (31), shows evidence of having a kind of sensitivity or perception other than normal vision. One might observe in regard to this that prophets and seers—those who can perceive in nonordinary dimensions—are sometimes depicted in myth as being physically blind (for example, Tiresias). Again, there is the coincidence involving the illusion of the triangular cloud and Plaskett's inadvertent photographing of the pediment resembling the symbol of the "third eye" (32): here a misperception results serendipitously in the evocation of a symbol of higher perception—suggesting perhaps that the transformation into higher forms of perception may require a temporary loss of accurate perception on normal levels.

In further support of this last suggestion, we can note that in one version of the Grail legend the knight Lancelot (a figure evoked by coincidences 4 and 5) at one point in his adventures actually caught sight of the Grail but approached too close to its radiance so that he was blinded and paralyzed for twenty-four days. When he eventually revived, he said, "I have seen so great marvels that my tongue may not describe them . . . and were it not for my great sins, I should have seen more."[26] This can be compared with one of Dante's experiences. In a section of the *Paradiso* reproduced by Plaskett (Canto XXVI),[27] Dante is depicted as having been blinded by the intensity of the love he encounters while being questioned by St. John. However, through answering St. John's questions satisfactorily he shows that he is capable of understanding the deeper nature of love. As a result, his sight is restored and, unlike Lancelot, he is enabled to "see more." Thus, in both cases, temporary blindness is the result of encountering a higher level of truth or reality. However, whereas Dante possesses the integrity and insight to pass into the corresponding higher level of perception and therefore eventually achieves the supreme vision of God, Lancelot lacks this integrity and so is unable to become a full achiever of the Grail and all that it represents spiritually.

Spirituality

The pervasiveness of the conceptual theme of spirituality should already be fairly clear. It is implied, for example, in the titles of two of the overarching content themes I have identified ("Celestial Phenomena" and "Dante's *Paradiso*") as well as in a number of other subthemes ("the Grail"—this being an object of spiritual quest; "coming up for air"—that suggests penetration into a higher dimension of reality;[28] and "new vision"—referring, above all, to a newly acquired form of spiritual perception).

Again, it is possible to differentiate several aspects of the spirituality theme. First, there are coincidences that draw attention simply to the existence of the spiritual dimension. Among these are the incident involving Plaskett's Star (2), which evokes the possibility of a spiritual aspect to one's identity; those involving meteorites (3, 18), which suggest the possibility of concrete effects originating from a transcendent source; and the Grail coincidence (10), which highlights this preeminent symbol of spirit.

Beyond drawing attention to the mere existence of the spiritual dimension, the coincidences suggest the importance of the process of developing toward fuller realization of spirit. This is especially the case in the apparent development of Plaskett's identification first with a crater on the moon that faces out into the heavens (1) and then with a star actually situated in the heavens (2), and the paralleling of this movement with Dante's journey through the heavens (11). We shall see later in this chapter that it is also implicit in the coincidences evoking the story of Parsifal and his quest for the Grail (4, 10).

A further aspect to the spirituality theme is the motif of bringing the spiritual into the psychophysical world. As I have already noted, the coincidences involving meteorites (3, 18) suggest, when interpreted symbolically, the entry of a tangible spiritual influence into the psychophysical dimension. A related interpretation might be put on the incident involving the image of the eagle in the context of the stealing and counterfeiting of coins (12). Here, through its association to Dante's *Paradiso* Cantos XVIII and XIX, the eagle suggests the notion of heavenly justice, while the coins readily suggest the realm of materiality. The implication is that the heavenly order of justice ought to prevail within the material world—which is to say, more broadly, that the spiritual ought to order the psychophysical. Again, we will see shortly that this idea is implicit also in the pattern of meaning evoked by the Arthurian legend coincidences (4–10).

Synchronicity

The final conceptual theme I wish to highlight from Plaskett's material is that of synchronicity itself. I have already mentioned a number of times what I call the self-referring nature of synchronicity, that is, the fact that the contents of synchronistic experiences not infrequently seem to refer, explicitly or implicitly, to the phenomenon of synchronicity itself. They do this either through having the concept of synchronicity (or an image symbolizing synchronicity) as their actual content, or else through having contents that express one or the other of the properties intrinsic to the general form of synchronistic experiences—for example, the kind of spiritual properties described in chapter 3 (numinosity, miraculousness, transformation, and so forth). Plaskett's material contains synchronicities that are self-referring in each of these senses.

The concept of synchronicity is especially evoked by the incident that centers around Plaskett's making of a symbolic association between meteorites and coincidences (3); but it is also readily suggested by the coincidence involving the two parallel dreams of synchronized swimming (23). In each of these cases, it is as though synchronicity is pointing toward itself and revealing certain aspects of its nature: its spiritual origin and the kind of proof to which it is susceptible (3), and the fact of its present unintegrated, submerged, largely unconscious status (23).

Regarding the self-referring nature of Plaskett's coincidences in the second of the senses mentioned, this can be explicated here specifically with reference to the preceding three conceptual themes of identity, transformation, and spirituality. Doing so will also illustrate how deeply the four themes I have been considering mutually implicate one another.

The factor of identity plays a crucial role in many if not most coincidences. For it is usually because there is at least one point of identity or near-identity between events that they are considered to form a coincidence at all.[29] Furthermore, inasmuch as many coincidences involve as one of their events an intimate psychic process of the experiencer that is then found to parallel a physical event seemingly very far removed from the area of influence of the experiencer's subjectivity, this can be considered to be establishing an unexpected form of identification between the experiencer and the world. When the identification is with not just a single isolated content but with several contents that together seem to evoke a dynamic pattern of meaning—perhaps with overtones of ritual, myth, or legend—then forms of spontaneous symbolic enactment may even take place. Thus, Plaskett's experiences can be understood to have led him to enact certain aspects of the legend of Parsifal (4, 5, 10) and of the symbolic journey of Dante (11–14). In the light of the Thornton case examined in chapter 4, it would seem possible that this potentiality for staging spontaneous enactments may be intrinsic to the very nature of synchronicity. In Plaskett's material it is specifically evoked by those coincidences whose content involves actors (4, 5, 9), and even more clearly by the incident whose content is Assagioli's psychosynthesis exercise with its technique of identifying with symbolic episodes from Arthurian legend and Dante's *Divine Comedy* (29).

The relationship to synchronicity of the concept of transformation was examined at length in chapter 3. That the contents of Plaskett's experiences so richly evoke this concept is thus another instance of synchronicity seeming to explicate an aspect of its own nature. In particular, we can note the incident involving the meteorites falling on the French town of L'Aigle (18). If we equate meteorites with coincidences and the eagle (*l'aigle*) with the transformative influence of heavenly justice, then the falling of the former on the latter suggests that a close connection may exist between these two ideas: in some sense, synchronicity may be an agent or vehicle for the transformative influence of heavenly justice.

Again, those of Plaskett's coincidences whose contents suggest the possibility of a new kind of perception (31–41) highlight another kind of transformation that is intrinsic to the very nature of synchronicity. Inasmuch as it directs our attention toward a kind of relationship between events that is usually unnoticed (namely, meaningful acausal paralleling), synchronicity encourages and requires us to look in a new way. In relation to one coincidence, Plaskett recalls thinking that the phenomenon may actually require us to develop a new science (38). More specifically, Jung presents the synchronistic relationship between events as *complementary to* the kinds of causal relationship of which we are normally aware. This balancing of one way of looking with a second complementary way may in part be what is suggested by the repeated emphasis in Plaskett's coincidences on the motif of one-eyedness (32, 36, 37, 39–41). Sometimes the implication of these one-eye incidents seems negative: being one-eyed means being partially sighted, limited, incomplete (36, 37, 40, 41). At other times, however, the tone is more positive: the "single eye" is the "third eye" of spiritual insight (32) or an unexpectedly appearing precious jewel (39). In these latter cases, the "single eye" may signify not one eye of two but rather a new kind of integrated or holistic perception. If so, it again reflects one of the intrinsic features of synchronicity, namely, its ability to effect temporary shifts from our usual mode of perception, based primarily on observer and observed separation, into a more holistic or centerless mode of perception, which involves additionally awareness of observer–observed unity.[30] The existence of both negative and positive connotations to the motif of one-eyedness may reflect the point suggested earlier, that it may be necessary to pass through a temporary impairment of one's normal perception in order to arrive at a new and higher form of perception.[31] Likewise, synchronicity, though it may be an important additional or new way of looking, can all too easily seem delusory nonsense to the unsympathetic.

Finally—and here the self-reference is at its most conspicuous—the contents of Plaskett's coincidences repeatedly and explicitly emphasize the concept of spirit, thereby reflecting the fundamentally spiritual nature of synchronicity as I have been elaborating on it throughout this work. In particular, that intelligible patterns of meaning, such as I have been presenting, can be plausibly extracted from the content of the coincidences suggests that synchronicity may be understood as a form of revelation. Further, considering that the specific "message" of the revelation concerns in large part the nature and status of synchronicity itself, the phenomenon should perhaps, at least on the basis of Plaskett's material, be viewed as self-revelatory. What it is revealing about itself includes many things but, as we are now seeing, important among them is its own spiritual nature. In other words, through Plaskett's material, one of the principal things we are enabled to witness is the self-revelation of synchronicity as spirit.

A MODERN GRAIL STORY

By way of illustrating more fully the kind of amplification and analysis on which the preceding interpretation has been based, I shall now present in greater detail the most salient features of the analysis I made specifically of the six coincidences grouped in the previous chapter under the thematic heading of "Arthurian Legend." Above all, this should illustrate how, through hypothesizing that there may be embedded or implicit levels of meaning within seemingly unpromising coincidence contents and then making the effort to uncover these meanings, it can happen that interesting and often quite remarkable patterns of meaning do emerge. Plaskett recognized this possibility and pursued it to a certain extent; what I have done is extend it more systematically.

Plaskett's coincidences highlight three central images from Arthurian legend: the knight Parsifal, the Round Table, and the Holy Grail. These images evoke various sections of the overall legend, each of which can be seen to have pertinent implications for the themes this work has been developing.

Parsifal

The first of the Arthurian legend coincidences (4) has as its principal content *a striking physical resemblance between Plaskett and the singer playing the part of Parsifal* in Wagner's opera. Previously Plaskett's identity was emphasized in terms of his surname (1, 2) and date of birth (1); here it is emphasized through his actual physical appearance. There may be a suggestion in this that the level of identification is here becoming more concrete, more physically embodied. Further, whereas before the identification was with images of the relatively static phenomena of a lunar crater and a distant star, here it is with the much more dynamic image of an actor or singer. A similar suggestion stems from incidents (5) and (9), in which the contents are the names of the actors *Lance Perceval* in the one instance and (Mel) *Ferrer* and (Stanley) *Baker* in the other. The emphasis on acting suggests a more intimate participatory relationship to the events, even that the experiencer may himself be involved in some kind of dramatic enactment.

Specifically, through the singer, Plaskett finds himself identified with the figure of Parsifal. Within most versions of Arthurian legend Parsifal is the knight who quests after and eventually discovers the Holy Grail. According to the legend, a certain king known as the Fisher King is suffering from a wound that will not heal until a knight of conspicuous excellence discovers his castle and, seeing the Grail there, immediately asks certain questions concerning it. So long as the king remains sick, the whole land suffers. But when the knight arrives and asks about the Grail, both the king and the land will be healed. Parsifal is the knight predestined to undertake and accomplish this task.

In the legend, Parsifal arrives at the Grail Castle twice. The first time he comes upon it with remarkable ease but without appreciating its significance. He views a number of marvelous things relating to the Grail and even the Grail itself, but, inhibited by the sense of decorum that he has been instructed to maintain, he omits to ask anything about them. The following morning all the marvels have disappeared, and he is informed subsequently that his omission to ask the relevant questions means that the curse on the king and the land remains in effect. His personal failure is thus the cause of continuing widespread suffering. Realizing this, he determines to find the Grail Castle again at any cost. After many years of seeking he eventually does so, this time he asks the all-important questions, and simultaneously the ailing Fisher King and the whole land recover from their plight.[32]

When Parsifal first sees the Grail he remains a passive observer, not appreciating his own crucial role in the events he is witnessing. However, by the time he sees it the second time, learning the significance of the Grail has become of burning personal relevance; indeed, it is the central goal of his life. There is a parallel to this in Plaskett's change of attitude toward coincidences. Before the extraordinary concentration of coincidences that occurred to him at the beginning of 1988, he had already noted a fair number of such events and had even been sufficiently interested to begin carefully recording them.[33] However, when the main clusters got under way, he became so fascinated that he began much more actively to consider their possible meaning and to pursue research associations.[34] Like Parsifal, he became engaged in a sort of quest. And it soon became clear that this active involvement was itself in some way leading to the occurrence of further incidents (the "triggering" effect to which Plaskett refers several times). In other words, Plaskett's participation in the coincidences—characterized primarily by his more inquiring attitude—appeared to result in more meaning manifesting in his environment (in the form of more meaningful coincidences). Thus, as in Parsifal's case, the asking of the right questions—questions ultimately concerning meaning—leads to a significant reanimation of the environment.

The Round Table

The first result of this more inquiring attitude appeared to be the triggering of the series of further coincidences involving Arthurian legend (6–10). The principal contents of the first four of these (6–9) evoke, directly or indirectly, the image of the Round Table. In one case (6), the content actually is *round table*; in another (8), it is *Knights of the Round Table*. In the other two cases, the contents are *Camelot* (7), the supposed location of the Round Table and of King Arthur's court; and *Ferrer* and *Baker* (9), the names of the two actors playing the film roles of King Arthur and his nephew Mordred, the conflict between whom resulted in the destruction of the fellowship of the Round Table.

The image of the Round Table evokes in several ways the problem of the integration of the spiritual aspect of reality with its more mundane aspect. According to the *Queste del Saint Graal*, the Round Table was the third of "three most important tables in the world."[35] The first table was that at which Christ and his Apostles ate the Last Supper. The second, "in the likeness and in remembrance of it,"[36] was the table of the Holy Grail, that is, the table in the Grail Castle upon which the Grail was placed or around which the Fisher King and his company sat eating food miraculously bestowed by the Grail.[37] Being the third, the Round Table is at a further remove again from the medieval author's conception of highest spirituality (Christ); used by King Arthur and his knights, it is very much in the material world. This gradation from more spiritual to more material contexts reflects what Emma Jung and Marie-Louise von Franz, following C. G. Jung, consider to have been one of the major impetuses behind the emergence of medieval alchemy, the legend of the Grail, and certain Holy Ghost movements such as that of Joachim of Floris: the psychic need to compensate the one-sidedness of Christianity through reconciling the conflicting opposites of spirit and matter; more specifically, through addressing "certain still unresolved problems, such as those of sexuality, the shadow and the unconscious in general."[38] (As we saw above, especially the latter two of these are among the ideas seemingly evoked by several of Plaskett's coincidences involving the theme of sea monsters.)

An important feature of the Round Table in the legend is that all the seats around it were occupied except one, the so-called *siège périlleux*. This "perilous seat" was supposed to represent the "empty place vacated by Judas when Christ said he would be betrayed."[39] It could only be occupied by "the predestined and most virtuous man who should one day find the Grail."[40] This is, of course, Parsifal. However, Jung and von Franz point out that "it is a remarkable fact that the discoverer of the Grail—who in his attribute of the redeemer is to some extent a reappearance of Christ or . . . represents an incarnation of the Holy Spirit—should have to occupy just precisely Judas's seat."[41] The reason for this, they suggest, is that "Perceval has been chosen to reunite the too widely sundered opposites of good and evil with the help of the Holy Spirit and the Grail."[42]

In the legend, contrary to what we are led to expect, Parsifal does not occupy the *siège périlleux* after discovering the Grail. Instead, he remains in the Grail Castle, renouncing chivalry to become a holy man; in some versions he even withdraws into the wilderness as an anchorite. Jung and von Franz see this as a failure on Parsifal's part and more generally as representing a failure on the part of medieval consciousness:

> Perceval should not have taken himself into the seclusion of the Grail Castle; in order to remain in the picture he should have brought the Grail to the Round Table, so that instead of the Spirit being divorced from the world the world would have been impregnated with the Spirit.[43]

As a result of this failure, the principal goal of the fellowship of the Round Table became worldly rather than spiritual. King Arthur and his knights left Britain on an expedition against Rome. During their absence, the regent, Arthur's nephew Mordred, seized power for himself. Arthur and his company returned as soon as they learned of this, but in the ensuing battles, all of the Knights of the Round Table, including King Arthur, met their death. Thus, Parsifal's failure to bring the spiritual and the worldly together resulted indirectly in the destruction of such worldly order as there was.

A number of features of the contexts of Plaskett's round table coincidences reflect this aspect of the legend. The phrase "round table" that he heard on the radio (6) referred to a meeting of *international politicians*. More specifically, as Plaskett further informs us, the politicians were due to discuss what policy they should adopt in regard to certain *countries in crisis* economically.[44] The implicit idea here of assessing or *evaluating* seems to be one of the motifs of the coincidence generally: the round table that Plaskett saw on the television program was being *evaluated* as an antique; and he himself was *evaluating* (as he says, "pondering intently") the possible coincidental status of seeing the round table when he did. All of this suggests the situation in regard to the Arthurian Round Table: at the conclusion of the Grail quest, the possible future *value* of the Round Table fellowship had to be assessed, and the fatal decision was made to direct its energies into specifically *political activities* (the expedition against Rome). The consequences of this decision are suggested by the next coincidence, when Plaskett learns that the composer of the musical *Camelot* has *died* (7). A composer is someone who, in this case working in sound, creates order and meaning. The death of the composer of *Camelot* suggests, then, the death of the one who ordered the Round Table fellowship located at Camelot, the death, that is, of King Arthur. More explicitly, the film

Knights of the Round Table (8) focused primarily on the *treachery* of Mordred and the *destruction* to which that led, including Arthur's death. Similarly, the coincidence involving the names Ferrer and Baker (9) alluded by association to the characters played by the actors Mel Ferrer and Stanley Baker, namely, King Arthur and Mordred, respectively—the two contestants in the *fatal struggle for worldly power*.

The Holy Grail

Besides this highlighting of the political dimension of Arthurian legend, there was emphasis on its spiritual dimension, as symbolized by the Holy Grail. Specifically, this comes into focus with Plaskett's discovery that one possible derivation of the word "Grail" was from the Latin (in fact originally Greek) word "*crater*" (10). Already I have noted how Plaskett's coincidences have brought about a spontaneous identification of him with the crater on the far side of the moon (1) and with Parsifal, the preeminent knight of the Grail legend (4). Each of these identifications can only have been reinforced by the unexpected equation of the two images, crater and Grail.

As we have seen, in most versions of the legend the Grail is considered to be a kind of vessel—the very one in which Joseph of Arimathea caught the blood dripping from the wounds of the crucified Christ. Wolfram von Eschenbach disagrees with this account and—almost certainly under the influence of alchemical thinking—portrays the Grail as a stone. But whether as a vessel or as a stone, all accounts agree in attributing to the Grail miraculous life-giving and life-sustaining powers of a spiritual nature.[45]

It is clear, then, that the Grail in itself is a resonant symbol of spiritual mystery and power, and, hence, also of the goal of spiritual striving. Indeed, for Parsifal the most important objective in his life becomes to find and ask about the Grail. Thus, it is not unlikely that when this symbol synchronistically emerges in Plaskett's life, it is also (at least in part) as a symbol of the spiritual goal toward which he is striving. Specifically, the goal that Plaskett saw himself as seeking was union of his normal self with his higher self or soul.[46] Interestingly, Jung and von Franz conclude their chapter on "The Grail as Vessel" with the suggestion that "in a special sense . . . the soul is that wondrous vessel which is the goal of the quest and in which the life-giving power inheres."[47]

Another object of Plaskett's quest was for some way of "proving the reality of the spiritual dimension of the universe."[48] This too is symbolized by the Grail. If Christ represents spiritual reality, then insofar as

Christ ascended to heaven with his body he left no traces of his physical life on earth apart from this very blood which remained on the lance [that had pierced his side] and in the Grail vessel. It is therefore the only permanent evidence of his *earthly* life and of the "substance of his soul."[49]

This problem of evidence and proof was for Plaskett initially found to center primarily on the coincidentally highlighted image of meteorites (3). Later, he had the realization "that really big meteorites not only produce samples of extra-terrestrial rock (the stuff that changed the scientists' minds [concerning the reality of there being such things as meteorites]), they also produce CRATERS! A crater is even clearer evidence!"[50] This suggests another line of connection. The image of the crater was found to be associated with the Grail. Now it turns out also to be associated with the image of meteorites. Finally, completing the circle of associations, Jung and von Franz relate information that enables the image of meteorites also to be associated directly with the Grail. In Wolfram von Eschenbach's *Parzival*, the Grail is, as has been said, not a vessel but a stone. Of this stone it is said:

> They [the Knights of the Grail] live from
> a stone
> of purest kind.
> If you do not know it,
> it shall here be named to you.
> It is called *lapsit exillis*.[51]

There is dispute as to what *lapsit exillis* means.[52] Some take it to be a corruption of either *lapis elixir* or *lapis exilis*, both of which expressions are found in alchemy to refer to the philosopher's stone. This is plausible, since there seems little doubt that Wolfram was strongly influenced by alchemical thought.[53] But there is also another intriguing possibility mentioned by Jung and von Franz: "Because of the reading, *lapsit ex coelis*, there was a wish [among some commentators] to interpret the Grail as a meteorite, for in antiquity meteorites were considered to be λίθοι ἔμψυχοι—stones with a soul."[54] This interpretation receives some support from the story, as Joseph Campbell relates, that

> [a]ccording to Wolfram's perhaps invented reference, the Provençal author Kyot discovered the legend of the Grail in Toledo, in the forgotten work of a heathen astrologer, Flegitanis

by name, "who had with his own eyes seen hidden wonders in the stars. He tells of a thing," states Wolfram, "called the Grail, whose name he had read in the constellations. 'A host of angels left it on the earth,' Flegitanis tells, 'then flew off, high above the stars.'"[55]

Again, Jung and von Franz relate another version of the story, according to which "the Grail was said to be a precious stone that fell out of Lucifer's crown when he was expelled from heaven. There the idea of the *lapsit ex coelis*, of its having fallen from heaven, is likewise expressed."[56]

The coincidences involving the images or ideas of the crater, meteorites, the Grail, and coincidence itself, together with the associations arising from them, have established the following connections:

a. the Grail is associated with a crater (10);
b. meteorites are associated with the phenomenon of coincidence (3);
c. meteorites are associated with craters (Plaskett's association, based on meteorological fact);
d. meteorites are associated with the Grail (in Wolfram von Eschenbach's *Parzival* and elsewhere; also by combining [a] and [c]);
e. the crater is associated with the phenomenon of coincidence (by combining [b] and [c])
f. the Grail is associated with the phenomenon of coincidence (by combining either [a] and [e] or [b] and [d]).

This tight nexus of associations is all the more striking in view of the fact that each of the images or ideas—crater, meteorites, Grail, coincidence—was already central to at least one incident impressive and suggestive in itself.

Plaskett's coincidences, then, have thrown into prominence the image of the Grail both as a vessel (crater) and as a stone (meteorite). The two versions are not strictly incompatible: the vessel could conceivably have been cut out of meteoric stone, perhaps even out of the jewel from Lucifer's crown. However, there may be a specific reason why both versions are evoked by Plaskett's material. In the case of a crater that has been produced by the impact of a meteorite, the meteorite would, at least initially, be contained in the crater. In a sense, then, the meteorite can be viewed as the content and the crater as the container. The fact that both images are equated here with the same thing, the Grail, suggests the paradox that "the container is the content." This in turn reflects the feature that we have several times observed about synchronicity: its self-referring nature whereby the meaning seemingly derivable from the content of a synchronicity is often basically the same as that which is derivable from consideration of the general form of any and every synchronicity. Thus, form and content express the same meaning, so that, in a sense, form and content are one.

In the light of all these connections, the speculation suggests itself that synchronicity, as it is revealing itself through Plaskett's coincidences, may itself be a form of the Grail. The Grail is something spiritual and bestowing of meaning. So, I have argued, is synchronicity. The Grail, though essentially spiritual, can manifest in the psychophysical world of normal experience, but elusively and evanescently. This, as we have seen, is just how synchronicity manifests. The Grail appears to Parsifal at first spontaneously and without requiring any special effort on his part, but before he can access its spiritualizing and regenerative power, he has to adopt an actively inquiring attitude in regard to it. The situation is similar with synchronicities, which appear spontaneously but require that the experiencer actively reflect on and inquire into them if they are to disclose the fuller dimensions of their meaningfulness. One of the reasons the Grail is such a sacred object is that, as Jung and von Franz noted, it is "the only permanent evidence of [Christ's] earthly life and of the 'substance of his soul,'" that is to say, the Grail constitutes physical proof of the spiritual reality represented by Christ.[57] Likewise, synchronicity can be experienced, as it was by Plaskett, as constituting a form of tangible proof both of the paranormal generally and, more specifically, of "the reality of the spiritual dimension of the universe."[58] Again, I just noted that the Grail, as both crater and meteorite, can be understood as both container and content, both outer vessel and inner substance. Synchronicity similarly has both its outer vessel-like aspect (its unvarying general form) and its inner substance of images and ideas (its variable specific content). Alternatively, one might consider the normal psychophysical events composing the synchronicity as the container and the anomalous and spiritually significant relationship between the events as the content. Finally, the symbolizing of the Grail as both meteorite and crater suggests that it is in some sense simultaneously both cause and effect and, hence, cause of itself (*causa sui*). Synchronicities by definition are not caused by any factor apart from themselves, and therefore can be viewed as uncaused or acausal phenomena; hence, as causes of themselves.

Within the context of Plaskett's experiences as a whole, the symbolism relating to Arthurian legend reiterates and develops motifs that have already been introduced by the celestial phenomena coincidences

(1–3) and that will be further developed by coincidences involving the other themes of Dante's *Paradiso*, sea monsters, and eyes and vision (11–41). In particular, the issue of identity and participation has been emphasized through the figure of Parsifal; the importance of the spiritual aspect of reality and of integrating it with the physical is expressed through the relationship between Parsifal as Grail seeker and the Round Table; and as we just saw, the relevance of the phenomenon of synchronicity itself to these issues is here suggested particularly strongly by a cluster of interconnections that may even lead to the thought that, in a sense, synchronicity is a form of the Grail.

Chapter 7

SYNCHRONICITY AND SPIRIT IN THE *I CHING*

> Many of us who have used [the *I Ching*] seriously over a number of years have been struck by its enigma. Although I have been familiar with it since my cradle days as an analytical psychologist I still feel equally disturbed and impressed by its efficacy. I am disturbed because it seems so utterly improbable that a book, several thousand years old and grown in such different cultural soil, should still prove so meaningful to us. If it *is* a genuine oracle, as I personally from my experiences have to accept, it cuts right across our Western scientific causalistic world-picture. It reveals an interdependence of subject and object, it stands against the accepted Western dogma of the division between the two, dictated by a limited ego-consciousness, and it reveals a profound correspondence between within and without. All this makes me wish that the riddle of the *I Ching* should be taken more seriously by us and systematically researched.
>
> I have mentioned the *I Ching* because I think that here we have the symbol of a possible development of man's consciousness in *the* or *a* next phase of history.
>
> Gerhard Adler, "C. G. Jung in a Changing Civilisation"

The preceding chapters have been concerned primarily with spontaneous synchronistic experiences. I have emphasized that they are spontaneous in order to distinguish them from another category of synchronistic experiences, namely, those that have been more consciously generated through involvement in one or another kind of divinatory procedure. What I wish to do in this chapter is to look in detail at one such divinatory procedure: the ancient Chinese Oracle of Change, the *I Ching*.

Though ancient, the *I Ching* is still very much alive today, with an especially thriving interest in Europe and America, where in fact it was only properly introduced during the twentieth century. It is relevant to the present study in several ways. First and foremost, the system of the *I Ching* has been explicitly claimed by Jung, and others following him, to be based primarily on the principle of synchronicity. Indeed, some of Jung's earliest public statements of his synchronicity principle were made specifically with reference to the *I Ching*.[1] If this claim is justified, it means that, in spite of the highly diverse and radically unpredictable nature of synchronicity, the phenomenon can nevertheless be systematized and put to orderly use. The possible implications of this are powerfully expressed by the quotation from Gerhard Adler at the head of this chapter. Jung earlier voiced similar sentiments in his memorial address for Richard Wilhelm:

> Anyone who, like myself, has had the rare good fortune to experience in association with Wilhelm the divinatory power of the *I Ching* cannot remain ignorant of the fact that we have here an Archimedean point from which our Western attitude of mind could be lifted off its foundations.[2]

We shall see, indeed, that the Chinese world, in which the *I Ching* arose in ancient times and for two and a half millennia continued to flourish, was imbued with an intricately worked out understanding of reality that bears important resemblance to the viewpoint of synchronicity. Of particular relevance to the present study is that in the Chinese world the *I Ching* would most often be understood against the backdrop of a worldview in which the spiritual aspect of reality was accorded an importance at least equal to that accorded to the physical and psychic aspects.[3] In other words, the principle of synchronicity underlying the functioning of the oracle was understood, as I also wish to understand it, in a spiritual light. Further, if in the *I Ching* we do indeed have a successful systematization of synchronicity, this should enable us to enrich our overall understanding of the phenomenon by comparing the systematically obtained synchronicities with those that arise spontaneously. Finally, inasmuch as I will be looking at the possible relationships between synchronicity and the *I Ching* more broadly, and in certain respects I hope also more deeply, than has hitherto been attempted, this chapter could also cast the odd ray of fresh light on our understanding of the *I Ching* itself.

In what follows, then, I shall first outline some of the historical background to the *I Ching*, from the alleged times of its composition in ancient China down to scholarly and psychological work being done on it in the contemporary West. I shall then briefly explain the various stages of the procedure for consulting the *I Ching* as an oracle, as this is still done by many people today. Next, I shall bring out in some detail the senses in which synchronicity can be understood to be involved in the working of the *I Ching*. In the light of this, I shall then examine the similarities and differences between oracular synchronicities and spontaneous synchronicities. At appropriate points within these discussions I shall use the oracle as a focus for exploring a number of key problems and issues intrinsic to synchronicity generally—problems such as: What constitutes or delimits the "moment" within which synchronistic patterning takes place? In what sense does the experiencer participate in the synchronistic moment? How do the various levels of concrete situation of a synchronicity relate to the abstract archetypal patterns that may underlie them? The chapter will conclude with a discussion of some of the ways in which the *I Ching* can be, and indeed has been, related to a spiritual dimension or aspect of reality.

HISTORICAL BACKGROUND

The *I Ching* as we find it is a collection of sixty-four, six-line figures ("kua" or "hexagrams": all possible combinations of whole and divided lines; see figure 7.1),[4] each figure having a name and being related to various textual matter. Some of this verbal material—the Judgment, Image, Lines, Commentary on the Decision, and so on—applies severally to the various hexagrams; other sections, namely, the Discussion of the Trigrams and the Great Treatise, are of a more general nature.[5]

According to ancient tradition,[6] the basic hexagrams themselves were discovered by the legendary culture hero Fu Hsi (third millenium B.C.E.), with the present arrangement and the Judgement texts being composed around 1150 B.C.E. by King Wên, father of the founder of the Chou dynasty (circa 1150–249 B.C.E.), during a period of political imprisonment. King Wên's son, the Duke of Chou, is supposed to have added the explanations of the individual lines (the Line texts). The remaining textual material, known collectively as the Ten Wings, is alleged to be the work of Confucius (circa 550 B.C.E.) or of his immediate disciples relating the master's expressed thoughts.

There are indications that hexagram figures may have existed and been used for oracular purposes as early as the second or even third millennium B.C.E. (though seemingly not in their present arrangement).[7]

FIGURE 7.1. Whole and divided lines.

However, modern scholarship demonstrates fairly convincingly that it is most unlikely that King Wên or the Duke of Chou, and certainly not Fu Hsi (if indeed such a person ever existed historically), had anything to do with the book's composition into its present form.[8] A more plausible account was proposed by the Russian scholar Iulian K. Shchutskii in the early 1930s: "the basic text of the *Book of Changes*," he suggested after a consideration of the then available evidence, "is originally a divinatory and subsequently a philosophical text which took shape from the materials of agricultural folklore in the Chin or Ch'in territories between the eighth and seventh centuries B.C."[9] Shschutskii also argued persuasively against Confucian authorship of the Ten Wings. Though some of this material was undoubtedly influenced by the Confucian school of thought, almost all of it actually dates (in Shchutskii's estimation) from well after Confucius's time and some of it definitely does not show his influence to any significant extent.[10] These chronological judgements of Shchutskii's have met with fairly wide (though certainly not universal) agreement among scholars in the sixty or so years since they were written.[11]

The *I Ching* enters more fully into history around 300 B.C.E. in the late Chou, Ch'in, and Early Han Dynasties, when it became established as one of the five Confucian Classics. From then until the end of the Ch'ing Dynasty (1644–1911), and even beyond, the work has continued to be a major influence on Chinese thinkers of many different orientations (especially Confucian and Taoist). Throughout this long history there have been numerous different schools of *I Ching* interpretation, but among these two principal orientations (in various forms) have predominated, often in explicit opposition to each other: the *i-li* or "meaning and principle" (or "moral principle") school, and the *hsiang-shu* or "image and number" school. As Joseph Adler explains:

> *I-li* commentaries are based on the textual elements of the I, i.e. the hexagram names and the texts. They represent attempts to derive moral guidance from the texts themselves, often apart from their oracular function. The *hsiang-shu* method of interpretation, on the other hand, is concerned with the hexagrams and trigrams, their genetic and transformational relations, their numerological values, and their symbolic correlations with a variety of cosmological categories.[12]

Both approaches are already present in the earliest commentaries (the Ten Wings): the *i-li* in the Commentary on the Decision, for example, and the *hsiang-shu* in the Image texts.[13] Subsequently the fates of the two schools seemed to oscillate somewhat. The *hsiang-shu* school had its first flowering among the Han scholar-magicians of circa 200 B.C.E. to circa 200 C.E. for whom the book provided the basis for increasingly esoteric numerological and symbolic speculations.[14] Then, in conscious opposition to this, Wang Pi (226–49) instigated a powerful and enduring version of the *i-li* approach, emphasizing the moral-philosophical component of the book above its divinatory aspect.[15] In fact, this interpretation received sanction as the official orthodoxy during the T'ang Dynasty (618–906). It was not until the time of the Northern Sung Dynasty (960–1127) that the *hsiang-shu* school was able to reassert itself in a major way, principally as a result of the work of Shao Yung (1001-77). His innovations included various numerological techniques for consulting the oracle without the use of yarrow stalks or coins,[16] and also "a history of the cosmos—past and future—derived *a priori* from the *I-ching*'s [sic] basic principle of *yin-yang* change."[17] His best-known contribution, however, is his presentation of the hexagram figures in linear, circular, and square arrangements in which the individual hexagrams stand in more logical relation to one another than they do in the traditional King Wên sequence (the sequence found in the texts as we now know them).[18]

Roughly parallel with this resurgence of the *hsiang-shu* approach, the *i-li* school was also gaining fresh impetus through the commentaries of Hu Yüan (993–1059) and his student Ch'eng I (1033–1107), who was to become the chief patriarch of the Neo-Confucian movement. It was left for the great Neo-Confucian synthesizer Chu Hsi (1130–1200), who "found merit in both approaches, but . . . considered neither one adequate in itself,"[19] to attempt to resolve the tension between them. He did this by, on the one hand, reasserting the importance of the divinatory aspect of the *I Ching*, while, on the other hand, arguing that the primary importance of this was to enable the candidate for sagehood, the *chün-tzu* (in Wilhelm–Baynes the "superior man"), to know in what specific time and context a particular moral-philosophical principle should be applied. For Chu Hsi the essential situation and the moral action it required were present in highly abstract form in the hexagram figure itself; the texts accompanying the hexagram were seen as verbal amplifications or concretizations of this basic meaning, and were in this sense secondary.[20] Chu Hsi's work on the *I Ching* had an immense influence on large numbers of subsequent commentators, but even so he was far from having established anything like a standard view.

In the seventeenth and eighteenth centuries alone nearly twenty different schools of interpretation can be identified.[21] From among this continuing diversity one final Chinese thinker we can single out here is Wang Fu-chih (1619–92), whom the sinologist Gerald Swanson has called "probably the most powerful writer on the *I Ching* in the entire Ch'ing period."[22]

Of primarily *hsiang-shu* orientation, he is relevant to the present study inasmuch as his theory of the numerical basis of the *I Ching* attracted the attention of some Jungian writers on synchronicity such as Marie-Louise von Franz.[23]

The first major event in the Western study of the *I Ching* was its impingement on the German philosopher Leibniz. Between 1697 and 1702 he was in correspondence with a Jesuit missionary in China, Fr. Joachim Bouvet. When in 1701 Leibniz sent Bouvet a table of numerals in the binary system that he (Leibniz) had worked out some twenty years previously, Bouvet responded by sending Leibniz two complete diagrams of the sixty-four *I Ching* hexagrams in the methodical arrangement worked out by Shao Yung. Counting a divided line as zero and a whole line as one, Shao Yung's sequence mirrored exactly the series of Leibniz's binary numbers from 63 to 0. Since Leibniz had worked out his system of binary arithmetic largely in an attempt "to validate spiritual truths in mathematical terms, thus making them, as he thought, irrefutable,"[24] the discovery of a parallel series of figures forming the foundation of a Chinese spiritual and philosophical system excited him tremendously. As Joseph Needham notes, "He continued to descant on his joint discovery with Bouvet for the rest of his life."[25] In fact, there is no indication that the Chinese ever conceived of the *I Ching* hexagrams as binary numbers or performed with them any arithmetical operations. However, there is no doubt that Leibniz's enthusiasm, even if based on a misunderstanding, stimulated him to develop and promote his own system further. This is significant in view of the enormously important role that binary arithmetic has come to occupy in the world of modern computers as well as in understanding neurophysiological and other phenomena.

Probably the most important step in the entry of the *I Ching* into the West was the publication in 1924 of a German translation by Richard Wilhelm, then in 1950 of a rendering of his German into English by Cary F. Baynes. A fairly accurate English translation by James Legge already existed (it was completed in 1855 but not published until 1882),[26] but by his own admission Legge understood little of the book's significance and could therefore do only so much to make it intelligible to the Western reader. Wilhelm's great achievement was not only to have translated the book (with considerable elegance) but also to have communicated, through his own extensive commentaries, its living spirit and application as a source of practical and psychological wisdom.

Jung was an enthusiastic user of the *I Ching* since around 1920—employing initially the Legge translation.[27] When in the early 1920s he met Wilhelm—then engaged in producing his translation—the result was a mutually enriching friendship, with Jung deepening his understanding of the *I Ching* and Wilhelm his understanding of psychology. For the remainder of his life, Jung was an unequivocal champion of the *I Ching*. The foreword he contributed to Baynes's English rendering of Wilhelm's translation and commentary has helped make the work almost a staple tool of analytical psychologists and, even more significantly, has precipitated it fully into the public domain where it has retained an extraordinary popularity ever since.[28]

In addition to this interest in the *I Ching* as a practical psychological tool and popular means of divination, the twentieth century saw a growth of scholarly interest in the work. One result of this has been to remove the tradition of four-sage authorship to the realm of legend where it belongs, and establish the work's undoubted multiple authorship on sounder philological and textual grounds. Other results have been to restore, with the help of new archaeological, historical, and textual evidence and techniques, the meaning of a number of passages that were impenetrable even to the earliest commentators, and in other cases to put a serious question mark over the traditional, millennia-old understanding of the meanings of certain hexagram titles themselves.[29]

An interesting fusion of detailed scholarship with depth psychological insight informed the Eranos I Ching Project (1988–94). Benefiting both from recent sinological research and the accumulated insights into the *I Ching* that have been gained through intimate involvement with it by Jungian and post-Jungian psychology over the last forty or so years, the project directors, Rudolf Ritsema and Stephen Karcher, produced a new and highly distinctive translation that, while paying particularly close attention to the nature of the oracle's language, nonetheless aims "to go behind historical, philological and philosophical analysis to revive the divinatory core, the psychological root of the book as a living practise."[30]

THE ORACULAR USE OF THE *I CHING*

As we have seen, at different periods and as understood by different thinkers, the *I Ching* has been treated sometimes primarily as an oracle and sometimes primarily as a book of wisdom. Historically speaking, it is fairly certain that its use as an oracle came first, and this is the aspect most relevant to the present study. Briefly, the oracular use of the *I Ching* involves three stages: making an inquiry, receiving a response, and then interpreting the response.

Typically, as with other oracular procedures, the *I Ching* is consulted when one is faced with a problem that cannot be resolved adequately by other means. Caught in an impasse, one seeks counsel from the oracle or from whatever power is supposed to operate through the oracle.

It is often stated, therefore, that when one consults the *I Ching* it should only be concerning matters that really are important to one and that have already defeated one's best efforts to deal with them by normal means.[31] Similarly, one is generally supposed to have respect for the oracle and integrity within oneself.[32] In this condition one frames a question, which preferably should be as specific and unambiguous as possible.[33]

Having formulated one's question, and while holding it firmly in mind, one then casts the actual hexagram. Traditionally, there are two principal methods for doing this. One, the more ancient, consists of a rather complex manipulation of a bunch of fifty yarrow stalks; the other, which is simpler and seems to be by far the commonest procedure used at the present, involves throwing a set of three coins six times.[34] Each manipulation of the stalks or fall of the three coins generates one of four possible kinds of hexagram lines: a divided moving (that is, changing) line, called an old yin; a whole resting (that is, unchanging) line, called a young yang; a divided resting line, called a young yin; or a whole moving line, called an old yang (see figure 7.2). The first manipulation or throw yields the bottom line of the hexagram, the next yields the second line, and so on until the hexagram is complete. Old or moving lines are especially important and have a propensity to change into their opposites—a moving yin into a resting yang, and a moving yang into a resting yin. If one's cast hexagram contains any such moving lines, these change into their opposites and a secondary or derived hexagram results, which is taken into consideration in addition to the primary hexagram. Each of the possible configurations of six lines that might be obtained by this procedure has attached to it a name and various sections of textual matter. It is also considered that there are certain symbolic implications in the abstract line configuration itself. Both of these aspects, text and structure, can contribute to one's actual interpretation of the oracular response.[35]

By way of illustration, consider the following experience of Gerhard Adler—the kind of experience that stimulated him to make statements such as that at the head of this chapter. This was actually his first encounter with

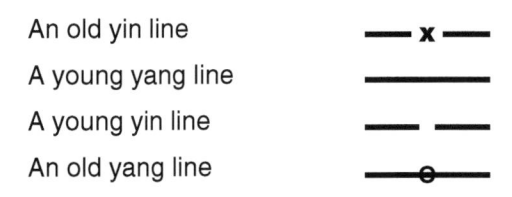

An old yin line	──x──
A young yang line	──────
A young yin line	── ──
An old yang line	──o──

FIGURE 7.2. The four kinds of lines.

FIGURE 7.3. Hexagram 44, Kou/Coming to Meet.

the *I Ching*, and he describes himself as being initially "rather incredulous" concerning the claims made for the oracle.[36] The context of his inquiry was the following "rather long-standing problem." He was in love with a girl who was very attractive and intelligent and whose background fitted his own; he would have considered marriage but was inhibited by the fact that she was also highly neurotic and "plagued by constant psychosomatic symptoms."[37] His question, accordingly, was: "Shall I marry her or not?" The *I Ching* responded with the configuration of lines in figure 7.3. This is Hexagram 44, Kou/Coming to Meet; there were no moving lines, so just this one hexagram was to be considered. The principal text to the hexagram, the Judgment, seemed to give Adler an explicit and unequivocal answer to his question: "Coming to meet. The maiden is powerful. One should not marry such a maiden."[38] Another text, the Commentary on the Decision (constituting a later stratum of the book), explains further: "'One should not marry such a maiden.' This means that one cannot live with her permanently."[39] The consultation had two major outcomes (implicit in Adler's account). First, his reservations concerning the possibility of marriage to the woman in question were strengthened to the point where he abandoned the idea. Thus, the oracle helped him become more conscious of his own state of doubt and on the basis of this to make a practical decision. Second, Adler's attitude to the *I Ching* was altered radically. It is, as he later came to appreciate, "rare to receive such an unequivocal answer to one's question." That such a thing happened to him on his first use of it was, he believed, "because it was necessary to break right through my rationalistic scepticism, to hit me with a hammer as it were."[40] From being skeptical and incredulous concerning the oracle, he became a lifelong and enthusiastic advocate of it.

Adler's interpretation here—as much of it as he has reported—is based solely on a couple of textual statements. Had the meaning not been so explicit from the texts, its general tenor might still have been inferred from the other main interpretative resource: the hexagram structure. As Richard Wilhelm explains, the one yin line entering at the bottom of the hexagram and encountering the five yang lines above represents "the dark principle, the feminine, which advances to meet the light principle, the masculine"; it is a dangerous situation in which the "inferior" or "weak" element takes the initiative and "becomes increasingly powerful."[41] Even such an abstract characterization as this might well have led Adler to interpret his situation in the same way he did on the basis of the texts.

To give a fuller idea of the range of interpretative resources that are available to the diviner, I shall briefly summarize, first the nature and significance of the various texts involved in the oracle, and then the most pertinent of the structural components of the hexagram figures. Finally, I shall show how, within the tradition, these two sources of meaning, text and hexagram structure, are considered to be intimately related.

The *I Ching* Texts

The *I Ching*'s verbal material is of a variety of kinds and was undoubtedly composed by several authors over quite a long period of time (possibly circa 700 B.C.E. to circa 100 C.E.).[42] Some layers of this textual matter might be considered more important than others, whether on historical, philological, or philosophical grounds. But while for certain purposes it can be vital to be aware of these differences in status, from the point of view of a modern-day diviner using the *I Ching*, it is more important to bear in mind that any aspect of this multilayered text might prove relevant to the inquiry made. Hellmut Wilhelm observes that

> the essential thing is to keep in mind all the strata that go to make up the book. Archaic wisdom from the dawn of time, detached and systematic reflection of the Confucian school in the Chou era, pithy sayings from the heart of the people, subtle thoughts of the leading minds: all these disparate elements have harmonized to create the structure of the book as we know it. Its real value lies in its comprehensiveness and many-sidedness. This is the aspect under which the book lives and is revered in China, and if we wish to miss nothing important, we must not neglect the later strata either. In these, many of the treasures of the very earliest origins are brought to light, treasures that up till then were hidden in the depths of the book, their existence divined rather than recognized.[43]

The principal text associated with each hexagram is the Judgment (*T'uan*). This incorporates the hexagram names themselves (almost certainly the earliest parts of the text); certain "mantic formulae" (as Shchutskii calls them), including especially the terms "sublime," "success," "furthering," and "perseverance"; and in most cases several lines of additional text. These

Judgment texts "refer in each case to the situation imaged by the hexagram as a whole,"[44] from which "it could be ascertained whether the course of action indicated by the images augured good or ill."[45] This is the part of the *I Ching* that legend claims to have been written by King Wên during his captivity at the hands of the last Shang ruler around 1150 B.C.E.

Next (or equal) in probable antiquity, and next in importance for one's appreciation of the hexagram, are the six texts attaching to each of the individual lines of a given hexagram. These were allegedly written by King Wên's son, the Duke of Chou, when he too was imprisoned. Called "The Lines" (*Hsiao*), each of these texts is, as Shchutskii puts it, "a concrete characterization of some stage in the development of the given situation."[46] When consulting the oracle one generally only pays specific attention, among the line-texts, to those associated with lines that are moving.[47]

The Lines and Judgments are, as it were, the core *I Ching* text. In addition to this, however, a number of sets of other textual matter—traditionally attributed to Confucius but in fact almost all post-Confucian in origin[48]—came to be so intimately associated with the basic text that they themselves were eventually considered integral parts of the classic. Known collectively as the Ten Wings (*Shih I*), these texts take various forms. Some are extended (though not very systematic) philosophical essays (the *Shuo Kua*, Discussion of the Trigrams, and the *Ta Chuan*, the Great Treatise); others are important commentaries on the structural aspects of the hexagrams (the *T'uan Chuan*, Commentary on the Decision, and the *Ta-Hsiang Chuan*, Great Image Commentary—in Wilhelm–Baynes called simply the Image); while others again are more in the nature of glosses (the *Wên Yen* or Commentary on the Words of the Text, the *Hsü Kua* or Sequence of the Hexagrams, the *Hsiao-Hsiang Chuan* or Small Image Commentary, and the *Tsa Kua* or Miscellaneous Notes). Of these texts, the Discussion of the Trigrams and, even more so, the Great Treatise, are of particular importance when considering the kinds of thinking implicit in the *I Ching* or how the oracle might actually have been perceived and understood by the ancient Chinese (or at least by some ancient Chinese). However, when actually using the *I Ching* for divining purposes, the texts that are usually most important are the Commentary on the Decision and the Image.

In general, as Richard Wilhelm notes, the Commentary on the Decision

> first explains the name of the hexagram, taking into consideration as occasion demands its character, its image, and its structure. Next it elucidates the words of King Wên [that is, the Judgment text], either using the sources just named or else

> starting from the situation of the ruler of the hexagram [that is, the line or lines considered most representative of the nature of the hexagram as a whole] or from the change of form that has given rise to the hexagram.[49]

The explanatory principles implied in this commentary are particularly suggestive with regard to the question, to be explored later, of how the verbal material associated with a hexagram might be related to the abstract figure of the hexagram itself.

As for the Image commentary, this, as Richard Wilhelm again explains,

> starting with the combination of the two trigrams, deduces from it the situation represented by the hexagram as a whole. With the attributes of the two trigrams as a basis, it then gives advice for correct behaviour in this situation.[50]

In fact, though actually belonging among the Ten Wings, these Image texts are, as Hellmut Wilhelm notes, "not to be considered commentaries on specific passages of the older texts . . . ; they constitute a third and independent approach, in addition to the judgments and the line texts, to the situations entailed by the hexagrams."[51]

As a supplement to the preceding, it should be noted that users of various translations and editions of the *I Ching* often find special relevance in the various elucidatory remarks added by the translator or editor. Sometimes these remarks hit the nail on the head with regard to a particular inquiry in a way that the classical texts themselves do not. Particularly rich in this respect are the commentaries of Richard Wilhelm. These are based, we are told, "on a careful reading of the later (postclassical) commentatory literature, on his discussions with Lao [his principal Chinese teacher and collaborator] and other friends and experts, on the modern scholarly literature then available, and on his own understanding and interpretation of the passages and situations involved."[52] That statements deriving from these kinds of secondary (or even tertiary) sources can nonetheless sometimes prove relevant seems to point toward a feature of the *I Ching* to which I will be drawing more specific attention shortly, namely, that it consists, both in the hexagram figures themselves and in their accompanying texts, only of paradigmatic representations of the situations prevailing at the time of consultation, not of exhaustive or point-for-point descriptions. There is thus plenty of scope for further elucidation of the situations, based on but going beyond what is actually stated in the texts and classical commentaries.

A final point that needs to be mentioned in regard to the textual matter of the *I Ching* is that the Chinese language used both in the earlier layers and in the later classical commentaries exhibits features that make it especially suited for oracular expression. The Great Treatise itself hints at this: "The names employed sound unimportant, but the possibilities of application are great. The meanings are far-reaching, the judgments are well ordered. The words are roundabout but they hit the mark."[53] As Ritsema and Karcher observe, the *I Ching* avails itself of a "special oracular language . . . made up of symbols with no rigid subject-verb, noun-adjective, pronoun or person distinctions. They combine and interact the way dream images do."[54] Such language "allows images and concepts to join in single words as well as in the sentences of the *I Ching*."[55] These image-concepts have a "wide and yet very precise" range of meanings that "our conceptual language cannot account for."[56] More generally, Richard Smith has commented of the use of language in the *I Ching*:

> In the earliest strata of the basic text we can already find a sensitivity to rhymes and homophony conducive to puns and double entendres, as well as a tendency to pair words and concepts with opposite or complementary meanings in such a way as to encourage associational or correlative thinking—a long-standing and integral feature of traditional Chinese thought. . . . [T]hese linguistic tendencies are particularly well developed in the Ten Wings—which together display a highly refined if rather diversified system of symbolic logic.[57]

Language that is so richly symbolic and so highly versatile and polysemantic lends itself to being molded to the expressive requirements of particular oracular occasions.

Hexagram Structure

As we have seen, the act of dividing the yarrow stalks or throwing the coins results in a six-line figure, the hexagram. Even in quite general terms, that is, before consideration is given to the character of the specific configuration of lines obtained by the consultation, this deceptively simple six-line figure has a tremendous wealth of internal structural significance. This basic structure is, as it were, the matrix or template within or upon which the chance event (that is, the actual configuration of lines resulting from one's act of consultation) is placed and in dynamic relationship to which it derives its meaning. The following is a summary of some of the most important of these structural features of the hexagram.[58]

First and foremost, there is significance in *the six lines as a whole*: together they depict, in highly abstract form, the overall situation or moment concerning which one has made one's inquiry. Beyond this, however, each hexagram can also be considered to consist of two (or four—see below) three-line figures, three pairs of lines, and six individual lines. In the case of each of these breakdowns, the component elements have special characteristics and interrelationships among themselves—though ultimately they all contribute back to the overall meaning of the hexagram as a whole.

Concerning the three-line figures or *trigrams,* there are eight possible kinds—every combination of whole and divided lines (see figure 7.4)—each of which has a wealth of concepts and imagery traditionally associated with it.[59] Within any hexagram there are two trigrams that are considered *primary* and consist of the bottom, second and third lines, and of the fourth, fifth, and top lines, respectively. There are also two further trigrams that are considered *nuclear* and consist of the second, third, and fourth lines, and of the third, fourth, and fifth lines, respectively. Importantly, trigrams derive certain significance simply from their position within the hexagram. Thus, for example, the lower primary trigram is considered to represent the inner aspect of a situation and to be lower, behind, earlier, and so on; while the upper primary trigram is considered to represent the outer aspect of the situation and to be upper, in front, later, and so on. These terms can be understood as having a potential bearing within practically any relational context: spatial, temporal, logical, ontological, social, and so on.

Less frequently appealed to but nonetheless part of the ancient Chinese interpretative tradition is the division of the hexagram into *pairs of lines*. These are understood to represent the three primal powers of earth or matter (bottom and second lines), humankind or psyche (third and fourth lines), and heaven or spirit (fifth and top lines).[60]

Considerable abstract significance also attaches to each of the *individual lines* and some of their interrelationships. Thus, certain line positions are considered to be *correct* or *incorrect* for each of the two kinds of line. A whole or yang line, for instance, is considered to be correctly placed if it is in the bottom, third, or fifth position but incorrectly placed if in the second, fourth, or top position; while the opposite positions are correct and incorrect for broken or yin lines. Again, certain lines within a hexagram can have a particularly close relationship. The two principal kinds of such relation-

Figure 7.4. The eight trigrams.

ships are *correspondence* and *holding together*. For two lines to correspond they must differ in kind (that is, one must be yang and one yin) and occupy analogous positions in the lower and upper primary trigrams. Thus, provided that they differ in kind, the first line corresponds with the fourth, the second with the fifth, and the third with the top. For two lines to hold together, they must again be different in kind but this time occupy adjacent positions.

Further, each *line position* was considered to characterize a different stage in the development of the situation represented by the hexagram as a whole. The first line is outside the situation or just entering. It is sometimes seen as the cause of the situation. In terms of people, it is a person without rank, a commoner. The second line characterizes the apogee of the inner aspect of the situation, since it occupies the center of the lower trigram. It is the official in the provinces, the wife, the son, the subordinate person in a relationship. The third line, at the top of the lower trigram but not yet having crossed into the upper trigram, characterizes "the moment of crisis, the transition from internal to external."[61] Hence, it usually depicts an unfavorable or difficult situation. As a person, it can represent someone with authority in a limited context. The fourth line characterizes the beginning of the external aspect of the situation. Though not typical of the situation, it is favorably influenced by its proximity to the fifth line. As a person, it is the minister or official at the court. The fifth line characterizes the maximal exposure of the situation externally. It is the position of the ruler, husband, father, or the dominant person in a relationship. At the center of the upper trigram, it represents the full fruit of the situation and is usually favorable. The sixth line, like the first, is outside the situation, but in the sense of just leaving. It characterizes "the completion or overdevelopment of the process of the given situation,"[62] its declining influence. It is the sage who has retired from active participation in the world.

Relationship of Text to Structure

We have seen, then, that there are two primary sources of meaning to which one can refer when attempting to interpret a cast hexagram: the various sections of textual material and the abstract figures themselves. The question remains of what might be the relationship between these two sources of meaning.

The most fruitful approach to this question may be to see the *I Ching*'s verbal material as an attempt (or, given the layered nature of the text, as several cumulative attempts) to elucidate the abstract meaning of the hexagram figures. This approach is wholly consonant with the ancient commentary tradition embodied in the Great Treatise and later reaching a particularly refined expression in the work of the Neo-Confucian philosopher Chu Hsi (1130–1200).[63] According to the presuppositions of the system, one's act of divination should access the particular hexagram that best depicts one's present situation. Most fundamentally, this depiction is in terms of abstract configurations of yin and yang forces. What the verbal material does is, as it were, "clothe" this abstract configuration in concrete form and thereby make it more readily intelligible. Insofar as it is a reflection of the same pattern of meaning that is also active within one's own situation, the verbal material may on occasion happen to contain words, images, and ideas that apply to one's own situation literally. This was the case with Adler's experience cited earlier. However, because the actual verbal material is just one out of numerous possible ways in which the abstract meaning of the hexagram figure might have been "clothed," it will often not apply so literally. Sometimes it will be fairly clear how it might nonetheless be applied after some degree of symbolic interpretation. But there will remain occasions when a straightforward symbolic understanding of the text may still not readily relate to one's situation. It then becomes necessary to use the verbal material simply as an aid to comprehending the essential abstract meaning of the hexagram, after which one can then reapply this abstract meaning to one's specific situation. That is, one thinks back from the abstract meaning of the hexagram figure (illuminated by the accompanying text) to the concrete circumstances that gave rise to the inquiry—which themselves may not obviously relate to the *I Ching* text.

The general idea here—that the hexagram figures express a more fundamental level of meaning than do the written texts—is contained in the following passage from the Great Treatise:

> The master said: Writing cannot express words completely. Words cannot express thoughts completely.
>
> Are we then unable to see the thoughts of the sages?
>
> The master said: The holy sages set up the images in order to express their thoughts completely; they devized the hexagrams in order to express the true and the false completely. Then they appended judgments and so could express their words completely.[64]

The tradition of attempting to explain the texts of hexagrams in terms of their structure is also very early and had already reached a fair level of sophistication by the time the *T'uan Chuan* (Commentary on the Decision) and *Hsiang Chuan* (Commentary on the Images) were composed. Basing himself on these, as well as on the postclassical commentatory traditions and his own intuitions, Richard Wilhelm was able (in Book III of his translation) to explain practically all the Judgment, Image, and Lines texts in terms of hexagram structure.

Synchronicity and Spirit in the *I Ching*

The key to the whole process here is the basic duality of whole and broken lines signifying the polarity between yang and yin, the masculine and the feminine, light and darkness, activity and passivity, the firm and the yielding, and so forth.[65] The eight possible combinations of these into stacks of three yields the trigrams. These in turn can be considered to be certain configurations of the basic polar forces (yang and yin), and from these configurations certain ideas and images are derived. A final stage in the generation of text from structure is represented by the hexagram figures themselves, which can be considered to be built up from a doubling of the trigrams. This doubling, as we have seen, generates a tremendous complexity of internal relationships among the various lines and line groupings within the resulting hexagram.

Thus, explanations of text in terms of structure can exploit sometimes the hexagram as a whole, sometimes its constituent trigrams (both primary and nuclear) along with their symbolic associations, and sometimes the relationship of individual lines. Always in the background is what I earlier called the essential matrix or template common to all the hexagrams and giving special nuances to the lines according to their position, correctness, and so on.

An example of how subtleties of structure can be related to textual expressions is provided by the third line of Hexagram 43, Kuai/Breakthrough (Resoluteness). The whole line text reads as follows:

> Nine in the third place:
> To be powerful in the cheekbones
> Brings misfortune.
> The superior man is firmly resolved.
> He walks alone and is caught in the rain.
> He is bespattered,
> And people murmur against him.
> No blame.[66]

When one looks at the hexagram figure containing this line (see figure 7.5), it seems most unlikely that the detailed imagery of this text could be derived from that inconspicuous third line that on the face of it seems almost lost and undifferentiated in the midst of the other yang

FIGURE 7.5. Hexagram 43, Kuai/Break-through (Resoluteness).

lines. However, by appealing to the various inner dynamics of the hexagram's structure, one can account for every concept and image in the line text. The phrase "To be powerful" is suggested by the trigram Ch'ien, which means "strong." This is especially so in view of the fact that the third line is not only at the top of the lower primary trigram Ch'ien but forms part of both of the two nuclear trigrams that are also Ch'ien. The image of "the cheekbones" is explained by Wilhelm as referring to the fact that Ch'ien can also mean "head"; the third line is at the top of this trigram and therefore high up on the head, as are the cheekbones.[67] The phrase "Brings misfortune" stems partly from the fact that the third line, being in the place of transition from the inner to the outer trigram, is generally dangerous and inauspicious. However, it also partly stems from an appreciation of the quality of the hexagram as a whole, according to which the attitude symbolized by the image of powerful cheekbones, namely, "showing strength outwardly," is not yet appropriate.[68]

"The superior man" refers to the diviner who is attempting, through the oracle, to harmonize his or her actions with the Tao. Such a person's presence is implied in all responses from the *I Ching*; the uncommon specific reference here (outside of an Image text) may again be due to the prominence of the trigram Ch'ien, another of whose meanings is superiority of person.[69] As for being "firmly resolved," Wilhelm relates this to the fact that the line "belongs to the strong primary trigram Ch'ien and also stands in the middle of the lower nuclear trigram Ch'ien, hence the redoubled resolution."[70] Next it is said that one "walks alone." According to Wilhelm, the line "is solitary because it alone is in the relationship of correspondence to the dark line at the top."[71] One is "caught in the rain" because one of the symbolic attributes of the upper primary trigram Tui is Lake and, hence, water and cloud, and this "suggests the idea of rain bespattering the line."[72] The negative connotation of "is bespattered" and of "people murmuring against one" derives partly from the difficult transitional position of the third line and partly from the dark yin line at the top with which this third line is in correspondence. The "murmuring" also relates to the trigram Tui, with its meaning of mouth and speaking.[73] Finally, the statement that there is "No blame" is explained by Wilhelm as follows: "The strength of [the third line's] nature protects it from contamination by the dark line above, hence despite evil appearances there is no mistake."[74]

Clearly, with this kind of analysis it is not a question of there being a fixed one-to-one correspondence between aspects of hexagram structure and the various units of verbalization (words, phrases, sentences). From one and the same structural element there are often derived two, three, or even more verbalized images and concepts. For example, in the above analysis, the trigram Ch'ien is variously taken to suggest strength, head, resolution, and superiority of person; while Tui is taken to suggest both rain and murmuring. This reflects the diversity of associations that attach to each of the trigrams. Add to this that there are in each hexagram not just two but four trigrams (primary plus nuclear) and that the line positions and relationships also supply a wide range of associations, and one can see that there are ample resources with which to explain any given word or phrase. However, this does not mean that the analysis of text in terms of structure is necessarily arbitrary. The range of associative and argumentative pathways leading from structure to text may be wide but it is not unlimited. The particular pathway followed, though it may seem arbitrary from the point of view of just the line or phrase under immediate consideration, can often be shown to be quite strongly conditioned by the wider context of the hexagram's overall meaning. Thus, the meaning of trigram Ch'ien as "resolution" is conditioned by the meaning of Hexagram 43 as a whole—"Resoluteness"—that derives from a number of other factors (for example, preponderance of massed yang lines) in conjunction with the forcefulness that attaches to the trigram Ch'ien considered individually.

Not only can one and the same structural feature, such as a trigram, yield a multiplicity of verbalized images and concepts but the reverse can also be true: one and the same verbal expression, recurring in several places throughout the book, can be considered to derive from different structural features in different contexts. The expression "crossing the great water," for instance, occurs in the Judgment and Lines texts twelve times.[75] For each occurrence (except one) Richard Wilhelm explains in Book III of his translation how the phrase derives from the structure of the related hexagram—always in terms of component trigrams. He does this, however, by appeal to no fewer that eight different combinations of trigram features.[76]

Implicit in the preceding discussion of the way the principal texts of the *I Ching* and the structure of the hexagram figures might be related to each other is the idea of a kind of spectrum running from the more concrete and specific levels of expression at one end to the more abstract and general levels of expression at the other. A given meaning can express itself anywhere along this spectrum. Thus, what is essentially the same meaning expresses itself more concretely in the images and ideas of the texts and more abstractly in the configurations of lines and their interrelationships that compose the hexagram figures. Moving further along the spectrum in one direction, toward greater concreteness and specificity, we encounter the actual set of circumstances within which one's inquiry has arisen: here the pattern of meaning present in the moment receives, as it were, a full-bodied instantiation. Correspondingly, if we move further along the spectrum in the other direction, toward even greater abstractness and generality than is represented by the hexagram figures, we begin to shift into a realm of abstract conception such as is represented by Jung's theory of archetypes.[77] More will be said about archetypes and their possible relationship to hexagrams later.[78] Here we can just note one suggestive parallel between Jungian archetypal expressions and the kinds of symbolism attached to, and supposedly derived from, the abstract structure of the *I Ching*—specifically from the trigrams.

Adrian Cunningham, in the context of a discussion of the notion of structure in the works of Jung and Lévi-Strauss, has highlighted that Jung described several different classes of material as archetypal. The classes Cunningham specifically mentions are that which has "a purely formal or geometrical character—the circle or square for instance"; that which "shows a consistent binary structure . . —for example, contrasts of inner-outer, high-low, centre-periphery, right-left, before-behind"; that which "consists of images whose Gestalt derives in part from common experience of the outer world—the tree, or fire, for instance, and perhaps those of male and female"; and finally—the most frequently occurring class in Jungian writing—that which "is composed of personal figures—the great mother, the hero, the wise old man, and so on."[79] This range of archetypal expressions—some highly abstract, others much more concrete—reflects the kind of spectrum mentioned earlier. Equally interesting, however, is the way it reflects the range of symbolism associated with the *I Ching* trigrams. The trigram Ch'ien/The Creative, for example, is associated with the formal quality of roundness; the binary pole of the male, the strong, the cold, and so on; such outer objects as jade, metal, tree fruit, and various kinds of horses; and such personal figures as the prince and father.[80]

SYNCHRONICITY IN THE *I CHING*

We are now in a position to look more closely at Jung's claim that the *I Ching* is based on the principle of synchronicity. There are a number of senses in which this can be shown to be the case, but also some restrictions that have to be made on the claim.

First and foremost, the very method of the oracle implies that meaningful acausal paralleling is possible. By means of a random procedure, an abstract configuration of lines—a hexagram—together with certain accompanying textual matter, is obtained. This is alleged to parallel one's real-life situation in a meaningful way without there being any normally

FIGURE 7.6. Hexagram 35, Chin/Progress.

comprehensible cause of this paralleling. Thus, in the example given earlier, Adler's real-life dilemma concerning the advisability of seeking to marry a particular woman was paralleled remarkably by the hexagram resulting from his act of consulting the oracle—a hexagram whose principal text seemed to offer him direct and unequivocal advice.

A couple of implications of the procedure for obtaining and interpreting a hexagram are worth highlighting. First, this procedure is a means of recording an event (consisting of a series of six subsidiary events) that is based essentially on chance. Assuming that the line configuration one obtains by following this procedure is the most apposite one possible in relation to one's question or situation (or at least is highly apposite, whereas others selected at random appear not to be), then this means that *by chance* one has accessed the one appropriate response (or one of the very few appropriate responses) out of a possible 4,096 (sixty-four hexagrams, each with sixty-four possibilities of combinations of changing and unchanging lines). What is being claimed is that (in the case of the most usual method employed) the coins, quite extraordinarily, manage to fall precisely in the appropriate way to yield this response. If, of the eighteen individual coin falls, just one had been different, if just one coin had bounced, spun, or rolled differently, a completely different result could have been obtained with possibly even a contrary meaning. For example, suppose in a consultation one obtained the generally very favorable Hexagram 35, Chin/Progress (see figure 7.6), representing a time of "rapid, easy progress" and "ever widening expansion and clarity."[81] If just one of the coins in one's fifth throw had landed differently, so that one obtained a total not of eight but of seven, then the fifth line would be yang instead of yin, and one would have accessed the generally very unfavorable Hexagram 12, P'i/Standstill (Stagnation) (see figure 7.7), representing a time in which "the creative powers are not in relation. It is a time of standstill and decline."[82] Thus, if the most apposite hexagram is obtained (and not only on one occasion but in relation to each properly conducted inquiry), this constitutes a truly astounding "chance" phenomenon. Richard Wilhelm, far from glossing over the factor of chance in the oracle, emphasizes its central importance:

FIGURE 7.7. Hexagram 12, P'i/Standill (Stagnation).

> Suprahuman intelligence has from the beginning made use of three mediums of expression—men, animals, and plants, in each of which life pulsates in a different rhythm. Chance came to be utilised as a fourth medium; the very absence of an immediate meaning in chance permitted a deeper meaning to come to expression in it. The oracle was the outcome of this use of chance.[83]

Ritsema and Karcher likewise recognize this: according to them, in divinatory systems such as the *I Ching* a "procedure using chance provides a gap through which . . . spirit expresses itself by picking out one of the available symbols."[84]

Furthermore, the paralleling that results from this chance event and that constitutes the synchronicity itself is considered to be possible because the hexagram is depicting the situation, moment, or "time" within which the inquirer's problem and consequent act of divination exist. As Jung put it, "the hexagram was understood to be an indicator of the essential situation prevailing in the moment of its origin."[85]

It should be noted that the concept here of a situation, moment, or "time" needs to be understood not just as measurable clock time but as something much more qualitative. Richard Wilhelm explains that "the time of a hexagram is determinative for the meaning of the situation as a whole" and, according to the character of the hexagram in question, can comprise such aspects as "the decrease or growth, the emptiness or fullness, brought about by [the] movement" expressed by a hexagram; "the action or process characteristic for a given hexagram"; "the law expressed through a certain hexagram"; or "the symbolic situation represented by the hexagram."[86] Hellmut Wilhelm clarifies the "very concrete" conception of time implicit in the *I Ching*:

> Here time is immediately experienced and perceived. It does not represent merely a principle of abstract progression but is

fulfilled in each of its segments. . . . Just as space appears to the concrete mind not only as a schema of extension but as something filled with hills, lakes, and plains—in each of its parts open to different possibilities—so time is here taken as something filled, pregnant with possibilities, which vary with its different moments and which, magically as it were, induce and confirm events. Time here is provided with attributes to which events stand in a relation of right or wrong, favourable or unfavourable.[87]

A cast hexagram, then, is considered to express a situation or a moment of time in the above sense, and it is this quality of the moment that characterizes and gives meaning to the various acausally paralleling elements that constitute the synchronicity.

There are two principal kinds of paralleling between states that can occur within *I Ching* synchronicities. On the one hand, the hexagram and its accompanying texts can be considered the outcome of a physical event, namely, the procedure of dividing the yarrow stalks or tossing the coins. This physical outcome can then parallel and cast light on the psychic condition stated or implied in one's inquiry. On the other hand, the hexagram and its texts can themselves be paralleled by outer physical events occurring subsequently to the act of consultation. Indeed, they can often seem actually to predict the likely occurrence of these outward patterns of events. Thus, the hexagram can serve both as the second, decisive term in one synchronicity, where it anomalously parallels the (usually) inner psychic state implicit in the inquiry, and also, perhaps even at the same time, as the initial term in a second synchronicity, where it is itself anomalously paralleled by subsequently occurring (usually) outer physical events. With this dual role, the hexagram often serves as the mediator enabling one to perceive acausal paralleling between the inner psychic and outer physical aspects of one's life—paralleling that otherwise one might have been much less likely to perceive.

Texts

There are also several senses in which the textual material associated with the hexagrams can be seen to involve a synchronistic relationship. Occasionally, an image or expression in one of the texts can be understood as implying the possibility of influence other than through normal causal means. The text to the second line of Hexagram 61, Chung Fu/Inner Truth (see figure 7.8), reads as follows:

> Nine in the second place means:
> A crane calling in the shade.
> Its young answers it.
> I have a good goblet.
> I will share it with you.[88]

According to Richard Wilhelm, this refers to "the involuntary influence of a man's inner being upon persons of kindred spirit."[89] He quotes an ancient commentary on the line (attributed to Confucius) that suggests that the kind of influence in question may be capable of operating nonlocally:

> The superior man abides in his room. If his words are well spoken, he meets with assent at a distance of more than a thousand miles. How much more then from near by![90]

More generally, it is possible to see the presence of a tacit synchronistic worldview in the fact that imagery within a single section of text can be so diverse and seemingly unrelated. Thus, Audrey Josephs, in the context of a discussion of *I Ching* divination, has argued that poetic metaphor is "one of the most obvious examples" of a synchronistic phenomenon:

> In the juxtaposition and apparent reconciliation of quite different or incompatible things, the imagination is stimulated to bridge the discontinuity between two images. The poet's ability to "see" such an analogical relation ... is an awareness of a synchronic [here = synchronistic] connection.[91]

In the text just mentioned, for example, what have the cranes to do with the goblet? Or in the text to the third line of Hexagram 43, what does getting caught in the rain and bespattered have to do with powerful

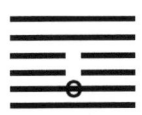

FIGURE 7.8. Hexagram 61, Chung Fu/Inner Truth.

cheekbones? There is no normal causal relationship here, but rather the implication that these diverse objects and states can be significantly related to one another through the meaning that they respectively embody. It is a pattern of such deep meaning, rather than a superficial naturalistic situation, that the lines and their texts are attempting to depict.

Again, a form of synchronicity is implied throughout in the Image texts (the *Ta-Hsiang Chuan*). Practically all of these texts begin by describing a relationship between the natural phenomena symbolized by the hexagram's primary trigrams (for example, the Image text to Hexagram 43 begins: "The lake has risen up to heaven"). Then they state that this provides the image of the situation as a whole signified by the hexagram title (in the case of Hexagram 43 the text continues: "The image of BREAK-THROUGH"). Finally, they draw a specific parallel with a kind of behavior appropriate to the *chün-tzu* or "superior man" within this situation (in Hexagram 43: "Thus the superior man Dispenses riches downward And refrains from resting on his virtue"[92]). As Shchutskii observes, "it is impossible not to see in the thinking of the author of the *Ta-hsiang chuan* the latent presence of parallelism."[93]

Elsewhere within the Ten Wings we occasionally find statements that might even more readily be understood to imply a synchronistic viewpoint. Thus, within the Commentary on the Words of the Text (*Wên Yen*) the following is said with reference to the fifth line of Hexagram 1, Ch'ien/The Creative: "Things that accord in tone vibrate together. Things that have affinity in their inmost natures seek one another."[94] Again, in the Great Treatise (*Ta Chuan*) it is said that when the superior man consults the *I Ching* "it takes up his communications like an echo; neither far nor near, neither dark nor deep exist for it, and thus he learns of the things of the future."[95]

Willard Peterson, in his excellent study of the Great Treatise (or, in the alternative title that he prefers, *Hsi Tz'u Chuan*, "Commentary on the Attached Verbalizations"), identifies several passages that imply a synchronistic relationship between the *I Ching* and the entire cosmos. As he sees it, these passages give expression to one of the major claims being made by the commentary—that "the technique, for which the text of the *Change* is the written repository, duplicates relationships and processes at work in the realm of heaven-and-earth."[96] In his own translation:

> The *Change* being the book that it is, it is broad and great and fully provided. It has in it the course traced by the ongoing processes in the heavens. It has in it the course traced by the ongoing processes among humans. It has in it the course traced by the ongoing processes on the earth.[97]

Elsewhere:

> Its broadness and greatness match heaven-and-earth's. Its flux and continuities match the four seasons'. Its impartial fittingness from [embodying] *yin* and *yang* matches the sun and moon's. What it is good at by being easy and simple matches that of the greatest potency.[98]

The relationship that Peterson tries to convey here with the expressions "has in it" and "matches" might, he suggests, better—but still inadequately—be conveyed by the term "duplicates."[99] As he understands it, the claim being made by the Great Treatise is not that the *I Ching* is "separate from but equal to the cosmos," nor that the relationship is "one of imitating, or being parallel to, or representing in microcosm, or . . . any other formulation which implies a gap between the *Change* and the realm of heaven-and-earth."[100] Rather, the *I Ching* and the cosmos

> are each "one of two things" exactly alike, each a double of the other, each "has in it" the other. Everywhere and always there is change, and the change everywhere and always is the same change, characterized by bipolarity and contained *in* the *Change*.[101]

Thus: "We must imagine, or perhaps believe, that the *Change* actually is a formal and processual duplicate of the realm of heaven-and-earth."[102]

Structure

Turning our attention to the more structural aspects of the system, we can note that, in the case of each hexagram, a synchronistic relationship may exist between its lower and upper trigrams: the lower trigram is considered to represent the inner aspect of the situation, while the upper trigram represents the outer aspect. This in itself suggests the paralleling of inner and outer events that is so characteristic of synchronistic experiences. More specifically, the tradition of the *I Ching*, as we have seen, highlights a relationship that exists between lines occupying the analogous position in the lower or upper trigrams, namely, the relationship of correspondence. Lines related through correspondence are not contiguous; hence, their sharing of characteristics is not due to a straightforward transmission of influence or significance from one line to the line immediately above it (representing the next stage in the situation). Rather, it appears that the relationship can best be understood as a kind of "action-at-a-distance." This "distance" could be spatial (between lower and higher), temporal (between earlier and later), logical (between cause and effect[103]), even psychological (between self and other[104]) or ontological (between psychic and physical). In any case, the relationship, both between the lower and upper trigrams as a whole and between analogous lines in each, appears more acausal than causal.[105]

The lines of a hexagram are viewed as entering (or "coming") from the bottom and moving upwards, eventually leaving (or "going") at the top.[106] Thus, as the Great Treatise puts it, "The Changes is a book whose hexagrams begin with the first line and are summed up in the last."[107] Significantly, the Great Treatise remarks further, "The beginning line is difficult to understand. The top line is easy to understand. *For they stand in the relationship of cause and effect.*"[108] This statement gives rise to a number of important considerations. First, if the vertical movement of the hexagram indicates a causal development, how are we to view the lateral movement represented by the fact that any given line can change into its opposite and is thereby related to the line occupying the same position in another hexagram? This again may be a form of acausal relationship. The lateral interchange of lines (called *Pang-t'ung* when it occurs to an entire hexagram, converting it into its line-for-line opposite)[109] is an expression of the inherent cosmic tendency for things in an extreme state to change into their opposites: the "law" of enantiodromia.[110] Enantiodromia is a principle of change that is not dependent on cause and effect in the normally understood sense. Without any discernible mediation or external influence, a state of affairs can convert into its opposite simply because there is an inherent tendency for it to do so. Hence, in the case of hexagram lines, as well as being caught in the vertical momentum of development from cause to effect, we can imagine them under the horizontal or lateral "pull" of enantiodromia. When the lines (that is, the situations—or aspects of situations—that they represent) are in a sufficiently extreme or unstable state, in other words, when the lines are "moving," the enantiodromial tendency can "pull" them into their opposites, effecting a change that is quite independent of the expected causal development. Since it is possible that any number of the six lines of a hexagram could change laterally like this, it is clear that any hexagram situation could convert into any other and therefore that each line of a hexagram is potentially related in this way to lines occupying the same place in all the other hexagrams. It might be suggested that, since the enantiodromial tendency constitutes a form of regular and, hence, potentially predictable connection between one state and another, it should therefore be viewed as a further form of causal relationship. However, inasmuch as the relationship is not a normally understood causal one, it qualifies for being considered acausal in the relative and provisional sense explained in chapter 2.

A second consideration is the following. If the relationship between the bottom and the top lines of a hexagram is a relationship of cause and effect, how are we to understand the significance of the four middle lines? From one point of view, we can see them as representing subtler stages of differentiation in the development from cause to effect: as the Great Treatise goes on to say, "if one wishes to explore things in their manifold gradation, and their qualities as well . . . , it cannot be done completely without the middle lines."[111] However, between the bottom and top lines there exist, as we have seen, three potential relationships of correspondence (between the first and fourth, second and fifth, and third and top lines)— a kind of relationship that we have already suggested is better understood as acausal rather than as causal. The picture we arrive at, then, is one in which, between a cause and its effect (the bottom and top lines) there exists a complexity of internal structural relationship that includes not only more finely graded causal relationships (that is, the step-by-step progression from one line up to the next) but possible acausal relationships as well (that is, correspondences). There may be some kind of abstract reflection here of the situation within our understanding of causality generally. Often, what at one scale of consideration appears to be a causal relationship can be shown to involve, at a subtler level of consideration, both a whole series of further causal interactions and also certain apparent elements of acausality.[112]

The mention in the Great Treatise of the relationship of cause and effect being implied within the hexagram structure should caution us against going too far in characterizing the *I Ching* as being based on synchronicity *as opposed to* causality. Jung, for example, sometimes seems to overstress this opposition: "What we call coincidence seems to be the chief concern of [the Chinese] mind, and what we worship as causality passes almost unnoticed."[113] In fact, the *I Ching* is very much concerned with causality. It is alleged to be a book that can help one participate in shaping one's circumstances through enabling one, as Richard Wilhelm says,

> to recognize situations in their germinal phases. The germinal phase is the crux. As long as things are in their beginnings they can be controlled, but once they have grown to their full consequences they acquire a power so overwhelming that man stands impotent before them.[114]

The implication here is that events develop in an orderly and, to some extent, predictable way; if certain conditions exist now, certain consequences will follow later. In other words, circumstances unfold according to some kind of intelligible and practicable principle of cause and effect. Thus, the *I Ching*'s understanding of how events unfold by no means necessarily contradicts or negates causal thinking; rather, it enriches it with a fuller picture of the kind of factors that can contribute to an understanding of events.

Correlative Thinking

There seems, however, no doubt that the *I Ching* is based on an overall view of reality and way of thinking that could be termed synchronistic, and it is from this that all the various hints of synchronicity we have been noting ultimately derive. Jung has specifically drawn attention to this in the context of his principal discussions of synchronicity.[115] He points out, for example, that "to the ancient Chinese view ... [t]he matter of interest seems to be the configuration formed by chance at the moment of observation and not at all the hypothetical reasons that seemingly account for the coincidence."[116] More formally, he spells out the difference between the causal view and the ancient Chinese "synchronistic" view as follows:

> Just as causality describes the sequence of events, so synchronicity to the Chinese mind deals with the coincidence of events. The causal point of view tells us a dramatic story about how D came into existence: it took its origin from C, which existed before D, and C in its turn had a father, B, etc. The synchronistic view on the other hand tries to produce an equally meaningful picture of coincidence. How does it happen that A', B', C', D', etc., appear all at the same moment and in the same place? It happens in the first place because the physical events A' and B' are of the same quality as the psychic events C' and D', and further because all are the exponents of one and the same momentary situation. The situation is assumed to represent a legible or understandable picture.[117]

Jung, as we have just had occasion to note, probably makes too strong a claim for the exclusiveness of the synchronistic mode of thinking among the Chinese, asserting that they were "not at all" interested in causality but let it pass "almost unnoticed."[118] With more specialist knowledge, Peterson surveys a range of connective concepts that can be shown to have been used in China in the fourth to the second centuries B.C.E. and concludes that

> there were strong arguments both . . . for and against understanding and explaining an event (1) by relating it to something external to it [that is, some form of causality], (2) by relating it to its own inherent qualities, or (3) by relating it to the bi-polar Great Harmony, the all inclusive Way of heaven-and-earth. The arguments show that there was no consensus. There was a range of views which—except for total schemes generated from binary oppositions—were at least vaguely similar to th[o]se found in the contemporary Mediterran[e]an world.[119]

With this qualification in mind, there is, however, no doubt that something very like what Jung understands by synchronicity did indeed receive prominent emphasis within Chinese thinking.

The kind of thinking in question has been independently elucidated by Joseph Needham in the wider context of a discussion of fundamental ideas in Chinese science.[120] Needham, following a number of previous scholars,[121] speaks of "coordinative," "associative," or "correlative" thinking, within which "conceptions are not subsumed under one another, but placed side by side in a *pattern,* and things influence one another not by acts of mechanical causation, but by a kind of 'inductance' . . . a kind of mysterious resonance."[122] The underlying idea is that for the ancient Chinese the universe was an organism in which "nothing was un-caused, but nothing was caused mechanically,"[123] a universe where

> organisation came about, not because of fiats issued by a supreme creator-lawgiver, which things must obey subject to sanctions imposable by angels attendant; nor because of the physical clash of innumerable billiard-balls in which the motion of the one was the physical cause of the impulsion of the other. It was an ordered harmony of wills without an ordainer; it was like the spontaneous yet ordered, in the sense of patterned, movements of dancers in a country dance of figures, none of whom are bound by law to do what they do, nor yet pushed by others coming behind, but cooperate in a voluntary harmony of wills.[124]

Needham makes a point of distinguishing this organismic view from the kind of "participative" thought that Lévy-Bruhl considered characteristic of primitive thinking.[125] The latter is, according to Lévy-Bruhl, insensitive to logical and physical absurdity, so that, to the "primitive" mind, anything can be the cause of anything else.[126] Chinese correlative thinking, by contrast, is based on a detailed system of correspondences whereby all the phenomena of experience are considered to belong to one or the other of a number of precisely defined categories: principally, the binary categorization of yin and yang and the five-"element" categorization of earth, metal, water, wood, and fire. The *I Ching*'s distribution of phenomena among the eight trigrams and sixty-four hexagrams is another instance.[127] As Needham notes in specific criticism of Lévy-Bruhl, "once a system of categorisation such as the five-element system is established, then anything can by no means be the cause of anything else";[128] on the contrary, one is left with "a picture of an extremely and precisely ordered universe."[129]

Needham contrasts this kind of coordinative thinking based on pattern with the "atomic" thinking that came to prevail in the West under the influence of Greek (more specifically, Democritean) philosophy and ultimately provided the conditions for the development of mechanistic science. Lacking a strong orientation in atomic thinking, he argues, the Chinese failed to develop comparable forms of modern science. But, as Needham also points out, modern science has by now, with quantum mechanics and astrophysics and new understandings in biology, begun to reach beyond the domain of applicability of mechanistic thought into realms where organismic thought becomes more relevant. This is not to say that the ancient Chinese worldview has all along been ahead of modern science and just waiting for the latter to catch up, but that the kind of coordinative thinking characteristic of the Chinese has a validity that is complementary to, rather than in contradiction with, mechanistic-atomic thought. Coordinative thinking is neither unscientific nor protoscientific, but an integral part of a more comprehensive form of scientific thinking that is perhaps still in the process of being developed.

It might be thought that this kind of correlative or coordinative thinking already has a long history in Western culture. One thinks immediately of Renaissance figures such as Paracelsus, Robert Fludd, and Agrippa of Nettesheim, and of the various traditions such as Kabbalah, alchemy, and astrology on which these thinkers drew and which stretched back many centuries before them. Is this not essentially the same as the Chinese view on which the *I Ching* is based? Jung appears to have thought so: "Only in astrology, alchemy, and the mantic procedures do we find no differences of principle between our attitude and the Chinese."[130] However, Needham suggests that an important distinction needs to be drawn between the two traditions. According to his reading of the history of ideas:

> Europeans could only think in terms either of Democritean mechanical materialism or of Platonic theological spiritualism. A *deus* always had to be found for a *machina*. Animas, entelechies, souls, archaei, dance processionally through the

> history of European thinking. When the living organism, as apprehended in beasts, other men, and the self, was projected on to the universe, the chief anxiety of Europeans, dominated by the idea of a personal God or gods, was to find the "guiding principle." . . .
>
> Yet this was exactly the path that Chinese philosophy had *not* taken. The classical statement of the organismic idea by Chang Chou in the -4th [that is, 4th B.C.E.] century . . . had set the tone for later formulations, expressly avoiding the idea of any *spiritus rector*. The parts, in their organisational relations, whether of a living body or of the universe, were sufficient to account, by a kind of harmony of wills, for the observed phenomena.[131]

It is true that a kind of organismic view closer to that of the Chinese can be found within Western philosophy, but Needham points out that the principal exponents of this can be traced back in a line that leads—through Whitehead, Hegel, Lotze, Schelling, and Herder—ultimately to Leibniz.[132] Now, as was pointed out earlier, through his connections with Jesuit missionaries, Leibniz had been able to study certain areas of Chinese thought, in particular the doctrines of the great Neo-Confucian philosopher Chu Hsi in which the organismic view receives one of its most refined expressions. Needham therefore suggests that the organismic view entered Western philosophy as a Chinese import via the Monadology of Leibniz.

Again, however, the basic distinction Needham is making in the preceding needs to be qualified. As Benjamin Schwarz has pointed out, in at least some versions of correlative cosmology the Chinese understanding of Heaven would not have been all that different from European conceptions of a heavenly "ruler," "father," and "sustaining principle."[133] Again:

> One cannot know exactly what Needham means by the term "guiding principle," but I think that the difference between the "world soul" of Western organismic thought is not as distinguishable from [the major correlative cosmologist] Tung Chung-shu's Heaven as he would have us believe.[134]

We can conclude from the whole of the preceding discussion of correlative thinking that Jung was indeed basically correct to emphasize the similarity between his concept of synchronicity and one of the major ancient Chinese modes of thought. However, this comparison needs to be made cautiously and with considerable sensitivity to the possible varieties and nuances of premodern thought, both Eastern and Western.

ORACULAR AND SPONTANEOUS SYNCHRONICITIES COMPARED

We are now also in a position to highlight some of the major similarities and differences between synchronicities that occur spontaneously and those that occur in relation to a systematic procedure such as consulting the *I Ching*. This task might help bring into sharper focus some of the characteristics of synchronicity generally.

The most obvious similarity, which in fact is the reason the two categories of occurrence are compared at all, is that both involve connections between events based on parallel meaning rather than on any normally recognizable form of causality. Naturally, a whole range of possible implications deriving from this basic fact (the implications explored throughout this book) will therefore also largely be held in common by the two kinds of happening. Both, for instance, are considered to express the particular psychophysical pattern of meaning active within a given situation or "time." This said, it does seem that with the *I Ching* one's attention is directed not just, or even primarily, to the acausality of the phenomenon; the presence and operation of this is virtually taken for granted by the implicit worldview of the *I Ching*. Paradoxically, what is of particular interest is often how the oracle can help one appreciate such causal elements within the *I Ching*'s field of operation as the lawfulness, and, hence (within certain bounds), the predictability, of the unfolding of events. With spontaneous synchronicities, by contrast, while these kinds of causal elements may be present, they usually are much less prominent, since attention tends to be on the conspicuously acausal character of the events, which is what gets the composite event of the synchronicity noticed at all.

When discussing spontaneous synchronicities I noted that the conscious attitude of the experiencer seems often to participate in generating, or at least affecting the character of, the experiences. Plaskett, for instance, refers frequently in his material to the "triggering effect" whereby his interest and intentions regarding a particular subject or idea preceded the occurrence of coincidences involving that subject or idea. With the *I Ching*, too, there is an important element of participation, though of a much more conscious, ordered, and controllable nature. This does not imply that synchronicities involving the *I Ching* can be precisely determined as to their form, content, and timing, but simply that these parameters are significantly more circumscribed than is the case with spontaneous synchronicities, where in most cases they are barely circumscribed at all. Thus, when one consults the *I Ching*, one formulates a specific question, or at the very least focuses on a specific subject of inquiry. With spontaneous synchronicities, by contrast, one does not usually formulate an inquiry consciously. An inquiry may be implied at the time of the synchronicity in the form of a major interest or intention, but it is not usual that it will have been formulated verbally in the expectation of receiving a response to it. In Plaskett's material there are many coincidences that could be interpreted as answers to implicit questions (instances of the "triggering effect") but none that can be seen as responses to explicitly formulated questions.

Again, when using the *I Ching*, one chooses the time at which the oracular response is to be given. The receiving of this response, as I have noted, can itself constitute a synchronicity with the already more or less known situation of the inquirer (the meaning of the hexagram and text parallels the meaning in the situation). In this case the response functions as the second term in a synchronicity. However, it is also possible that the *I Ching* response can prefigure events, in which case it is functioning as the first term in a future synchronicity. Thus, in choosing the time at which the *I Ching* response is received one can be both choosing the time at which one synchronicity actually occurs and also fixing a temporal reference point for the occurrence of another subsequent synchronicity. With spontaneous synchronicities, none of this happens by conscious choice, since by definition one has no real say in when the synchronistic event is going to take place.

With the above contrast, certain qualifications are again required. Principally, it needs to be noted that there is much middle ground between systematically generated synchronicities and spontaneous synchronicities. It is, for example, theoretically quite possible to formulate a question for oneself and then consider the next spontaneously occurring synchronicity as the answer to that question. Again, it is sometimes possible to create conditions that past experience has shown to be conducive to the likely occurrence of synchronicity (conditions of emotional intensity, perhaps).[135] In such cases, however, there is no certainty or even likelihood, comparable to that experienced when using the *I Ching*, that any synchronicity will in fact occur, and if it does, when precisely.

A further ambiguous category of events would be answers to prayers or results of magical procedures. These are meaningful happenings that occur other than by normally understood causal means, and as such might qualify as synchronicities. On the one hand, they are generated events in the sense that they are related to a deliberate intention on the part of the experiencer. On the other hand, they are spontaneous events in the sense that when or even whether they will occur remains highly uncertain. Furthermore, the fact that they are intended or willed distinguishes them from synchronicities based on the *I Ching*, which are the result of an inquiry into how things are and are likely to become rather than of an active desire to make things otherwise.

With the *I Ching* there is a more or less systematic procedure for interpreting the synchronicity represented by the oracular response. This means that the psychophysical pattern of meaning, the "time," is on the whole much more easily accessed and defined than is the case with the spontaneous experiences. Again, while both kinds of synchronicity can give direction to the experiencer, with the *I Ching* this is much more explicit, based as it is on texts that in part are specifically intended to provide counsel for action. With spontaneous synchronicities one can, as Plaskett not infrequently did, allow oneself to follow a train of associations suggested by one's experiences and get direction from it. However, if one does this, it generally requires considerable ingenuity to construe the experience as providing this direction, and it is not often proffered directly as is the case with the texts of the *I Ching*.

The language of the *I Ching* texts is, as I have noted, often very obscure, with imagery and concepts from a wide variety of contexts juxtaposed enigmatically to create a highly polysemantic overall texture. This is characteristic of oracular language generally (witness the notoriously ambiguous responses of the Delphic Oracle in ancient Greece). It is also, however, characteristic of the content of spontaneous synchronicities when this is construed as possibly communicating meaning to (or through) an experiencer. The tantalizing nature of Plaskett's material provided ample illustration of this. On the one hand, the degree of intelligibility within and between the contents of his various experiences was such as to suggest at least areas of underlying coherent meaning. On the other hand, determining with any precision what this meaning might actually be proved extremely difficult, if not ultimately impossible, not least because the contents often seemed to direct attention with equal plausibility in several directions at once. Because of this obscurity of language, the interpretation both of *I Ching* responses and of spontaneous synchronicities usually requires symbolic analysis, which is therefore a further point of similarity between the two kinds of experience.

It might be thought that because the *I Ching* consists largely of fixed textual matter, the meaning of these texts would, over the centuries, also have become more or less fixed, and that this feature of the oracle needs to be distinguished from the totally open nature of the content of spontaneous synchronicities, which can consist of any kind of image or idea and, hence, of an unlimited range of possible meanings. However, there are a number of considerations that make this distinction less sharp than might initially be supposed.

First, as has already been argued at length, although the text has in most respects remained more or less the same for two millennia, throughout that period it has always been subject to diverse forms of interpretation. This is no doubt partly due to the polysemantic nature of the language and imagery of the texts. However, a further reason is that the texts may be only an approximate expression of the deeper abstract meaning depicted by the hexagram figures. These hexagram figures, as we have seen, have an extraordinary structural richness that gives them a wide-ranging, not to say unlimited, field of applicability. The texts, when appreciated as expressions of this underlying structural meaning and as pointers toward it, begin to lose something of their superficially fixed character.

Even so, one might ask, how can a mere sixty-four hexagram figures with their accompanying texts possibly come close to competing with the total freedom and infinite variability of contents expressible through spontaneous synchronicities? In answer to this, we can note first that, although there are indeed only sixty-four hexagrams, there are separate texts for each hexagram line, which means that there are $6 \times 64 = 384$ sections of textual matter in addition to the sixty-four Judgment texts. Furthermore, because in an actual consultation there might be any number of moving lines in one's hexagram response (anything from none to all six) and, hence, one's primary hexagram could change into any of the other hexagrams (or remain unchanging), it follows that there are in fact $64 \times 64 = 4,096$ possible responses to each act of consultation. To be sure, these 4,096 responses have to make use of the more limited range of $64 + 384 = 448$ sections of principal textual matter. However, in each case they will combine different selections of text, with the result that the overall meaning, even if sometimes similar, will nonetheless be different each time. Then there is the fact that in each case the response is obtained in relationship to a definite inquiry, and this inquiry has emerged out of a situation (the circumstances of the inquirer) that in the last analysis is unique. Thus, whichever of the 4,096 responses one obtains will be further individualized by its relationship to one's specific and unique inquiry. We have to conclude, then, that the range of meanings accessible through *I Ching* divination is, in spite of the system's highly structured nature, in its own way infinite.[136]

If the *I Ching* is thus less restricted than might at first appear, it is also arguable that spontaneous synchronicities, for their part, are less unrestricted than might first appear. According to Jung's understanding, synchronistic experiences generally only occur when an archetype is constellated. Underlying the varied detail of the experiences described by Jung—a dream of jewelery and an insect flying in through a window, birds alighting on the roof of a house, above-random guessing in ESP experiments—one or another archetype was considered to be active: in these cases, the archetypes of rebirth, of death, and of magical effect, respectively.

Thus, the multiplicity of phenomena involved in synchronicities is considered to be ordered by a limited range of much more basic factors. Quite how limited this range is never becomes clear in Jung's writings. In one place, he writes, "There are as many archetypes as there are typical situations in life."[137] Elsewhere he writes that "just as certain biological views attribute only a few instincts to man, so the theory of cognition reduces the archetypes to a few, logically limited categories of understanding."[138] Whether his estimate of the actual number of typical situations and, hence, of archetypes would be somewhere in the region of sixty-four or nearer 4,096, nevertheless it is certain that it would be a manageable number rather than one close to infinity.[139] Spontaneous synchronicities, then, when viewed from a Jungian perspective as expressions of activated archetypes (or from the perspective of any non-Jungian but analogous model), appear much less free and open than might initially be supposed. In the way we have just been considering them, there is a movement from obvious multiplicity to the discerning of a finite range of inner structures (archetypes) informing that multiplicity. With the *I Ching*, precisely the opposite was the case: we saw first the limited range of structures (the sixty-four hexagrams) and then how these could nonetheless be related to an infinite multiplicity of phenomena. Thus, while *I Ching* synchronicities and spontaneous synchronicities seem on the surface to be very different—the former extremely limited in their expression, the latter extremely free—arguably, when viewed more closely, both involve the same relationship between a finite set of basic structures and an infinity of phenomenal expressions. It is just that, in the way we happen to encounter the two kinds of synchronicity, they appear to converge toward this common ground from opposite directions.

SPIRIT IN THE *I CHING*

Most traditional accounts of how the *I Ching* works attributed a central role to the factor of spirit or *shen*.[140] However, it is possible to acknowledge that the system works without invoking the concept of spirit. Before discussing the spiritual perspective, I shall briefly review some ancient and modern explanations in which this is the case.

A Working *I Ching* without Spirit

The system of correlative cosmology, so central to an understanding of the apparently synchronistic way in which the *I Ching* operates, can be understood as not requiring any spiritual underpinnings. Benjamin Schwarz expresses this view:

> To the extent that the entire system [of correlative cosmology] is conceived of as working through a vast network of correspondences and resonances among natural and human phenomena, its key terms do not refer to acts of spirits and gods. *Yin/yang* and the five elements are presumably abstract entities ... and thus presumably not spirits or gods.[141]

The possibility of understanding how the *I Ching* operates in terms of an abstract system rather than in terms of spirit or spiritual agencies remained an option throughout the long history of the work, even for theorists wholly believing in its efficacy. For instance, Wang Fu-chih in the seventeenth century could understand the system—for which he had tremendous respect—in terms of an ordered continuum underlying all of reality. Hellmut Wilhelm recapitulates his theory as follows:

> His premise is an ordered continuum of existence, which is governed by laws and is all embracing. This continuum "lacks appearance"—that is, it is not immediately accessible to sense perception. But through the dynamism inherent in existence, images are differentiated out of the continuum which by their structure and position partake of the laws of the continuum; they are, in a sense, individuations of this continuum. On the one hand, these images—that is, the sixty-four situations of the Book of Changes—can be perceived and experienced; on the other hand, as embodiments of the law and therefore governed by it, they are open to theoretical speculation. With this they enter into the field of numbers and may be numerically structured and ordered as objects of theory governed by law. Thus each situation can be apprehended in two ways: through direct experience as a consequence of the dynamism of existence, and through theoretical speculation as a consequence of the continuousness of existence and its government by laws. The oracle serves to bring the two aspects into harmony with each other, to co-ordinate a question resulting from immediate, differentiated experience, with the theoretically correct—and only correct—answer. The questioner thus obtains access to the theoretically-established aspect of his own situation, and by reference to the texts set forth under this aspect in the Book of Changes he obtains counsel and guidance from the experience of former generations and the insights of the great masters. Thus the synchronicity disclosed by the oracle is merely the apprehension of two different modes of experiencing the same state of affairs.[142]

Jung expresses a similar notion, though framed in more psychological terms. He believed that, through the principle of synchronicity, the oracle is "grasping a situation as a whole and thus placing the details against a cosmic background—the interplay of Yin and Yang."[143] For him the technique accesses and reveals something of the "absolute knowledge" of the unconscious or objective psyche. It therefore provides "a method of exploring the unconscious."[144]

A more reductive psychological explanation would be that there is no objective factor at work in obtaining the particular hexagram one does, and that the significance discerned in it is projected there from one's unconscious. Jung expressed acute awareness of this possibility: "any person of clever and versatile mind," he remarks, after summarizing the impressive results of his own experiment in consulting the oracle, "can turn the whole thing around and show how I have projected my subjective contents into the symbolism of the hexagrams." However, he also notes that "such a critique, though catastrophic from the standpoint of Western rationality, does no harm to the function of the *I Ching*," since the important thing, from the Chinese standpoint, is simply "that the intelligent individual realizes his own thoughts."[145]

Common to each of these three characterizations of what the *I Ching* does—expresses networks of correspondences within a situation, formulates numerically the law-governed order underlying a situation, or discloses the unconscious background to a situation—is the basic fact that in some way it makes the unknown known. It enhances one's appreciation of one's present situation and its inherent potentialities. In practical terms, this gives one a new perspective onto one's situation—a perspective that is often significantly broader than that which one had prior to consulting the oracle. The result, when the oracular procedure is successful, is that one's blocked energy (the impasse that caused one to turn to the oracle) is released.

The *I Ching*, and similar divinatory procedures, could be useful even if they do not work in any of the senses mentioned above but simply because they introduce an element of randomness into decision making. As the Belgian mathematician David Ruelle remarks with reference to the theory of games, "in a competitive situation, the best strategy often involves random, unpredictable behavior."[146] For example:

> In everyday life you will find that your boss, your lover, or your government often try to manipulate you. They propose to you a "game" in the form of a choice in which one of the alternatives appears definitely preferable. Having chosen this alternative, you are faced with a new game, and very soon you find that your reasonable choices have brought you to something

you never wanted: you are trapped. To avoid this, remember that acting a bit erratically may be the best strategy. What you lose by making some suboptimal choices, you make up for by keeping greater freedom.[147]

Thus, without even engaging with the question of whether reality might be structured so as to allow for the possibility of relationships of synchronicity, a contemporary mathematician can conclude that the "clever use of oracular unpredictability by an intelligent leader may have been a good way to reach optimal probabilistic strategies."[148]

Contrary to the assumptions underlying the above kinds of explanation, a number of parapsychological experiments carried out in regard to the *I Ching* suggest that a factor may be operating in the oracle other than, or in addition to, projection or randomness. In 1971, Charles Honorton and Lawrence Rubin reported on an experiment that indicated that subjects who did not believe in ESP were less able than those who believed in it to distinguish between a response obtained from the *I Ching* according to the traditional procedure and a control response selected randomly.[149] When, twenty years later, Michael Thalbourne and some colleagues attempted to replicate the experiment, they failed to reproduce the specific finding in regard to belief in ESP. However, they found instead that "those who believed in the efficacy of the *I Ching* did in fact tend to rate their actual reading as more relevant than their control reading, in the absence of any normal information as to which was really the correct one."[150] Such results suggest that the efficacy of the *I Ching* cannot entirely be accounted for in terms of either projection or the theory of games.

Shen

As for what additional factor there might be that could account for the apparent efficacy of the *I Ching* in producing distinctly meaningful responses, traditionally this would most often be identified as one or another understanding of spirit or *shen*. Jung summarizes that "according to the old tradition, it is 'spiritual agencies,' acting in a mysterious way, that make the yarrow stalks give a meaningful answer. These powers form, as it were, the living soul of the book."[151] Jung is alluding in particular to a statement at the beginning of the Discussion of the Trigrams (*Shuo Kua*), according to which the ancient sages "invented the yarrow-stalk oracle in order to lend aid in a mysterious way to the light of the gods [*shen ming*]."[152] In drawing attention to this, Jung remarks that more impersonal understandings of how the *I Ching* works, such as his own argument concerning synchronicity, "of course never entered a Chinese mind."[153] This, however, is far from true. We have already seen how sophisticated the implicit understandings of correlative cosmology could be. What Richard Lynn says about the concept of Tao applies equally to that of *shen*:

> [T]hroughout traditional Chinese society . . . a spectrum of opinion existed, at one end of which, the Dao [Tao]—especially when it was understood as the manifestation of the will of Heaven—was seen as an unconscious and impersonal cosmic order that operated purely mechanistically, and, at the other, as something with a consciousness that heeded the plights of both human kind as a whole and the individual in particular and could answer collective and individual pleas for help and comfort. Although intellectual, elite culture tended to hold to the former view and popular culture favored the latter, much ambivalence concerning this issue can be found in the writings of many a sophisticated thinker.[154]

The word "*shen*" has connotations that enable it to be related to both personal and impersonal understandings. Peterson, discussing the use of the word in the Great Treatise, points out that sometimes it "can be understood and translated as 'divinities' without much risk of being misled or misleading." More often, however, the word is used adjectivally and "in a more extended sense than 'partaking of the defining quality or characteristic of divinities.'"[155] To approximate the broader meaning of the adjectival use of *shen*, Peterson therefore adopts Rudolf Otto's term "numinous." This term,

> if we reduce or neglect its intended religious overtones, points to a certain quality, state or condition which cannot be fully apprehended and which some of us today might acknowledge as present more in an abstract and depersonalized manner than was perhaps characteristic of the divinities, spirits, demons, and *numen* (and *shen*) which some of our ancestors recognized.[156]

Peterson emphasizes that, in contradistinction to Kant's notion of the "noumenon," to which his own understanding of *shen* as numinosity bears certain similarities, "in the usage of the 'Commentary', what is *shen* is present 'out there' and can be taken on by a person; it impinges on our lives as well as our mental processes."[157] This accords with the understanding of spirit favored in the present work.

Indeed, the concept of "*shen*" as used in the Great Treatise is in many ways synonymous with my earlier characterization of spirit in chapter 2. In addition to being numinous and directly experienceable, *shen* is considered to have a transcendent nature, as suggested by statements such as "that aspect of [the Tao] which cannot be fathomed in terms of the light and the dark is called spirit."[158] Its transgressive or miraculous quality is evoked by claims that "spirit is bound to no one place,"[159] and "only through the divine can one hurry without haste and reach the goal without walking,"[160] and again "when a man comprehends the divine and understands the transformations, he lifts his nature to the level of the miraculous."[161] *Shen* is considered intrinsically beneficial and purposive: "That which furthers on going out and coming in, that which all men live by, they called the divine."[162] In particular its intelligible nature is emphasized: "Perfect concepts come about by entrance into the numinous, which, once had, allows one to extend their application to the utmost" (Lynn's translation).[163] Again: "Heaven creates divine things; the holy sage takes them as models."[164]

The Great Treatise makes very strong and explicit claims about the relationship of *shen* to the I Ching. The book can "penetrate all situations under heaven" precisely because it is "the most divine thing on earth."[165] Thus, "whoever knows the tao of the changes and transformations, knows the action of the gods."[166] We are told that contact with a spiritual dimension was involved when the ancient sages first invented the I Ching: "they fathomed the tao of heaven and understood the situations of men. Thus they invented these divine things in order to meet the need of men."[167] The instruments utilized in consulting the oracle, the yarrow stalks, are themselves described as "round and spiritual."[168] And finally, the actions and effects intended to be brought about by involvement with the I Ching are also characterized as spiritual: "By virtue of its numinous power, it lets one know what is to come"; the sages "used it to make their virtue numinous and bright"; "they made a drum of it, made a dance of it, and so exhausted the potential of its numinous power."[169]

A Modern Integration

The work on the I Ching by Rudolf Ritsema and Stephen Karcher picks up on this ancient understanding of the spiritual aspect of the oracle as implied in the Great Treatise and integrates it with the insights of Jung's analytical psychology. For Karcher, as for Peterson, *shen* is understood to encompass the meanings "spirit, spirits, what is numinous or spiritually potent."[170] The I Ching, as Ritsema and Karcher see it, "gives voice to a spirit concerned with how we can best live as individuals in contact with both inner and outer worlds."[171] Proper use of the oracle brings about "an intuitive clarity traditionally called *shen ming* or the *light of the gods*. It is a bright spirit that is creative, clear-seeing and connected."[172] With implicit reference to the statement in the Great Treatise about drumming and dancing, they view the *I Ching* as performing a quasi-shamanic role:

> Like the shamans and sages of old, this tradition maintains, the person who uses these symbols to connect with *I* [that is, change or versatility] will have access to the numinous world and acquire a helping-spirit, a *shen*. The *I Ching* is more than a spirit, it channels or connects you to spirit. It puts its users in a position to create and experience their own spirit as a point of connection with the forces that govern the world.[173]

Thus, engaging with the oracle can be "an epiphanic experience of that golden age when the Gods and humans met. In the irrational and subversive encounter with the demons of divination, we experience ourselves once again ensouled, as spirits in an imagined world."[174] In fact, "it is this creation of a dynamic field of meaning between the individual and the 'spirits,' re-established in each consultation through the oracle's image-clusters, that is the real heritage of the text."[175]

The traditional elements in this understanding of the *I Ching* are clear enough. Ritsema and Karcher also make explicit the modern psychological elements. The *I Ching*, they write, is "a particular kind of imaginative space set off for a dialogue with the gods or spirits, the creative basis of experience now called the unconscious."[176] The *shen ming* or "light of the gods" is understood as "the unconscious forces creating what you experience."[177] Divination involves a "dynamic interchange between conscious and unconscious" in which "both are moved";[178] it relies on "occulted *daimones*, the *imagines agentes* or 'living units of the unconscious psyche' which Jung called the 'architects of dreams and symptoms.' . . . In modern terms '*daimones*' have much in common with 'complexes.'"[179]

This integration of the ancient understanding with modern psychology clearly accommodates the concept of spirit. However, Ritsema and Karcher's epistemological position regarding the direct experience-ability of spirit is essentially the same as Jung's. In an attempt to summarize the main currents of thought informing the work of Eranos, including his and Karcher's own work on the *I Ching*, Ritsema formulates seven points, two of which are that "Matter and Spirit, the essence of the world, are transcendental and in themselves unknowable," and that "the psyche is the only realm of immediate experience. It is the realm in which the Spirit constellates images and Matter constellates concepts."[180] This epistemological position differs both from the ancient Chinese understanding and from that of the present work.[181] However, this position of Ritsema and Karcher's can readily enough be modified into conformity with the view I am proposing by making the same kind of epistemological maneuvers as were made in chapter 2 in regard to Jung.

Spirit and Synchronicity

That a system of thought based on the principle of synchronicity should so readily lend itself to being understood in spiritual terms suggests again the congruence between synchronicity and spirit that has been elaborated throughout this book. It would be otiose to run through again, in the context of the *I Ching*, all the various specific connections between synchronicity and spirit. However, there is one connection that is worth highlighting, both because of its central importance and because it is arguably being made by the Great Treatise itself.

In his study of the Great Treatise, Peterson draws on various passages, including some of the ones quoted above, to provide a rich account of how the spiritual or numinous was understood in the ancient world to be related to the *I Ching*. He notes, as I have, that the *I Ching* was understood both to connect us to the numinous and to be itself numinous. Concerning the first of these points, he remarks:

> The "Commentary" itself wants us to recognize that the *Change* is the means by which we can have access to the powerful, numinous presence which is hidden and difficult, perhaps even impossible, to perceive, just as it gives us access to knowledge of the subtle origins of change in heaven-and-earth and in human society.[182]

Concerning the *I Ching*'s being itself numinous, he says, largely on the basis of passages I have already quoted,[183] that "the *Change* is numinous in the same way that it *is* change";[184] or again that "according to the 'Commentary,' the *Change* goes and is everywhere, for it is numinous presence."[185] Putting these two points together, Peterson concludes further that "by being numinous, the *Change* is the medium giving us access to all that is numinous."[186]

Earlier in this chapter, when discussing the synchronistic nature of the *I Ching*, I noted that Peterson interprets the Great Treatise to be implying that the book "duplicates relationships and processes at work in the realm of heaven-and-earth."[187] Passages such as have been quoted and referred to previously now put him in a position in which he can make a similar claim regarding the spiritual or numinous: that "the *Book of Change* is a mysterious and potent duplicate of that which is numinous."[188] From this one might make either of two inferences. On the one hand, one could infer that it is the synchronistic power of the *I Ching*, its capacity to "duplicate" all relationships and processes, that enables it also to duplicate the numinous or spiritual. In this case, the *I Ching* would be spiritual by virtue of synchronicity. On the other hand, one could infer that it is because the *I Ching* is numinous or spiritual that it is capable of establishing and elucidating the kind of anomalous connections between events that are the essence of what is meant by synchronicity. In this case, the *I Ching* would be synchronistic by virtue of spirit. Probably, however, the implied view is that both factors, synchronicity and spirit, operate within the book together, and together contribute, in equally unfathomable ways, toward its efficacy. As Peterson concludes: "As far as I can discern, we are being asked to accept that the Book and its technique duplicate change in heaven-and-earth, in the realm of that which is numinous, and in our minds. There are no strict rules or guides for how it does it."[189]

A Sacred Vessel

The Great Treatise, as one of the appendices incorporated in the *I Ching*, provides a particularly intimate and authoritative account of how the book is to be understood. There exists, however, a further and possibly even more intimate source of testimony to the nature of the work. Given that the book is an oracle, capable in a sense of speaking for itself, one might wonder how, when questioned to this effect under suitably important circumstances, it might elect to characterize its own nature. It happens that the oracle has indeed been prompted to make a couple of such self-characterizations at important moments during its entry into Western culture.

When C. G. Jung was writing his foreword to the Wilhelm–Baynes translation of the *I Ching*, he took the bold step of "personif[ying] the book in a sense" and asking its own "judgment about its present situation, i.e., my intention to introduce it to the English-speaking public."[190] The answer he obtained was Hexagram 50, Ting/The Cauldron (see figure 7.9). He comments:

FIGURE 7.9. Hexagram 50, Ting/The Cauldron.

> In accordance with the way my question was phrased, the text of the hexagram must be regarded as though the *I Ching* itself were the speaking person. Thus it describes itself as a cauldron, that is, as a ritual vessel containing cooked food. Here the food is to be understood as spiritual nourishment.[191]

He quotes some of Richard Wilhelm's commentary:

> The *ting*, as a utensil pertaining to a refined civilization, suggests the fostering and nourishing of able men, which redounded to the benefit of the state. . . . Here we see civilization as it reaches its culmination in religion. The *ting* serves in offering sacrifice to God. . . . The supreme revelation of God appears in prophets and holy men. To venerate them is true veneration of God. The will of God, as revealed through them, should be accepted in humility.[192]

Jung then adds: "Keeping to our hypothesis, we must conclude that the *I Ching* is here testifying concerning itself."[193] In other words, the *I Ching* is effectively describing itself as "a ritual vessel containing . . . spiritual nourishment" and as a medium through which the will of God can be revealed.[194]

Interestingly, Ritsema and Karcher, in the introduction to their recent translation, report a very similar experience as the first of eight examples of "Encounters with the Oracle." The anonymous questioner is said to have encountered the *I Ching* for the first time twenty-five years previously (that is, in the late 1960s) during a period of profound personal crisis and collective disorientation. He asked the *I Ching*: "Who are you? How should I use you?" Here again, the answer was Hexagram 50, called by Ritsema and Karcher "The Vessel/Holding."[195] Thus, according to their commentary and glosses, the book was describing itself and the experiencer's relation to it "in terms of the imaginative capacity of a sacred vessel. It emphasizes that securing and imaginatively transforming the material at hand is the adequate way to handle [the situation]."[196] They further explicate the hexagram title through the following "Associated Contexts":

> **Vessel/holding,** TING: bronze cauldron with three feet and two ears, sacred vessel used to cook food for sacrifice to gods and ancestors; founding symbol of family or dynasty; melting pot or receptacle; hold, contain, transform; establish, secure; precious, respectable.[197]

They conclude that the experiencer's realization that the *I Ching* was "offer[ing] itself to him personally as an imaginative process . . . was like putting on a new fate, entering an imaginal world," giving him "the personal experience of meaning" and "the feeling of being in touch with the hidden spirit of the time."[198]

That the nature of the *I Ching*, the *Book of Changes*, may indeed be appositely symbolized by the *ting*, the cauldron or vessel, is suggested already by the early commentator Wang Pi (226–49 C.E.), who writes: "The Cauldron is a hexagram concerned with the full realization of the potential in change."[199] It is therefore quite remarkable that Jung, when he invited the book to speak concerning itself, should have obtained precisely this hexagram; and even more remarkable that an independent request for the oracle to characterize itself, as reported by Ritsema and Karcher, should likewise have yielded Hexagram 50.[200] Finally, in the light of this symbolic equation of the *I Ching* with a cauldron or vessel of spiritual transformation, it is tempting to recall from the previous chapter the apparent self-revelation of synchronicity as being symbolically equivalent to the spiritually transformative vessel of the Holy Grail.

NOTES

CHAPTER 1: INTRODUCTION

1. This incident is reported by Gilles Quispel, "Gnosis and Psychology," in *The Gnostic Jung*, ed. Robert A. Segal (Princeton, NJ: Princeton University Press, 1992), 247.

2. Paul Auster, *The Red Notebook and Other Writings* (London: Faber and Faber, 1995), 28–29.

3. Bob Bloomfield, *Synchronistic Images* (Cheddar, UK: Charles Skilton Ltd., 1987), 102–4.

4. Marie-Louise von Franz, "Matter and the Psyche from the Point of View of Jung," in *Psyche and Matter* (Boston: Shambhala, 1992), 24–25.

5. See, for example, Eric J. Sharpe, *Comparative Religion: A History* (London: Duckworth, 1975).

6. C. G. Jung, "Synchronicity: An Acausal Connecting Principle" (1952), in *The Collected Works of C. G. Jung*, ed. Sir Herbert Read, Michael Fordham, and Gerhard Adler, exec. ed. William McGuire, trans. R. F. C. Hull [hereafter *Collected Works*], vol. 8, *The Structure and Dynamics of the Psyche*, 2nd ed. (London: Routledge and Kegan Paul, 1969), 417–519; and "On Synchronicity" (1951), in *Collected Works*, vol. 8, *The Structure and Dynamics of the Psyche*, 2nd ed. (London: Routledge and Kegan Paul, 1969), 520–31.

7. C. G. Jung, "Foreword to the 'I Ching'" (1950), in *Collected Works*, vol. 11, *Psychology and Religion: West and East*, 2nd ed. (London: Routledge and Kegan Paul, 1969), 589–608.

8. Many of Jung's statements on synchronicity, apart from those in his essay "Synchronicity: An Acausal Connecting Principle," are gathered in Roderick Main, ed., *Jung on Synchronicity and the Paranormal* (London: Routledge; Princeton, NJ: Princeton University Press, 1997).

9. See Marie-Louise von Franz, *Number and Time: Reflections Leading Towards a Unification of Psychology and Physics*, trans. Andrea Dykes (London: Rider, 1974); *On Divination and Synchronicity: The Psychology of Meaningful Chance* (Toronto: Inner City Books, 1980); and *Psyche and Matter*.

10. For some possible connections between the spiritual and scientific implications of synchronicity as elaborated by von Franz, see Roderick Main, "Magic and Science in the Modern Western Tradition of the *I Ching*," *Journal of Contemporary Religion* 14, no. 2 (1999), 263–75.

11. For the source of the Jungian use of this term, see Henry Corbin, "*Mundus Imaginalis* or the Imaginary and the Imaginal," *Spring* (1972): 1–19.

12. For Hermes, see Allan Combs and Mark Holland, *Synchronicity: Science, Myth, and the Trickster* (New York: Paragon House, 1990; repr. Edinburgh: Floris Books, 1994). The authors also refer to trickster gods from other cultures, such as Ictinike, Coyote, Rabbit, and others from Native American mythology; Maui of the Polynesian Islanders; Loki of the old Germanic tribes of Europe; and Krishna from India (ibid., 82). For Pan, see James Hillman, "An Essay on Pan," in *Pan and the Nightmare*, by W. H. Roscher and James Hillman (Zürich: Spring Publications, 1972), esp. lvi–lix; for Dionysus, see Andrew F. Burniston, "Synchronicity: A Dionysian Perspective," *Harvest* 40 (1994): 118–27.

13. Arnold Mindell, "The Golem: An Image Governing Synchronicity," *Quadrant* 8, no. 2 (1975): 5–16; also Sidney Handel, "Mirabile Dictu," in *Chicago 92: The Transcendent Function: Individual and Collective Aspects: Proceedings of the Twelfth International Congress for Analytical Psychology Held in Chicago 23–28 August 1992*, ed. Mary Ann Mattoon (Einsiedeln, Switzerland: Daimon Verlag, 1993), 387–94.

14. For example, see Michael Fordham, "Reflections on the Archetypes and Synchronicity," in *New Developments in Analytical Psychology* (London: Routledge and Kegan Paul, 1957), 35–50; "An Interpretation of Jung's Thesis about Synchronicity," *British Journal of Medical Psychology* 35 (1962): 205–10; Mary Williams, "An Example of Synchronicity," *Journal of Analytical Psychology* 2, no. 1 (1957): 93–95; Rosemary Gordon, "Reflections on Jung's Concept of Synchronicity," in *In the Wake of Jung: A Selection from* "*Harvest*," ed. Molly Tuby (London: Coventure, 1983), 129–46; James F. McHarg, "An Enquiry into the Ostensibly Synchronistic Basis of a Paranoid Psychosis," in *Research in Parapsychology 1972: Abstracts and Papers from the Fifteenth Annual Convention of the Parapsychological Association, 1972*, ed. W. G. Roll, R. L. Morris, and J. D. Morris (Metuchen, NJ: Scarecrow Press, 1973), 87–89; Barbara

Wharton, "Deintegration and Two Synchronistic Events," *Journal of Analytical Psychology* 31, no. 3 (July 1986): 281–85; Jan Marlan, "Beyond Projection and Introjection: The Archetypal and Unitary Field of the Transference" (Chicago: C. G. Jung Institute of Chicago, 1996); and George Bright, "Synchronicity as a Basis of Analytic Attitude," *Journal of Analytical Psychology* 42, no. 4 (1997): 613–35.

15. For example, see C. A. Meier, "Psychosomatic Medicine from the Jungian Point of View," *Journal of Analytical Psychology* 8, no. 2 (1963): 103–21; and Ira Progoff, *Jung, Synchronicity, and Human Destiny* (New York: Dell, 1973; repr., New York: Julian Press, 1987).

16. Aniela Jaffé, "Synchronistic Phenomena," in *Apparitions: An Archetypal Approach to Death, Dreams and Ghosts* (Irving, TX: Spring, 1978), 187–206; Mary Gammon, "'Window into Eternity': Archetype and Relativity," *Journal of Analytical Psychology* 18, no. 1 (1973): 11–24; Carolin S. Keutzer, "The Power of Meaning: From Quantum Mechanics to Synchronicity," *Journal of Humanistic Psychology* 24, no. 1 (Winter 1984): 80–94; Sandra Brenneis and Frederic Boersma, "Typology and Trance: Developing Synchronicity in Hypnotic Induction," *Medical Hypnoanalysis Journal* 8, no. 2 (June 1993): 45–56; Robert S. McCully, "The Rorschach, Synchronicity, and Relativity," in *Toward a Discovery of the Person*, ed. Robert Wm. Davis (Burbank, CA: Society for Personality Assessment, 1974), 33–45; and Lavonne H. Stiffler, "Adoptees and Birthparents Connected by Design: Surprising Synchronicities in Histories of Union/Loss/Reunion," *Pre- and Perinatal Psychology Journal* 7, no. 4 (Summer 1993): 267–86.

17. C. A. Meier, ed., *Atom and Archetype: The Pauli/Jung Letters, 1932–1958* (London: Routledge, 2001). Also see in *Journal of Analytical Psychology* 40, no. 4 (1995), Beverley Zabriskie, "Jung and Pauli: A Subtle Asymmetry," 531–53; and David Lindorff, "One Thousand Dreams: The Spiritual Awakening of Wolfgang Pauli," 555–69, and "Psyche, Matter and Synchronicity: A Collaboration between C. G. Jung and Wolfgang Pauli," 571–86. Also see David Lindorff, *Pauli and Jung: The Meeting of Two Great Minds* (Wheaton, IL: Quest Books, 2004); Herbert van Erkelens, "Wolfgang Pauli's Dialogue with the Spirit of Matter," *Psychological Perspectives* 24 (1991): 34–53; and Marialuisa Donati, "Beyond Synchronicity: The Worldview of Carl Gustav Jung and Wolfgang Pauli," *Journal of Analytical Psychology* 49, no. 4 (2004): 707–28.

18. Joseph Cambray, "Synchronicity and Emergence," *American Imago* 59, no. 4 (2002): 409–35 and "Synchronicity as Emergence," in *Analytical Psychology: Contemporary Perspectives in Jungian Analysis*,

ed. Joseph Cambray and Linda Carter (Hove, UK: Brunner-Routledge, 2004), 223–48; and George Hogenson, "The Self, the Symbolic, and Synchronicity: Virtual Realities and the Emergence of the Psyche," *Journal of Analytical Psychology* 50, no. 2 (2005): 271–84.

19. Jean Shinoda Bolen, *The Tao of Psychology: Synchronicity and the Self* (1979; repr., New York: Harper and Row, 1982); Robert Aziz, *C. G. Jung's Psychology of Religion and Synchronicity* (Albany: State University of New York Press, 1990); and Victor Mansfield, *Synchronicity, Science, and Soul-Making: Understanding Jungian Synchronicity through Physics, Buddhism, and Philosophy* (Chicago: Open Court, 1995). Also see Mansfield's *Head and Heart: A Personal Exploration of Science and the Sacred* (Wheaton, IL: Quest Books, 2002).

20. Bolen, *The Tao of Psychology*, 24.

21. On the ethical dimension of synchronicity, see Robert Aziz, "Synchronicity and the Transformation of the Ethical in Jungian Psychology," in *Asian and Jungian Views of Ethics*, ed. Carl B. Becker (Westport, CT: Greenwood Press, 1999), 65–84.

22. See Marilyn Nagy, *Philosophical Issues in the Psychology of C. G. Jung* (Albany: State University of New York Press, 1991), for a carefully argued case that "the conceptual structure of Jung's psychology is based on philosophical postulates which express an idealist and a metaphysical view of reality" (265).

23. Roderick Main, *The Rupture of Time: Synchronicity and Jung's Critique of Modern Western Culture* (Hove, UK: Brunner-Routledge, 2004).

24. Paul Bishop, *Synchronicity and Intellectual Intuition in Kant, Swedenborg, and Jung* (Lampeter, UK: Edwin Mellen Press, 2000).

25. Alice Johnson, "Coincidences," *Proceedings of the Society for Psychical Research* 14 (1899): 158–330.

26. Arthur Koestler, *The Roots of Coincidence* (London: Hutchinson, 1972); and Alister Hardy, Robert Harvie, and Arthur Koestler, *The Challenge of Chance: Experiments and Speculations* (London: Hutchinson, 1973). Also significant for the study of coincidence is Arthur Koestler, *The Case of the Midwife Toad* (London: Picador 1975), which contains an appendix (pages 133–42) summarizing the book on coincidence by the Austrian biologist Paul Kammerer, *Das Gesetz der Serie* (Stuttgart: Deutches Verlags-Anstalt, 1919).

27. Koestler, *The Roots of Coincidence*, 111–14.

28. Ibid., 122.

29. Ibid., 119.

30. Hardy, Harvie, and Koestler, *The Challenge of Chance*, 159–60.

31. More fully the Koestler, Inglis, Bloomfield (or KIB) Foundation.

32. Brian Inglis, *Coincidence: A Matter of Chance—or Synchronicity?* (London: Hutchinson, 1990).

33. Jane Henry, "Coincidence Experience Survey," *Journal of the Society for Psychical Research* 59, no. 831 (April 1993): 97–108.

34. Ibid., 101.

35. Ibid., 104, 108. I mention here only the results that bear most directly on the subject of the present work.

36. Alan Vaughan, *Incredible Coincidence: The Baffling World of Synchronicity* (New York: Harper and Row, 1979, repr., New York: Ballantine Books, 1989); John Beloff, "Psi Phenomena: Causal Versus Acausal Interpretation," *Journal of the Society for Psychical Research* 49, no. 773 (September 1977): 573–82; Ivor Grattan-Guinness, "What Are Coincidences?" *Journal of the Society for Psychical Research* 49, no. 778 (December 1978): 949–55, and "Coincidences as Spontaneous Psychical Phenomena," *Journal of the Society for Psychical Research* 52, no. 793 (February 1983): 59–71; Lila L. Gatlin, "Meaningful Information Creation: An Alternative Interpretation of the Psi Phenomenon," *Journal of the American Society for Psychical Research* 71, no. 1 (January 1977): 1–18; Charles Tart, "Causality and Synchronicity: Steps towards Clarification," *Journal of the American Society for Psychical Research* 75 (1981): 121–141; and Stephen Hladkyj, "A Comparative Analysis of the Experience of Synchronicity as a Possible Spontaneous Mystical Experience" (master's diss., University of Manitoba, Canada, 1995).

37. Sigmund Freud, "Dreams and Telepathy," in *The Standard Edition of the Complete Psychological Works of Sigmund Freud* [hereafter *Standard Edition*], vol. 18, trans. and ed. James Strachey (London: Hogarth Press, 1964); "Psycho-analysis and Telepathy," in *Standard Edition*, vol. 18; "The Occult Significance of Dreams," in *Standard Edition*, vol. 19, trans. and ed. James Strachey (London: Hogarth Press, 1964); and "Dreams and Occultism," in *Standard Edition*, vol. 22, trans. and ed. James Strachey (London: Hogarth Press, 1964).

38. George Devereux, ed., *Psychoanalysis and the Occult* (New York: International Universities Press, 1953; repr., London: Souvenir Press, 1974).

39. Jule Eisenbud, *Parapsychology and the Unconscious* (Berkeley, CA: North Atlantic Books, 1983); and "Of Mice and Mind, or The Sorcerer's Apprentice: A Cautionary Tale," *Journal of the American Society for Psychical Research* 84, no. 4 (October 1990): 345–64.

40. Mel Faber, *Synchronicity: C. G. Jung, Psychoanalysis, and Religion* (Westport, CT: Praeger, 1998).

41. See Main, *The Rupture of Time*, 32–35.

42. George Spencer Brown, "Statistical Significance in Psychical Research," *Nature*, July 25, 1953, 154–56; and *Probability and Scientific Inference* (London: Longmans, 1957).

43. Persi Diaconis and Frederick Mosteller, "Methods for Studying Coincidences," *Journal of the American Statistical Association* 84, no. 408 (December 1989): 853–61. For a summary, see Main, *The Rupture of Time*, 27–28.

44. See Inglis, *Coincidence*, 98–99.

45. C. G. Jung, "Letters on Synchronicity" (1950–55), in *Collected Works*, vol. 18, *The Symbolic Life* (London: Routledge and Kegan Paul, 1977), 504; and von Franz, *On Divination and Synchronicity*, 50.

46. See Caroline Watt, "Psychology and Coincidences," *European Journal of Parapsychology* 8 (1990–91): 73–74; Combs and Holland, *Synchronicity*, 158; and Brian McCusker and Cherie Sutherland, "Probability and the Psyche I: A Reproducible Experiment Using Tarot, and the Theory of Probability," *Journal of the Society for Psychical Research* 57, no. 822 (January 1991): 344–53.

47. Watt, "Psychology and Coincidence," 66–84. For a summary of her arguments as well as other psychological considerations that can be invoked to account for the experience of meaningful coincidence, see Main, *The Rupture of Time*, 28–32. Also see Peter Brugger et al., "Coincidences: Who Can Say How 'Meaningful' They Are?" in *Proceedings of the Parapsychological Association 34th Annual Convention Held in Heidelberg 8–11 August 1991* (Heidelberg: Parapsychological Association, 1991), 65–72.

48. Watt, "Psychology and Coincidences," 82.

49. Diaconis and Mosteller, "Methods for Studying Coincidences," 859.

50. See, for example, Combs and Holland, *Synchronicty*, 15, 18, 20–31; Inglis, *Concidence*, 178–85; F. David Peat, *Synchronicity: The Bridge between Matter and Mind* (New York: Bantam, 1987), 168–73; Louis Zinkin, "The Hologram as a Model for Analytical Psychology," *Journal of Analytical Psychology* 32 (1987): 1–21; and Carolin Keutzer, "Archetypes, Synchronicity, and the Theory of Formative Causation," *Journal of Analytical Psychology* 27 (1982): 255–62. The principal texts referred to by these writers are David Bohm, *Wholeness and the Implicate Order* (London: Routledge and Kegan Paul, 1980); and Rupert Sheldrake, *A New Science of Life: The Hypothesis of Formative Causation* (London: Blond and Briggs, 1981), and *The Presence of the Past* (London: Collins, 1988).

51. Von Franz, *Number and Time*, 192–93, 209–11, and *Psyche and Matter*, 50–51, 305–6. Also see Gatlin, "Meaningful Information Creation"; and Jacques Vallée, *Messengers of Deception* (Berkeley, CA: And/Or Press, 1979), 210–17.

52. See, for example, Robert Hopcke, *There Are No Accidents: Synchronicity and the Stories of Our Lives* (London: Macmillan, 1997); and Phil Cousineau, *Soul Moments: Marvelous Stories of Synchronicities—Meaningful Coincidences from a Seemingly Random World* (Berkeley CA: Conari Press, 1997).

53. Wayne McEvilly, "Synchronicity and the I Ching," *Philosophy East and West* 18, no. 3 (1968): 137–49; Willard Peterson, "Making Connections: 'Commentary on the Attached Verbalizations' of the *Book of Change*," *Harvard Journal of Asiatic Studies* 42, no. 1 (1982): 67–116, and "Some Connective Concepts in China in the Fourth to Second Centuries B.C.E.," *Eranos* 57 (1988): 201–34; Michael Thalbourne et al., "A Further Attempt to Separate the Yins from the Yangs. A Replication of the Rubin-Honorton Experiment with the *I CHING*," *European Journal of Parapsychology* 9 (1992–93): 12–23; and Stephen Karcher, "Divination, Synchronicity, and Fate," *Journal of Religion and Health* 37, no. 3 (1998): 215–28, and *Total I Ching: Myths for Change* (London: Time Warner, 2003), 67. Also see Roderick Main, "Synchronicity and the *I Ching*: Clarifying the Connections," *Harvest: Journal for Jungian Studies* 43, no. 1 (1997): 51–64, and "Magic and Science".

54. I am grateful to Stuart Rose for supplying me with these figures from the survey he conducted as part of his doctoral thesis within the Department of Religious Studies at Lancaster University. See his "Transforming the World: An Examination of the Roles Played by Spirituality and Healing in the New Age Movement," Ph.D. thesis, Lancaster University, 1997. The figures were supplied when the thesis was still in progress in November 1995. The kinds of psi experience reported as occurring more frequently than synchronicity were (in descending order) telepathy, 52.3 percent; precognition, 44.1 percent; and past life, 40.7 percent. Of equally frequent occurrence was clairvoyance, 40.6 percent. Of less frequent occurrence were clairaudience, 25.3 percent; cosmic intelligence, 20.3 percent; psychokinesis, 8.8 percent; and out-of-body experiences, 5.7 percent. A more detailed breakdown of those reporting experiences of synchronicity shows male, 46 percent; female, 38 percent; under 35 years of age, 39 percent; between 35 and 55, 43 percent; over 55, 38 percent; and therapists, 55 percent.

55. See, for example, Combs and Holland, *Synchronicity*; Peat, *Synchronicity*; Vaughan, *Incredible Coincidence*; Bolen, *The Tao of Psychology*; and even Bohm, *Wholeness and the Implicate Order*; and Sheldrake, *A New Science of Life* and *The Presence of the Past*. Indeed, the survey by Stuart Rose revealed Jung was mentioned second most frequently as a major influence on the lives of respondents.

56. Typical of this tendency is Wayne Dyer, *You'll See It When You Believe It* (London: Arrow, 1993), in which we find in chapter 6, titled

"Synchronicity," statements such as the following: "Acknowledgment of synchronicity in our lives nurtures our divine connection to the invisible, formless world. It allows us to begin the awakening process and to see that we can use our ability to think and be thought, to reshape and redirect our entire lives" (210). See also James Redfield, *The Celestine Prophecy* (London: Bantam, 1994), esp. 11–28.

57. The relationship between the New Age and Jung's theory of synchronicity is addressed in Main, *The Rupture of Time*, 144–74.

58. Edward Thornton, *Diary of a Mystic* (London: George Allen and Unwin, 1967), 124–33.

59. The material was subsequently included in a book published by the experiencer. See James Plaskett, *Coincidences* (Hastings, UK: Tamworth Press, 2000).

60. See especially, C. G. Jung, *Collected Works*, vol. 12, *Psychology and Alchemy*, 2nd ed. (London: Routledge and Kegan Paul, 1968), 43–46.

CHAPTER 2:
SYNCHRONICITY AND SPIRIT

1. See Anthony Flew, "Coincidence and Synchronicity," *Journal of the Society for Psychical Research* 37, no. 677 (November 1953): 199, in which he argues that there is no special category of events—other than just coincidences generally—to which the term "synchronicity" applies. On the alleged vacuity of "spirit" and related terms, see Alfred J. Ayer, *Language, Truth, and Logic* (Harmondsworth, UK: Penguin, 1980), 41–42, 151–58.

2. Stephen Jenkins, *The Undiscovered Country* (Sudbury, UK: Neville Spearman, 1976), 108–9.

3. Zechariah 1:8; 6:1–8.

4. Jenkins, *The Undiscovered Country*, 108.

5. Ibid.

6. Ibid., 108–9.

7. *Chambers Twentieth Century Dictionary*, 1977 ed., s.v. "coincidence." Different dictionaries capture slightly different nuances within the concept. For example, *The Oxford English Dictionary*, 1989 ed., s.v. "coincidence," emphasizes that the absence of causal connection may be only apparent: a coincidence is "the notable occurrence of events or circumstances without apparent causal connection." On the other hand, this does not make explicit that the parallel occurrence may be either simultaneous or consecutive.

8. Note the plural "horses" in each case in Zechariah 6:2–3: "In the first chariot were red horses; and in the second chariot black horses; And in the third chariot white horses; and in the fourth chariot grizzled and bay horses."

9. See, for example, Arthur Koestler, *The Roots of Coincidence*. (London: Hutchinson, 1972). Also see Ivor Grattan-Guinness, "Coincidences as Spontaneous Psychical Phenomena," *Journal of the Society for Psychical Research* 52, no. 793 (February 1983): 59–71.

10. See, for example, Alan Vaughan, *Incredible Coincidence: The Baffling World of Synchronicity* (New York: Harper and Row, 1979; repr., New York: Ballantine, 1989); F. David Peat, *Synchronicity; The Bridge between Matter and Mind* (New York and Bantam, 1987); and Brian Inglis, *Coincidence: A Matter of Chance—or Synchronicity?* (London: Hutchinson, 1990).

11. Jenkins, *The Undiscovered Country*, 108.

12. C. G. Jung, "Synchronicity: An Acausal Connecting Principle" (1952), in *Collected Works*, vol. 8, *The Structure and Dynamics of the Psyche*, 2nd ed. (London: Routledge and Kegan Paul, 1969), 426.

13. C. G. Jung, *Memories, Dreams, Reflections* (London: Collins, 1979), 405.

14. As in the subtitle of Jung, "Synchronicity: An Acausal Connecting Principle."

15. Ibid., 441.

16. C. G. Jung, "On Synchronicity" (1951), in *Collected Works*, vol. 8, *The Structure and Dynamics of the Psyche*, 2nd ed. (London: Routledge and Kegan Paul, 1969), 525.

17. Ibid.

18. Ibid., 525–26.

19. Jung, "Synchronicity," 436.

20. Ibid., emphasis added.

21. Ibid., 439.

22. Ibid., 440.

23. Ibid., 439–40.

24. Ibid., 439.

25. For a more detailed discussion of how synchronicity relates to analytical psychology, see Roderick Main, *The Rupture of Time: Synchronicity and Jung's Critique of Modern Western Culture* (Hove, UK: Brunner-Routledge, 2004), 14–26.

26. Jung, "On Synchronicity," 526. In the "Résumé" added to the 1955 English edition of his principal essay, Jung attempts to refine this tripartite definition in the light of his view that the coinciding events of a

synchronicity should both be considered psychic. See C. G. Jung, *Synchronicity: An Acausal Connecting Principle* (London: Ark Paperbacks, 1987), 144–45; see also his, "Synchronicity," 444–45. However, as I have demonstrated in detail elsewhere (see Main, *The Rupture of Time*, 44–47), this attempted refinement generates more problems than it solves, so that the version given here remains the more satisfactory. For a further detailed discussion of Jung's definitions, see Main, *The Rupture of Time*, 12–14, 39–47.

27. Jung, "Synchronicity," 481, 483.

28. Jung, "On Synchronicity," 522.

29. This is appreciated by Ivor Grattan-Guinness who observes, "The usual understanding of coincidence is that two or more events take place in some strikingly correlative way (*for example, more or less simultaneously* [emphasis added]), but each event inhabits its own causative framework, disjoint from the frameworks of the other event(s)" ("What Are Coincidences?" *Journal of the Society for Psychical Research* 49, no. 778 [December 1978]: 949). Jane Henry is also sensitive to this point: "Typically [coincidences] concern simultaneous (or near-simultaneous) experiences, though extremely improbable events may be related much more distantly in time" ("Coincidence Experience Survey," *Journal of the Society for Psychical Research* 59, no. 831 [April 1993]: 97).

30. Only then did I begin to explore what possible symbolic meaning the image of "origami" might have for me.

31. James Plaskett, revised presentation of coincidence narrative, typewritten manuscript, July 2, 1992, present writer's personal collection, 33–34.

32. Each of these terms—psychic, physical, inner and outer—I use in nontechnical, common-sense ways. Dreams, thoughts, and memories are examples of the psychic; trees, books, and bodies are examples of the physical. By "inner" is meant having to do primarily with oneself; for example, a thought in one's own mind or a sensation or action of one's own body. By "outer" is meant not having to do primarily with oneself; for example, a dream of someone else's, an action by someone else, or a state of affairs in the environment independent of oneself. I also acknowledge that perhaps no event is wholly one thing or the other, and that there can be areas of ambivalence as to whether certain given events are primarily physical or psychic, inner or outer.

33. Edward Thornton, *The Diary of a Mystic* (London: George Allen and Unwin, 1967), 125. See chapter 4 of this study for a full discussion of Thornton's synchronistic experiences.

34. C. G. Jung, "Letters on Synchronicity: To Michael Fordham, 1st July 1955," in *Collected Works*, vol. 18, *The Symbolic Life* (London: Routledge and Kegan Paul, 1977), 508.

35. C. G. Jung, *Collected Works*, vol. 14, *Mysterium Coniunctionis* (London: Routledge and Kegan Paul, 1963), 464–65.

36. This said, Jung's development of the concept synchronicity should not be viewed solely as an attempt to resolve the dualism between psyche and matter. This is how Roger Brooke seems to view it. He considers that Jung's psychology generally, for all that it attempts to sustain the view that "psyche and body are not separate entities but one and the same life" (see C. G. Jung, "On the Psychology of the Unconscious" [1917/1926/1943], in *Collected Works*, vol. 7, *Two Essays on Analytical Psychology*, 2nd ed. [London: Routledge and Kegan Paul, 1966], 115) nevertheless perpetuates a Cartesian dualism by assuming that psyche is "an interior locality outside of which is the body and the world" (Roger Brooke, *Jung and Phenomenology* [London: Routledge and Kegan Paul, 1991], 68). In this light Brooke sees the concept of synchronicity primarily as "a magical attempt on Jung's part to jump over the chasm that his separation of subject and object had already created" (ibid., 175). What such an interpretation overlooks is the radically anomalous nature of the events that Jung was designating as synchronistic. He was not just looking for a concept that would enable psyche and matter to be seen ubiquitously as "one and the same life." He was also, even more importantly, offering a descriptive and explanatory category for a very specific kind of experience.

37. A case could be made for adopting an understanding of acausality that likewise reflects common experience. One can readily enough become aware of events within the field of one's normal experience that seem to be connected meaningfully but not in any obvious causal way. To be sure, one may be fairly confident that with a modicum of serious reflection one could account for the connection as being either causal in some way or else totally spurious, the result of projection. But the fact remains that prima facie, as immediately experienced, the event strikes one as acausal. Indeed, if the same kind of mental rigor that was used to discern the hidden causal relationships in such cases was also used to search for deeper forms of acausality—for example, the fact that the laws of physics should be as they are and not otherwise might be considered an instance of deep acausality, Jung's "general acausal orderedness"—one might find that at each level of understanding both causal and acausal relationships were capable of remaining in the picture, neither of them being fully explicable in terms of the other. This, presumably, is why Jung conceived of them as being complementary concepts.

38. Charles Tart, "Causality and Synchronicity: Steps towards Clarification," *Journal of the American Society for Psychical Research* 75 (April 1981): 130–31.
39. Ibid., 131.
40. Ibid., 132.
41. Ibid., 135.
42. Ibid.
43. *Macmillan Dictionary of Religion*, 1994, s.v. "Spirit." However, even this definition may be less neutral than intended. As Robert Segal points out, the anthropologist Edward Tyler insists that for primitives "soul" and "spirit" are material, the metaphysical notion of immateriality having no meaning for primitives (see Robert Segal, *Theorizing about Myth* [Amherst: University of Massachusetts Press, 1999], 8).
44. *New Catholic Encyclopedia*, 1967, s.v. "Spirit," by A. J. McNicholl; C. G. Jung, "Spirit and Life" (1926), in *Collected Works*, vol. 8, *The Structure and Dynamics of the Psyche*, 2nd ed. (London: Routledge and Kegan Paul, 1969), 319–20.
45. Jung, "Spirit and Life," 329.
46. C. G. Jung, "The Phenomenology of the Spirit in Fairytales" (1945/1948), in *Collected Works*, vol. 9i, *The Archetypes and the Collective Unconscious*, 2nd ed. (London: Routledge and Kegan Paul, 1968), 209.
47. *Concise Dictionary of Religion*, 1993, s.v. "Spirit."
48. Ibid. Cf. *New Catholic Encyclopedia*, s.v. "Spirit: Christian Concept," by A. J. McNicholl, in which Christian thought is said to recognize "three main kinds of spirit: (1) the human soul, incomplete in its mode of subsisting and extrinsically dependent on the body; (2) pure finite spirit, i.e., the angel, perfectly subsisting and independent of matter; and (3) Absolute Spirit, or God, infinite, utterly pure, and fully actual being (subsistent existence) without any limitation."
49. *Encyclopedia of Religion*, 1987, s.v. "Soul: Christian Concept: Soul and Spirit," by Geddes MacGregor. On the interchangeability of the terms "soul" and "psyche," also see Victor White, *Soul and Psyche: An Enquiry into the Relationship of Psychotherapy and Religion* (London: Collins and Harvill Press, 1960), esp. 11–31; also 217–25.
50. *Encyclopedia of Religion*.
51. *New Catholic Encyclopedia*, s.v. "Spirit."
52. Ibid.
53. Ibid., s.v. "Spirit: Christian Concept."
54. Ibid.
55. Ken Wilber, Jack Engler, and Daniel P. Brown, *Transformations of Consciousness* (Boston: Shambhala, 1986), 74.

56. Ken Wilber, *Eye to Eye: The Quest for the New Paradigm*, exp. ed. (Boston: Shambhala, 1990), 209.

57. Ibid., 212.

58. Jung's primary reference in these discussions is to the German word "*Geist*" that, as was noted previously, has a different root metaphor from that of *ruah, pneuma, spiritus*, and so forth. However, it is clear that Jung is also aware of, and taking into account, the words from the other languages with their metaphorical associations to breath (see, for example, "Spirit and Life," 319–20).

59. Jung, "Spirit and Life," 320.

60. Ibid., 330.

61. Ibid., 335.

62. Ibid., 336.

63. Jung, "The Phenomenology of the Spirit in Fairytales," 208.

64. Ibid., 212.

65. Ibid.

66. This is, in effect, part of the strategy both of Jung ("The Phenomenology of the Spirit in Fairytales," 210–12) and of Wilber (Ken Wilber, "The Great Chain of Being," *Journal of Humanistic Psychology* 33, no. 3 [Summer 1993]: 59–60).

67. This strategy also informs both Jung's approach ("The Phenomenology of the Spirit in Fairytales," 209–10) and Wilber's (Ken Wilber, "Reply to Schneider," *Journal of Humanistic Psychology* 29, no. 4 [Fall 1989]: 494–98).

68. See, for example, Wilber, "The Great Chain of Being," 53.

69. See, for example, *Encyclopedia of Religion*, s.v. "Soul: Christian Concept: Soul and Spirit," in which the Pauline understanding of spirit is said to be effectively of a "dimension . . . in which the human participates in the divine"—the divine thus clearly being something "beyond" spirit.

70. Cf. the last of the quotations from the *New Catholic Encyclopedia* above.

71. Cf. Jung, "The Phenomenology of the Spirit in Fairytales," 208, where one characterization given is of "spirit as a higher and psyche as a lower form of activity."

72. Cf. Wilber's "spectrum of consciousness" model in Ken Wilber, *The Spectrum of Consciousness* (Wheaton, IL: Quest, 1977) and throughout his writings. However, as I explain later, I do not see the relationship between the phases of the spectrum as hierarchical in as strong a sense as does Wilber.

73. Both points of view are registered by Jung, "The Phenomenology of the Spirit in Fairytales," 208.

74. See Rudolf Otto, *The Idea of the Holy*, trans. John W. Harvey, 2nd ed. (Oxford: Oxford University Press, 1958). For a fuller discussion of numinosity, see chapter 3 of the present study, subsection on "Numinosity: *Mysterium Tremendum et Fascinans*."

75. Cf. Andrew Samuels, Bani Shorter, and Fred Plaut, *A Critical Dictionary of Jungian Analysis* (London: Routledge and Kegan Paul, 1986), s.v. "Spirit": "the usual response [to the activity of spirit] is one of affect, whether positive or negative"; they also refer to spirits' "numinous power and the effectiveness of their interventions."

76. Cf. the quotations above from the *New Catholic Encyclopedia* (spirit is "not subject to determinations of time and space") and from Wilber (spirit is "a point where the soul touches eternity").

77. Cf. the further quotations above from the *New Catholic Encyclopedia* (spiritual reality is "not composed of parts spatially distinct from one another") and from Wilber (absolute spirit involves "nondual awareness or unity consciousness").

78. See Ken Wilber, "Odyssey: A Personal Inquiry into Humanistic and Transpersonal Psychology," *Journal of Humanistic Psychology* 22, no. 1 (Winter 1982): 66, 84–85.

79. Cf. the *New Catholic Encyclopedia*'s inclusion of "intelligence, reason, knowledge of universals" as among the factors that have been identified as "the radical and essential manifestation of spirit" (quoted previously).

80. See Wilber, *Eye to Eye*, 97.

81. This kind of understanding is clearly expressed already in Plato's *Republic*, for example, 506d–518b.

82. See Wilber, "The Great Chain of Being," 52–65.

83. Ibid., esp. 54–55.

84. C. G. Jung, "The Undiscovered Self (Present and Future)," in *Collected Works*, vol. 10, *Civilization in Transition*, 2nd ed. (London: Routledge and Kegan Paul, 1970), 257–58.

85. Jung, "The Phenomenology of the Spirit in Fairytales," 212.

86. Jung, "Spirit and Life," 328.

87. Ibid.

88. C. G. Jung, "Basic Postulates of Analytical Psychology" (1931), in *Collected Works*, vol. 8, *The Structure and Dynamics of the Psyche*, 2nd ed. (London: Routledge and Kegan Paul, 1969), 353.

89. Ibid.

90. Ibid., 353–54.

91. Edward C. Whitmont, "Prefatory Remarks to Jung's 'Reply to Buber'," *Spring* (1973): 192.

92. Ibid.

93. Ibid., 189.
94. Ibid.
95. Ibid., 193.
96. For a summary of Kant's philosophy and its relationship to Jung's psychology, see Stephanie de Voogd, "Fantasy versus Fiction: Jung's Kantianism Appraised," in *Jung in Modern Perspective*, ed. Renos K. Papadopoulos and Graham S. Saayman (Hounslow, UK: Wildwood House, 1984), 204–28. For more depth, see Paul Bishop, *Synchronicity and Intellectual Intuition: Kant, Swedenborg, and Jung* (Lampeter, UK: Edwin Mellen, 2000).
97. Ibid., 204, citing C. G. Jung, "On the Nature of the Psyche" (1947/1954), in *Collected Works*, vol. 8, *The Structure and Dynamics of the Psyche*, 2nd ed. (London: Routledge and Kegan Paul, 1969), 171.
98. Stephanie de Voogd, "C. G. Jung: Psychologist of the Future, 'Philosopher' of the Past," *Spring* (1977): 180.
99. Ibid., 180–81. The implied epistemological stance is the one explicated by James Hillman wherein "the archetype is wholly immanent in its image" (cited in Roberts Avens, *Imagination Is Reality: Western Nirvana in Jung, Hillman, Barfield, and Cassirer* [Dallas, TX: Spring, 1980], 45; also see 93).
100. De Voogd, "Fantasy versus Fiction," 225.
101. Ibid., 227.
102. Wolfgang Giegerich, "The Rescue of the World: Jung, Hegel, and the Subjective Universe," *Spring* (1987): 107–14.
103. Ibid., 110.
104. Ibid.
105. Ibid. With these words Giegerich cuts through one of the great controversies surrounding Jung's psychology of religion. Also see James W. Heisig, *Imago Dei: A Study of C. G. Jung's Psychology of Religion* (London: Associated University Presses, 1979).
106. Giegerich, "The Recue of the World," 111.
107. Ibid., 110.
108. Ibid., 111.
109. Ibid. That there could be "land beyond Kant" is, according to Giegerich, demonstrated by the case of Hegel who, "because he had paid the entire toll Kant demands, was free of Kant" (ibid.).
110. Ibid., 108.
111. Whitmont, "Prefatory Remarks," 193.
112. Ibid., 192.
113. Ibid.
114. Ibid., 194.
115. Ibid.

116. Jung, "The Phenomenology of the Spirit in Fairytales," 212.
117. Whitmont, "Prefatory Remarks," 195.
118. One could just as well argue that all psychic experience is inescapably colored by spirit; indeed, that any experience at all, whether predominantly spiritual or psychic or physical, inevitably also involves the other two aspects and so is bound to be colored by them to some degree. Psyche, according to this view, is not unique in being pervasive.
119. See again Wilber, "Reply to Schneider," 494–498.
120. Jung, "Spirit and Life," 319.
121. Ibid., 335–36.
122. Ibid.
123. Jung, "The Phenomenology of the Spirit in Fairytales," 214; emphasis added.
124. Ibid.
125. The main weight of Jung's argument here has to be carried by dreams, since fairytales are in many cases demonstrably much less spontaneous than he supposed. See John M. Ellis, *One Fairy Story Too Many: The Brothers Grimm and Their Tales* (Chicago: University of Chicago Press, 1983).

CHAPTER 3:
THE SPIRITUAL DIMENSION OF SPONTANEOUS SYNCHRONICITIES

1. On Jung's understanding and use of the idea of the numinous, see Leon Schlamm, "The Holy: A Meeting-Point between Analytical Psychology and Religion," in *Jung and the Monotheisms: Judaism, Christianity, and Islam*, ed. Joel Ryce-Menuhin (London: Routledge, 1994), 20–32.
2. Rudolf Otto, *The Idea of the Holy*, trans. John W. Harvey, 2nd ed. (Oxford: Oxford University Press, 1958).
3. Ibid., 6.
4. Ibid., 12.
5. Ibid., 11.
6. Ibid., 12.
7. Ibid., 13–24.
8. Ibid., 25–30.
9. Ibid., 26.
10. Ibid., 31–40.
11. Ibid., 31.
12. Ibid., 27.
13. Ibid.

14. Ibid., 28.
15. Ibid., 29.
16. Ibid., 28–29.
17. Ibid., 16–17.
18. Persi Diaconis and Frederick Mosteller, "Methods for Studying Coincidences," *Journal of the American Statistical Association* 84, no. 408 (December 1989): 859. Freud, too, considered coincidences a possible source of the experience of the uncanny. See his "The Uncanny" (1919), in *Standard Edition*, vol. 17, trans. and ed. James Strachey (London: Hogarth Press, 1964), 237–40, 247–48.
19. Otto, *The Idea of the Holy*, 22.
20. William James, *The Varieties of Religious Experience: A Study in Human Nature*, 38th impression (London: Longmans, Green, 1935), 381–82.
21. Otto, *The Idea of the Holy*, 24.
22. Ibid., 31.
23. See, for example, Alan Vaughan, *Patterns of Prophecy* (London: Turnstone Books, 1974), 23–24.
24. This point was noted specifically by Robert Aziz in his *C. G. Jung's Psychology of Religion and Synchronicity* (Albany: State University of New York Press, 1990), 80.
25. Friedrich Nietzsche, *Ecce Homo: How One Becomes What One Is*, trans. R. J. Hollingdale (Harmondsworth, UK: Penguin, 1979), 93.
26. R. F. Holland, "The Miraculous," in *Religion and Understanding*, ed. D. Z. Phillips (Oxford: Basil Blackwell, 1967), 167.
27. Colin Brown, *Miracles and the Critical Mind* (Grand Rapids, MI: William B. Eerdmans, Exeter, UK: Paternoster Press, 1984), 174–76.
28. Holland, "The Miraculous," 157.
29. Ibid.
30. Jung, too, sometimes referred to synchronicities as miracles. See, for example, C. G. Jung to Dr. H., August 30, 1951, in *C. G. Jung Letters 2: 1951–61*, ed. Gerhard Adler and Aniela Jaffé, trans. R. F. C. Hull (London: Routledge and Kegan Paul, 1976), 21–23. However, see also letter to A. D. Cornell, February 9, 1960, 537–43, in which, after seeming to call synchronicities miracles (537, 539), Jung later remarks that the synchronistic event "is not 'miraculous' but merely 'extraordinary' and unexpected" (540). See also Roderick Main, *The Rupture of Time: Synchronicity and Jung's Critique of Modern Western Culture* (Hove, UK: Brunner-Routledge, 2004), 146.
31. See Alan Vaughan, *Incredible Coincidence: The Baffling World of Synchronicity* (New York: Harper and Row, 1979; repr., New York: Ballantine, 1989), 147, citing Warren Weaver, *Lady Luck: The Theory of*

Probability (New York: Anchor Books, 1963), 280; the story was originally published in *Life* magazine (March 27, 1950).

32. Holland, "The Miraculous," 157.
33. Vaughan, *Incredible Coincidence*, 147.
34. Holland, "The Miraculous," 157.
35. See Brian Inglis, *The Unknown Guest: The Mystery of Intuition* (London: Chatto and Windus, 1987), 172–73, citing Guy Lyon Playfair, *If This Be Magic* (London: Jonathan Cape 1985).
36. See in chapter 2 the subsection "Some Differentiating Attributes of Spirit," in which I speak, more specifically, of repatterning or restructuring contents within the fields of the psychic and physical.
37. See, for example, C. G. Jung, "Foreword to Suzuki's 'Introduction to Zen Buddhism'" (1939), in *Collected Works*, vol. 11, *Psychology and Religion: West and East*, 2nd ed. (London: Routledge and Kegan Paul, 1969), 545–48.
38. This idea has been explored at length by David Curtis, "The Synchronistic Continuum," typewritten manuscript, February 1994, present writer's personal collection.
39. Cited in F. W. Happold, *Mysticism* (Harmondsworth, UK: Penguin, 1970), 67.
40. Jiddu Krishnamurti, *The First and Last Freedom* (London: Gollancz, 1954), 108.
41. Ibid.
42. Alister Hardy, *The Spiritual Nature of Man* (Oxford: Oxford University Press, 1979), 26, 143.
43. On integration see, for example, C. G. Jung, "The Relations between the Ego and the Unconscious" (1928), in *Collected Works*, vol. 7, *Two Essays on Analytical Psychology*, 2nd ed. (London: Routledge and Kegan Paul, 1966).
44. C. G. Jung, "Flying Saucers: A Modern Myth of Things Seen in the Skies" (1958), in *Collected Works*, vol. 10, *Civilization in Transition*, 2nd ed. (London: Routledge and Kegan Paul, 1970), 409.
45. Ibid.
46. C. G. Jung, *Collected Works*, vol. 14, *Mysterium Coniunctionis* (1955–56) (London: Routledge and Kegan Paul, 1963), 464–65.
47. Marie-Louise von Franz, *Number and Time: Reflections Leading towards a Unification of Psychology and Physics*, trans. Andrea Dykes (London: Rider, 1974), 247; emphasis in original.
48. Wolfgang Pauli, "The Influence of Archetypal Ideas on the Scientific Theories of Kepler," in C. G. Jung and W. Pauli, *The Interpretation of Nature and the Psyche*, trans. R. F. C. Hull (London: Routledge and Kegan Paul, 1955), 209–10; emphasis in original.

49. Cited in John Honner, *The Description of Nature: Niels Bohr and the Philosophy of Quantum Physics* (Oxford: Clarendon Press, 1987), 186.

50. David Bohm, "A New Theory of the Relationship of Mind and Matter," *Journal of the American Society for Psychical Research* 80, no. 2 (April 1986): 129.

51. C. G. Jung, "Synchronicity: An Acausal Connecting Principle" (1952), in *Collected Works*, vol. 8, *The Structure and Dynamics of the Psyche*, 2nd ed. (London: Routledge and Kegan Paul, 1969), 512.

52. Von Franz, *Number and Time*, 247.

53. *Macmillan Dictionary of Religion* (1994), s.v. "Transcendence."

54. See Alister Hardy, Robert Harvie, and Arthur Koestler, *The Challenge of Chance: Experiments and Speculations* (London: Hutchinson, 1973), 157–204.

55. Stephen Jenkins, *The Undiscovered Country* (Sudbury, UK: Neville Spearman, 1976), 73.

56. St. Thomas Aquinas, *Philosophical Texts*, sel. and trans. by Thomas Gilby (London: Oxford University Press, 1951), 117–18 (from Opusc. XII, *Compendium Theologiae*, 137).

57. This inference to a transcendent level of operation resembles and is compatible with the previously discussed inference to a level of unity. Relative to the level of normal psychic and physical differentiation, any higher level activity might well appear unitary—without necessarily being so in any absolute sense.

58. *Chambers Dictionary of Beliefs and Religions* (1992), s.v. "Transcendence and immanence."

59. Ibid. Of course, those more favorably disposed to pantheism would not consider it to be degenerate.

60. Ibid.

61. Ibid., s.v. "Providence."

62. John Polkinghorne suggests that highly significant coincidences may fall into a borderline area between special providence and miracles. See his *Science and Theology: An Introduction* (London: SPCK, 1998), 85.

63. Jenkins, *The Undiscovered Country*, 73.

64. Ira Progoff, *Jung, Synchronicity, and Human Destiny* (New York: Dell, 1973; repr., New York: Julian Press, 1987), 170–72.

65. Ibid., 171.

66. See, for example, Jean Shinoda Bolen, *The Tao of Psychology: Synchronicity and the Self* (1979; repr., New York: Harper and Row, 1982), esp. chap. 5, "Significant Meetings and the Synchronistic Matchmaker."

67. See, for example, Brian Inglis, *Coincidence: A Matter of Chance—or Synchronicity?* (London: Hutchinson, 1990), 33–41, subsection titled "Providence."

68. *Chambers Dictionary of Beliefs and Religions*, s.v. "Revelation."

69. This said, I do not discount the possibility that what appear primarily or initially as "revelations" of importance only to one or a few individuals could also turn out to be of importance more collectively.

70. Note that the expression "essential form" is used here simply in the sense explained and is not meant to carry Platonic, Aristotelian, or any other kind of extraneous philosophical overtones.

71. C. G. Jung, *Collected Works*, vol. 6, *Psychological Types* (1921) (London: Routledge and Kegan Paul, 1971), 474; emphasis in original.

72. Ibid., 475, 474.

73. Avery Dulles, *Models of Revelation* (Dublin: Gill and Macmillan, 1983), 132.

74. Ibid., 143.

75. Ibid., 136.

76. Ibid.

77. Ibid., 137.

78. Ibid.

79. Ibid., 136.

80. Ibid., 1–128.

81. Ibid., 131–53.

82. Ibid., 131, 141.

83. Ibid., 33.

84. Ibid., 141–45.

85. Ibid., 33.

86. Ibid., 145.

87. Examples of synchronicities that might be experienced as revelatory on a more collective scale are the kind of astrological coincidences mentioned by Jung, such as that "between the life of Christ and the objective astronomical event, the entrance of the spring equinox into the sign of Pisces." See his *Memories, Dreams, Reflections* (London: Collins, 1979), 248.

88. Dulles, *Models of Revelation*, 33.

89. Ibid., 148.

90. Ibid., 149.

91. Ibid., 33.

92. Ibid., 85.

93. Ibid., 152.

94. Ibid., 150.

95. Ibid., 33.

96. Ibid., 153.

97. Coincidence experiences have been explicitly viewed in this light by Brian Cocksey, "Coincidence and Divine Revelation," typewritten manuscript, March 1990, present writer's personal collection.

CHAPTER 4:
SYMBOL, MYTH, AND SYNCHRONICITY:
THE BIRTH OF ATHENA

1. See, for example, Alister Hardy, Robert Harvie, and Arthur Koestler, *The Challenge of Chance: Experiments and Speculations* (London: Hutchinson, 1973); Alan Vaughan, *Incredible Coincidence: The Baffling World of Synchronicity* (New York: Harper and Row, 1979; repr., New York: Ballantine, 1989); and Brian Inglis, *Coincidence: A Matter of Chance—or Synchronicity?* (London: Hutchinson, 1990).

2. Edward Thornton, *The Diary of a Mystic* (London: George Allen and Unwin, 1967).

3. Ibid., 124.
4. Ibid., 125.
5. Ibid.
6. Ibid.
7. Ibid.
8. Ibid.
9. Ibid.
10. Ibid., 125–26.
11. Ibid., 126.

12. Thornton records this dream initially as having occurred on May 9 (ibid.). Later, it transpires that it actually occurred in the early hours of May 10 (ibid., 132).

13. Ibid., 126. As Thornton mentions (ibid.), this dream was included in C. A. Meier, *Ancient Incubation and Modern Psychotherapy*, trans. Monica Curtis (Evanston, IL: Northwestern University Press, 1967), 88–89, in which Thornton's account says, more specifically, "an operation is to be performed, *I think by Jung*" (emphasis added).

14. Thornton, *The Diary of a Mystic*, 126.
15. Ibid.
16. Ibid.

17. Ibid., 127, quoting from Karl Kerényi, *The Gods of the Greeks* (London: Thames and Hudson, 1951), 120. Matter in brackets is correction of Thornton's careless quoting. He has "hammer" for "a hammer," "mortals" for "immortals," "afraid of" for "afraid and astonished at," and "out of the front of" for "in front of."

18. Thornton, *The Diary of a Mystic*, 126.
19. See C. G. Jung, *Collected Works*, vol. 14, *Mysterium Coniunctionis* (1955–56) (London: Routledge and Kegan Paul, 1963).
20. Thornton, *The Diary of a Mystic*, 127.
21. Ibid., 128.
22. Ibid., 128–29.
23. Ibid., 129.
24. Ibid.
25. Ibid.
26. Ibid.
27. Ibid., 129–30.
28. Ibid., 130.
29. Ibid., 127.
30. Ibid., 129–31.
31. Rudolf Otto, *The Idea of the Holy*, trans. John W. Harvey, 2nd ed. (1917; Oxford: Oxford University Press, 1958), 16–17.
32. Thornton, *The Diary of a Mystic*, 125.
33. Ibid., 130.
34. Ibid., 131.
35. Ibid., 134. The bronze owl and the statue of Athena were accounted for, he later discovered, by the fact that the Leeds coat of arms "consists of two large owls with a small one above them."
36. Ibid.
37. Ibid., 131.
38. Ibid., 132.
39. Ibid.
40. Ibid.
41. Ibid. The religious community was a Trappist order based in Hertfordshire.
42. Ibid., 133.
43. Marie-Louise von Franz, *On Divination and Synchronicity: The Psychology of Meaningful Chance* (Toronto: Inner City Books, 1980), 105–8. Also see C. G. Jung, "Synchronicity: An Acausal Connecting Principle" (1952), in *Collected Works*, vol. 8, *The Structure and Dynamics of the Psyche*, 2nd ed. (London: Routledge and Kegan Paul, 1969), 503–4;
44. Thornton, *The Diary of a Mystic*, 133. A further point, which Thornton himself does not explicitly relate to the theme of unity, is that the osteopath told him how once when she had doubts concerning her role as a healer she dreamed that she saw written on a frieze the words: "Together we stand, divided you fall"—with the word "fall" underlined very thickly four times (ibid., 128). This suggests the importance of maintaining some kind of unitive contact with a higher dimension of reality, in

her case, with the "power . . . working through her" (ibid.). The theme of unity and division is curiously evoked also, though in a different sense, by the names of the first two doctors mentioned by Thornton: "Asked which doctor I would like, I insisted on Dr. Isaac *Cainer* whom I had not met, in preference to Dr. *Abel* my mother's doctor" (ibid., 129; emphasis added). In the light of this, note again the dream (10) involving Thornton's *brother chopping him on the head with an axe* (ibid., 126).

45. A closer examination of Thornton's narrative might uncover even more synchronistic events. I am focusing on the most salient, which are sufficient for my purposes.

46. Ibid., 125.
47. Ibid., 126.
48. Ibid.
49. Ibid.
50. Ibid., 127.
51. Ibid.
52. Ibid., 129–30.
53. Ibid., 130.
54. Ibid., 125.
55. Ibid., 126. This and the preceding event are not yet synchronistic, but they do illustrate the pattern of Thornton's thinking. My point is that synchronicity can enhance the revelatory character of events, not that synchronicity is a necessary condition of revelation.
56. Ibid., 127.
57. Ibid., 130.
58. Ibid.
59. Ibid., 131.
60. Ibid., 126, 133.
61. Cf. the second of the three stages of the alchemical conjunction as understood by Gerhard Dorn and discussed by Jung in *Mysterium Coniunctionis*, 457–553. The first stage is the *unio mentalis*, a state of "interior oneness . . . of equanimity transcending the body's affectivity and instinctuality" (ibid., 471). The second stage is "the re-uniting of the *unio mentalis* with the body" (ibid., 476). The third stage, the "complete conjunction," is "union [of the individual] with the *unus mundus*" (ibid.).
62. Cf. the third of Dorn's stages of alchemical conjunction (see preceding note).
63. Thornton, *The Diary of a Mystic*, 133.
64. Ibid., 130–31.
65. See the review of statistical and psychological work in chapter 1 of this study.
66. Thornton, *The Diary of a Mystic*, 130.

CHAPTER 5:
MULTIPLE SYNCHRONICITIES OF A CHESS GRANDMASTER

1. My work on this material was originally done between 1991 and 1995. The experiencer himself subsequently published the material in substantially the form in which I had seen it. See James Plaskett, *Coincidences* (Hastings, UK: Tamworth Press, 2000). In the following, I retain the references to the actual manuscripts from which I worked.

2. The experiencer generally refers to his experiences as coincidences rather than as synchronicities. To avoid misrepresentation or confusion I too shall tend to use the word "coincidence" in this chapter, though in a sense that implies my usual understanding of synchronicity as outlined in chapter 2.

3. I was put in touch with Plaskett through contacts in the field of psychical research, specifically through Dr. H. Breederveld who had been informed of my interest in synchronicity by Dr. John Beloff.

4. The questionnaire administered was the Gray-Wheelwright. See Joseph B. Wheelwright, Jane H. Wheelwright, and John A. Beuhler, *Jungian Type Survey: The Grey-Wheelwright Test Manual*, 16th rev. ed. (San Francisco: Society of Jungian Analysts of Northern California, 1964). I am grateful to Adrian Cunningham for doing the scoring. The actual results were as follows: introversion 24 (71 percent) as compared to extraversion 10 (29 percent); thinking 12 (57 percent) as compared to feeling 9 (43 percent); intuition 14 (54 percent) as compared to sensation 12 (46 percent).

5. James Plaskett, revised presentation of coincidence narrative, typewritten manuscript, July 2, 1992, present writer's personal collection, 3, 41–44, 66–72, 84–86, 104–10, 126–28.

6. Ibid., 2–3, 52, 62, 73, and more.
7. Ibid., 2.
8. Ibid., 130.
9. Ibid., 29.
10. Ibid., 39–41.
11. Ibid., 26.
12. Ibid., 3, 128.
13. Ibid., 6, 8, 11–12.
14. Ibid., 62.
15. Ibid., 28.
16. Ibid., 129.
17. Ibid., 56.
18. Ibid., 117.

19. Ibid., 129.
20. Ibid.
21. Ibid., 29.
22. Ibid., 11. He does not specify exactly when he drew up and began following this program, but it was probably in the mid-1980s.
23. Ibid., 60.
24. Ibid., 63.
25. Ibid., 26–27, 17, 58. Plaskett mistakenly refers to Ian Wilson's book as *"The Near-Death Experience."*
26. Plaskett, revised presentation, 1, 39, 74.
27. Ibid., 131.
28. Ibid.
29. The precise number of coincidences in the narrative is uncertain, since it is debatable whether some incidents should be considered coincidences proper or just associative connections, and in other cases where an initial event is paralleled by several subsequent events it is debatable whether this should be counted as one coincidence with several aspects or as several independent coincidences. However, a precise count is not essential for any of my purposes; in general, when I invoke numbers, it is simply in order to draw attention to an impression of surprising quantity.

Plaskett also sent me substantial selections from his nonnarrative collection. "These examples," he says, "are either directly concerned with the main text or I have included them just to give you an idea of the sundry coincidences that form those lists" (James Plaskett to Roderick Main, autographed letter signed, August 8, 1991, 5). For the sake of simplicity I have left these additional coincidences out of consideration (except occasionally when referring to the quantity of Plaskett's material as a whole). The additional coincidences are also gathered in Plaskett, *Coincidences*.

30. Plaskett, revised presentation, 86.
31. Plaskett mentions that, before it came my way, he had shown his material, at varying stages of preparation, to the parapsychologists Susan Blackmore, Brian Inglis, and Dr. H. Breederveld, as well as to the writer Colin Wilson and to a number of friends within the chess world, such as William Hartston (Plaskett to Main, 5).
32. Plaskett, revised presentation, 133.
33. Plaskett to Main, 5.
34. Ibid., 6.
35. A coincidence has been assessed as expressing a particular theme if the coincidence content is either the actual image being used to designate the theme (for example, Dante's *Paradiso*, sea monsters) or else is strongly associated to the image designating the theme (for example, the eagle is strongly associated to Dante's *Paradiso*, the idea of "coming

up for air" is strongly associated to the theme of sea monsters). Some of the theme titles are not actual contents themselves but phrases that adequately embrace a range of related themes (for example, celestial phenomena embraces moon, stars, and meteorites; Arthurian legend embraces Parsifal, the Holy Grail, and the Round Table).

36. The precise number depends on how much latitude of association one allows. See note 29.

37. Italicizing has been used to highlight the specific points of paralleling involved in the coincidences, even within quoted material. No explanation of italicizing is given in individual cases unless there is the likelihood of confusion arising. As Plaskett subsequently learned, Plaskett's Crater was so named after two Canadian astronomers, father and son. Plaskett's Star, figuring in the next coincidence, was also named after them.

38. The map that gave rise to this belief in Plaskett appeared in *The Times*, March 19, 1960. He consulted this in order to read about the newsworthy events of the previous day—the day of his birth.

39. Plaskett, revised presentation, 2, 10. When he checked further, he discovered that Plaskett's Crater did not in fact receive its name until ten years after the publication of the first map of the far side of the moon. Nevertheless, the coincidence still seemed striking.

40. Ibid., 3.

41. Ibid., 2–3.

42. Ibid., 41, reproducing an extract from Arthur C. Clarke's *World of Strange Powers* (details of publication and page number(s) not given; emphasis in original); also Plaskett, revised presentation, 85–86.

43. Ibid., 64, reproducing Alister Hardy, Robert Harvie, and Arthur Koestler, *The Challenge of Chance: Experiments and Speculations* (London: Hutchinson, 1973), 198; emphasis added by Plaskett.

44. Plaskett, revised presentation, 35, quoting van der Post's "introduction to William Plomer's novel Turbott Wolffe" [sic].

45. Plaskett, Revised presentation, 1, 3, 95–101.

46. Ibid., 4–5.

47. Ibid., 5–8.

48. Ibid., 6.

49. Ibid., 6–7.

50. Ibid., 7.

51. Ibid.

52. Ibid., 5, reproducing *The Caxton World of Knowledge*, 1963 ed., s.v. "GRAIL"; italics in original.

53. Plaskett, revised presentation, 11.

54. Ibid., 12–13.

55. Ibid., 14.

56. There is no indication that the sweater involved in the previous coincidence was given to Plaskett because of the connection between the image of the eagle and his former school.
57. Ibid., 14–15.
58. Ibid., 16.
59. Ibid., 16–17.
60. Ibid., 17.
61. Ibid., 85.
62. Ibid. The eagle here, as on the coins in incident (12), is presumably a symbol of the United States.
63. Ibid., 17–23, reproducing Arthur C. Clarke, *Chronicles of the Strange and Mysterious* (details of publication not given), 94–98.
64. Plaskett, revised presentation, 25.
65. Ibid., 29–32.
66. Ibid., 32–33.
67. Ibid., 33–34.
68. Ibid., 34.
69. Ibid., 36. Octopuses, of course, do not come up for air.
70. Ibid., 37–38. The people responsible for the Greenpeace mailing might also have been influenced by this approaching anniversary.
71. Ibid. Plaskett writes that he accepted the offer.
72. Ibid., 112–14.
73. Ibid., 27.
74. Ibid., 116, reproducing and quoting Colin Wilson, *New Pathways in Psychology: Maslow and the Post-Freudian Revolution* (1972; other details of publication and page number(s) not given); Wilson in turn is quoting (without visible reference in Plaskett) a work of Assagioli's.
75. Plaskett, revised presentation, 27–28.
76. Ibid., 55–56. Cryptomnesia suggests itself as a particularly likely explanation for this apparent coincidence—the experiencer could so easily have seen in a guide or newspaper that this episode was going to be shown. However, while a theoretical possibility, there is nothing positively to support this suggestion. A further association to the theme of blindness, and one Plaskett himself does not specifically note, is that in a later canto of the *Paradiso*, Canto XXVI, a translation of which Plaskett reproduces in relation to another coincidence, Dante is depicted as having been *temporarily blinded* by the intensity of the love he encounters (see Plaskett, revised presentation, 24).
77. Ibid., 45–51. The (unreferenced) source Plaskett reproduces (ibid., 50) seems to equate the originally probably distinct symbols of the eye in the triangle and the third eye—a common conflation in twentieth-century eclectic esotericism.

78. Ibid., 54–55.
79. Ibid., 60, 63.
80. Ibid., 61.
81. Ibid., 60. This incident belongs thematically in the subsection entitled "Sea Monsters" but has been included here because of its close relationship to the preceding incident. One can glimpse from this something of the tight interconnectedness between the themes—a point to which I shall draw specific attention later.
82. Ibid., 62.
83. Ibid., 63. Out of context, this also seems rather unimpressive, especially since, as Plaskett mentions, it was something that had happened before (ibid.).
84. Ibid., 66. This was a piece of junk mail, to be sure, and there is probably nothing too remarkable about Plaskett's name and address having found their way onto a database of potential subscribers; but the *timing* of the offer's arrival is nonetheless quite impressive.
85. Ibid., 65.
86. Ibid., 52.
87. Ibid., 51.
88. Ibid.
89. Ibid.
90. Ibid.
91. Ibid., 1.
92. Ibid.
93. Ibid., 39.
94. Ibid., 17.
95. Ibid., 132.
96. Ibid., 5.
97. Ibid., 16.
98. Ibid., 40–41.
99. Ibid., 74.
100. Ibid., 128.
101. Ibid., 6.
102. Ibid., 8.
103. Ibid., 83.
104. Ibid., 82.
105. Ibid., 8.
106. Ibid., 11; see also ibid., 51.
107. Ibid., 73.
108. Ibid., 35.
109. Ibid.; see note 44.
110. Ibid.

111. Ibid., 133.
112. Ibid., 73, 77.
113. Ibid., 28.
114. Ibid., 101–2.
115. Ibid., 129.
116. Ibid., 49.
117. Ibid., 115–25.
118. Ibid., 28.
119. Ibid., 39–40.
120. Ibid., 40.
121. Ibid., 66–70, 70–72.
122. Ibid., 131.
123. Ibid., 132.
124. Ibid., 41–44.
125. Ibid., 84.
126. Ibid., 58–59.
127. Ibid., 126–28.
128. Ibid., 41, reproducing an extract from Arthur C. Clarke's *World of Strange Powers* (details of publication and page number(s) not given); emphasis in original.
129. Plaskett, revised presentation, 85–86, 88–89.
130. These parallels between the cases of meteorites and of coincidences were made more explicit to me in personal communications with Plaskett.
131. Ibid., 61, reproducing Laurens van der Post, *The Heart of the Hunter* (details of publication not given), 182–83.
132. Plaskett, revised presentation, 67–70.
133. Ibid., 104.
134. Ibid., 109.
135. Ibid., 83, 70–72.
136. Ibid., 74.
137. Ibid., 75.
138. Ibid. For a brief discussion of the Gauquelins's work and the ensuing scandal, see Brian Inglis, *Coincidence: A Matter of Chance—or Synchronicity?* (London: Hutchinson, 1990), 142–47.
139. Plaskett, revised presentation, 80.
140. Ibid., 75.
141. Ibid.
142. Ibid., 76.
143. As Plaskett explains: "The title of Grandmaster (GM) is the highest and most prestigious in the game (apart from World Champion of course). It is achieved by a player acquiring at least two and sometimes

three GM norms. A GM norm is achieved by a player who scores a certain % of points in an event where at least three Grandmasters are participating" (ibid., 77).

144. Ibid.
145. Ibid.
146. Ibid.
147. Ibid. There may be a slight confusion here either in the math or in Plaskett's reporting: surely the margin would have been narrower if not "each of the competitors" but only some or one of them had been rated just one point higher. But the point can be taken nonetheless.
148. Ibid. These personal details were widely reported in the press at the time; there is no suggestion in Plaskett's account that he feels he is being indiscreet in mentioning them.
149. Ibid.
150. This last detail is included only in James Plaskett, earlier presentation of coincidence narrative, typewritten manuscript, August 8, 1991, present writer's personal collection, 77.
151. Plaskett, revised presentation, 77.
152. Ibid.
153. Ibid., 78.
154. Ibid.
155. Ibid.
156. Ibid., reproducing Stan Gooch, *The Paranormal* (London: Fontana, 1979), 149.
157. Plaskett, revised presentation, 78.
158. Ibid., 80.
159. Ibid.
160. Ibid.
161. Ibid.
162. Ibid., 81(a). Unusually, Plaskett used the verso of page 81, numbering it 81(a).
163. Ibid., 82. The expression "the limits of intelligence [or knowledge]" is itself probably not all that uncommon; thus, the impressiveness of the present coincidence depends very much on the accurate timing and on the fact that it was precisely Hartston who here used the expression.
164. Ibid.
165. Ibid. I understand Plaskett to mean by this not that we project subjective meaning onto a world that is objectively meaningless, but that our subjectivity can participate with the world in the creation of a dimension of meaning that is an objective feature of the world—a world from which we ourselves are not ultimately separable.
166. Ibid., 80.

167. Plaskett told me in 1993 that by then Hartston's position regarding coincidences had, in spite of his experiences and admission relating to them, reverted to one of skepticism—publicly at least.

CHAPTER 6:
THE SELF-REVELATION OF SYNCHRONICITY AS SPIRIT: A MODERN GRAIL STORY

1. When Plaskett did eventually self-publish his material, he did not greatly revise it. See his *Coincidences* (Hastings, UK: Tamworth Press, 2000).

2. I am referring here to Plaskett's revised narrative rather than to the selection of forty-odd incidents presented in the previous chapter or to his collection as a whole that may comprise some six hundred or so incidents.

3. All numbers in this chapter refer to Plaskett's experiences as related in the previous chapter.

4. This kind of coincidence has received attention from Alan Vaughan, *Incredible Coincidence: The Baffling World of Synchronicity* (New York: Harper and Row, 1979; repr., New York: Ballantine, 1989), 23, who referred to them as "The Synchronicity of Synchronicity"; as well as from Ivor Grattan-Guinness, "Coincidences as Spontaneous Psychical Phenomena," *Journal of the Society for Psychical Research* 52, no. 793 (February 1983): 60.

5. Cf. my loosening of Jung's definitions of synchronicity in chapter 2 of this study.

6. James Plaskett, revised presentation of coincidence narrative, typewritten manuscript, July 2, 1992, present writer's personal collection, 104.

7. Ibid., 132.

8. See the works in statistics and mainstream psychology briefly surveyed in chapter 1. See also Roderick Main, *The Rupture of Time: Synchronicity and Jung's Critique of Modern Western Culture* (Hove, UK: Brunner-Routledge, 2004), 27–35.

9. Others, however, I found rather tenuous, such as the ones involving the image of the bird of prey on the sweater (13) or the lens falling out of Plaskett's glasses (37).

10. If one takes into consideration not just conspicuous but also subtler associative connections, the web of interrelatedness becomes progressively more entangled.

11. The theme of celestial phenomena is connected because the image of the rose is suggested by the Rosette nebula; the theme of sea monsters is implicit because it provides the overall context for the incident and, more particularly, because of the incident's essential relation to the coincidence immediately following (30).

12. Plaskett, revised presentation, 1.

13. That is, from Plaskett's narrative as a whole, not just from my selection presented in the previous chapter.

14. See, for example, C. G. Jung, *Collected Works*, vol. 12, *Psychology and Alchemy* (1944), 2nd ed. (London: Routledge and Kegan Paul, 1968); *The Visions Seminars*, from the complete notes of Mary Foote, postscript by Henry A. Murray, 2 vols. (Zürich: Spring Publications, 1976); and *Dream Analysis: Notes of the Seminar Given in 1928–1930*, ed. William McGuire (London: Routledge and Kegan Paul, 1984). Also see Gerhard Adler, *The Living Symbol* (London: Routledge and Kegan Paul, 1961).

15. On the importance of this, see, for example, Marie-Louise von Franz, *Introduction to the Interpretation of Fairy Tales* (Dallas, TX: Spring Publications, 1982), 7–8.

16. Jung, *Collected Works*, vol. 12, *Psychology and Alchemy*, 43.

17. Ibid., 44.

18. Ibid., 45.

19. Ibid., 45–46; emphases in original.

20. The importance of each of these themes within his material was registered by Plaskett, but he was much less systematic than I hope to have been in tracing their pervasiveness, interrelationships, and subtler implications.

21. Plaskett, revised presentation, 131.

22. Attention has also been drawn to this potentiality of synchronicities by Allan Combs and Mark Holland. See their *Synchronicity: Science, Myth, and the Trickster* (New York: Paragon House, 1990; repr., Edinburgh: Floris Books, 1994), 73.

23. Plaskett, revised presentation, 116, citing Colin Wilson who in turn is citing Assagioli (see note 74 in the preceding chapter); emphasis added.

24. Plaskett, revised presentation, 28, reproducing Assagioli (without reference).

25. Plaskett, revised presentation, 37, reproducing a letter from Greenpeace dated March 1988.

26. Joseph Campbell, *The Masks of God*, vol. 4, *Creative Mythology* (London: Souvenir Press, 1974), 544, quoting the *Queste del Saint Graal*.

27. See coincidence (31) in chapter 5 and its note.

28. Cf. the notion of the *spiraculum aeternitatis* (airhole into eternity) or *spiraculum vitae aeternae* (airhole to eternal life) of the alchemist Gerhard Dorn, which is specifically related to synchronicity by Marie-Louise von Franz in her *Number and Time: Reflections Leading towards a Unification of Psychology and Physics*, trans. Andrea Dykes (London: Rider, 1974), 261.

29. It is, however, possible for a coincidence to be registered between events that do not have points of identity, either obvious or symbolic. As Robert Aziz has pointed out, the coinciding events can stand to one another in a relation of compensation. See his *C. G. Jung's Psychology of Religion and Synchronicity* (Albany: State University of New York Press, 1990), 59–67, 84–90.

30. See chapter 3, the sections on "Transformation" and "Unity."

31. See in this chapter, the section on "Transformation" above.

32. This summary of the legend is based on Emma Jung and Marie-Louise von Franz, *The Grail Legend* (London: Hodder and Stoughton, 1972).

33. Plaskett, revised presentation, 2–3, 132.

34. Ibid., 5.

35. Quoted in Jung and von Franz, *The Grail Legend*, 162.

36. Ibid.

37. Ibid., 161.

38. Ibid., 19.

39. Ibid., 342.

40. Ibid.

41. Ibid., 342–43.

42. Ibid., 343.

43. Ibid., 389.

44. Plaskett, revised presentation, 6.

45. See, for example, Jung and von Franz, *The Grail Legend*, 118–19, 122, 123.

46. Plaskett, revised presentation, 131.

47. Jung and von Franz, *The Grail Legend*, 140–41.

48. Plaskett, revised presentation, 132.

49. Jung and von Franz, *The Grail Legend*, 97; emphasis in original.

50. Plaskett, revised presentation, 86.

51. Quoted in Jung and von Franz, *The Grail Legend*, 148.

52. Or at least there was dispute at the time Jung and von Franz were writing (the original German edition was published in 1960).

53. See, for example, Jung and von Franz, *The Grail Legend*, 149.

54. Ibid., 148.
55. Joseph Campbell, *The Masks of God*, 429, quoting Wolfram von Eschenbach, *Parzival*, IX 454:17–25.
56. Jung and von Franz, *The Grail Legend*, 151.
57. Ibid., 97.
58. Plaskett, revised presentation, 132.

CHAPTER 7: SYNCHRONICITY AND SPIRIT IN THE I CHING

1. See C. G. Jung, "Richard Wilhelm: In Memoriam" (1930), in *Collected Works*, vol. 15, *The Spirit in Man, Art, and Literature* (London: Routledge and Kegan Paul, 1966), 56; and "Foreword to the 'I Ching'" (1950), in *Collected Works*, vol. 11, *Psychology and Religion: West and East*, 2nd ed. (London: Routledge and Kegan Paul, 1969), 591–93. See also Roderick Main, *The Rupture of Time: Synchronicity and Jung's Critique of Modern Western Culture* (Hove, UK: Brunner-Routledge, 2004), 77–79.
2. Jung, "Richard Wilhelm," 55.
3. In particular, these three aspects of the spiritual, physical, and psychic would be articulated as heaven, earth, and man. See Richard Wilhelm, trans., *The I Ching or Book of Changes*, rendered into English by Cary F. Baynes, 3rd ed. (London: Routledge and Kegan Paul, 1968 [hereafter cited as Wilhelm–Baynes]), 351–52.
4. Note that the component three-line figures (trigrams) within the hexagrams are also called "kua." (Transcriptions from the Chinese are in the Wade-Giles rather than the Pinyin system—thus, for example, "kua" and not "gua." On the rare occasions when Pinyin phrases occur in quoted matter, the Wade-Giles equivalent is given in brackets.)
5. Unless otherwise stated, all translations of terms used in the *I Ching* are from Wilhelm–Baynes.
6. For a summary of this, see, for example, Wilhelm–Baynes, lviii–lix.
7. See ibid., lviii.
8. See Joseph Needham, *Science and Civilisation in China*, vol. 2 (Cambridge: Cambridge University Press, 1962), 306; also see Hellmut Wilhelm, "Preface to the Third Edition," in Wilhelm–Baynes, xiv–xvi.
9. Iulian K. Shchutskii, *Researches on the I Ching* (Princeton, NJ: Princeton University Press, 1979), 195.
10. Ibid., 197.
11. See, for example, Needham, *Science and Civilization in China*, 306–7; Hellmut Wilhelm in Wilhelm–Baynes; Greg Whincup, *Rediscover-*

ing the I Ching (Wellingborough, UK: Aquarian Press, 1987). Much of this agreement constitutes independent corroboration, since Shchutskii's work was suppressed by the then Soviet authorities, only appearing in Russian in 1960 and in English translation in 1979; Shchutskii himself had met an early death in the 1930s in a Soviet prison camp; see his *Researches on the I Ching*, ix.

12. Joseph Adler, "Divination and Philosophy: Chu Hsi's Understanding of the *I Ching*" (Ph.D. diss., University of California, Santa Barbara, 1984), 41–42.

13. Ibid., 42–45. Unless otherwise referenced, the following historical sketch is based on ibid., 45–57.

14. Wilhelm–Baynes, xlvii, lx.

15. See especially Richard John Lynn, trans., *The Classic of Changes: A New Translation of the "I Ching" as Interpreted by Wang Bi* (New York: Columbia University Press, 1994).

16. See Da Liu, *I Ching Numerology* (London: Routledge and Kegan Paul, 1979).

17. Joseph Adler, "Divination and Philosophy," 47.

18. See the diagrams in, for example, Diana ffarington Hook, *The I Ching and You* (London: Routledge and Kegan Paul, 1974), 83.

19. Joseph Adler, "Divination and Philosophy," 42.

20. See ibid., 135–267.

21. Richard Smith, *Fortune-tellers and Philosophers: Divination in Traditional Chinese Society* (Boulder, CO: Westview Press, 1991), 94.

22. Gerald W. Swanson, "Introduction to the English Edition," in *Researches on the I Ching*, by Iulian K. Shchutskii, (Princeton, NJ: Princeton University Press, 1979) xxxviii.

23. Marie-Louise von Franz, *Number and Time: Reflections Leading towards a Unification of Psychology and Physics*, trans. Andrea Dykes (London: Rider, 1974), 10.

24. Hellmut Wilhelm, *Change: Eight Lectures on the I Ching* (London: Routledge and Kegan Paul, 1961), 91.

25. Needham, *Science and Civilisation in China*, 342.

26. James Legge, trans., "The Yi King," in *The Sacred Books of the East*, vol. 16, ed. Max Müller (Oxford: Clarendon Press, 1882; repr. Delhi: Motilal Banarsidass, 1966).

27. C. G. Jung, *Memories, Dreams, Reflections* (London: Collins, 1979), 405; and "Richard Wilhelm," 54.

28. The Wilhelm–Baynes *I Ching* "continue[s] to this day as the best selling book ever published by the Princeton University Press" (Willard Peterson, "Some Connective Concepts in China in the Fourth to Second Centuries B.C.E.," *Eranos* 57 [1988]: 234).

29. Important Western work along some of these lines has been carried out by Arthur Waley (see Needham, *Science and Civilisation in China*, 308–9 and the references cited there); Shchutskii, *Researches on the I Ching;* Hellmut Wilhelm, *Change,* and *Heaven, Earth, and Man in the Book of Changes* (Seattle: University of Washington Press, 1977); Gerald Swanson, *The Great Treatise: Commentary Tradition to the Book of Changes* (Ann Arbor, MI: University Microfilms, 1974); Willard J. Peterson, "Making Connections: 'Commentary on the Attached Verbalizations' of the *Book of Change,*" *Harvard Journal of Asian Studies* 42, no. 1 (1982): 67–116, and "Some Connective Concepts in China;" Edward Shaughnessey, *The Composition of the "Zhouyi"* (Ann Arbor, MI: University Microfilms International, 1983); and Richard Kunst, *The Original "Yijing": A Text, Phonetic Transcription, Translation, and Indexes, with Sample Glosses* (Ann Arbor, MI: University Microfilms International, 1985).

30. Rudolf Ritsema and Stephen Karcher, *I Ching: The Classic Chinese Oracle of Change* (Shaftesbury, UK: Element, 1994). The same work was also serially published, with an alternative title, as *Chou Yi: The Oracle of Encompassing Versatility,* 3 vols., *Eranos* 58–60 (1989–91). For a fuller evaluation of this translation, see Roderick Main, "Review of *I Ching: The Classic Chinese Oracle of Change,*" by Rudolf Ritsema and Stephen Karcher, in *Journal of the Society for Psychical Research* 60, no. 839 (April 1995): 278–81; also see Main's "Magic and Science in the Modern Western Tradition of the *I Ching,*" *Journal of Contemporary Religion* 14, no. 2 (1999): 263–75. Karcher has also published individual translations, extending his original collaborative work with Ritsema. See, for example, Karcher's *Total I Ching: Myths for Change* (London: TimeWarner Books, 2003).

31. See, for example, Hook, *The I Ching and You,* 11–12; also see Rudolf Ritsema, "The Great's Vigour: A Study of the 34th Hexagram in the *I Ching,* with a Note on Consulting the *I Ching,*" *Spring* (1978): 183.

32. See, for example, Wilhelm–Baynes, 349; also see Hellmut Wilhelm, "The Concept of Time in the Book of Changes," in *Papers from the Eranos Yearbooks,* vol. 3, *Man and Time,* ed. Joseph Campbell (New York: Bollingen, 1957), 220–21.

33. See Ritsema, "The Great's Vigour," 184.

34. For details of the procedures involved see Wilhelm–Baynes, 721–24.

35. It was largely the different emphases given to these two aspects of the system that distinguished the *i-li* and the *hsiang-shu* schools of interpretation mentioned in the historical sketch above.

36. Gerhard Adler, "Reflections on 'Chance' and 'Fate,'" in *The Shaman from Elko: Papers in Honor of Joseph L. Henderson*, ed. Garth Hill (Boston: Sigo Press, 1991), 94.
37. Ibid.
38. Ibid., citing Wilhelm–Baynes, 171.
39. Ibid., 94–95, citing Wilhelm–Baynes, 609.
40. Ibid., 95.
41. Wilhelm–Baynes, 608–9.
42. Shchutskii, *Researches on the I Ching*, 195, 197.
43. Hellmut Wilhelm, *Change*, 38.
44. Wilhelm–Baynes, 291.
45. Ibid., 288.
46. Shchutskii, *Researches on the I Ching*, 226.
47. In the not uncommon event of there being more than one moving line, there are special rules that can be followed for determining to which aspects of one's reading one should then give most attention. See W. A. Sherrill and W. K. Chu, *An Anthology of I Ching* (London: Arkana, 1989), 27–28.
48. See, for example, F. M. Doeringer, "Oracle and Symbol in the Redaction of the *I Ching*," *Philosophy East and West* 30, no. 2 (April 1980): 195–209.
49. Wilhelm–Baynes, 370.
50. Ibid., 372.
51. Hellmut Wilhelm, "Preface to the Third Edition," in ibid., xviii. Because of this independence, the Wilhelm–Baynes presentation of the *I Ching* gives the section titled "The Image" a status equal to that given to the precommentary texts of the Judgment and the Lines.
52. Ibid., xviii.
53. Ibid., 345.
54. Ritsema and Karcher, *I Ching*, 16.
55. Rudolf Ritsema, "The Corrupted: A Study of the 18th Hexagram of the *I Ching*," *Spring* (1972): 90–91. See also Hellmut Wilhelm, *Heaven*, 190–221.
56. Ritsema, "The Corrupted," 91.
57. Smith, *Fortune-Tellers and Philosophers*, 121.
58. This summary is based primarily on Wilhelm–Baynes and Shchutskii, *Researches on the I Ching*.
59. See the *Shuo Kua,* Discussion of the Trigrams, in Wilhelm–Baynes, 262–279.
60. Ibid., 351–52; see also Richard Wilhelm, *Lectures on the I Ching: Constancy and Change* (London: Routledge and Kegan Paul, 1980), 27.

61. Shchutskii, *Researches on the I Ching*, 226.
62. Ibid., 227.
63. See the earlier section on "Historical Background."
64. Wilhelm–Baynes, 322.
65. See Hellmut Wilhelm, *Change*, 23–34.
66. Wilhelm–Baynes, 168.
67. Ibid., 606.
68. Ibid., 168.
69. Ibid., 275.
70. Ibid., 606.
71. Ibid.
72. Ibid.
73. Ibid., 279.
74. Ibid., 606.
75. It occurs in the Judgment texts of Hexagrams 5, 6, 13, 18, 26, 42, 59, and 61, and in the Lines texts of Hexagrams 15 (line 1), 27 (lines 5 and 6), and 64 (line 3).
76. See Wilhelm–Baynes, Book III, commentaries to each of the hexagrams mentioned in the preceding note.
77. Wayne McEvilly, exploring the relationship between synchronicity and the *I Ching* primarily from a Western philosophical perspective, has also emphasized the archetypal nature of the hexagrams. His understanding of the archetype is, however, essentially Platonic and he does not seriously engage with possible differences between the Platonic conception and Jung's. See his "Synchronicity and the I Ching," *Philosophy East and West* 18, no. 3 (1968): 146: "[The] structural aspects of the *I Ching* may conveniently be understood, without doing a great deal of violence to the system, as a highly articulated and specified working out of a Platonic type of metaphysic"; again: "The *I Ching* stands as . . . the most impressive working out of the principle of synchronicity as the clue to the meaningful interaction of the world of phenomena with that unseen world of guiding universal archetypes" (ibid., 148).
78. See the section on "Oracular and Spontaneous Synchronicities Compared" later in the chapter.
79. Adrian Cunningham, "Structure in Jung and Lévi-Strauss," in *Traditions in Contact and Change: Selected Proceedings of the XIVth Congress of the International Association for the History of Religions*, ed. Peter Slater and Donald Wiebe, with Maurice Boutin and Harold Coward (Waterloo, Ont.: Wilfred Laurier University Press, 1983), 632–33.
80. See, for example, Wilhelm–Baynes, 273, 275.

81. Ibid., 136.
82. Ibid., 52.
83. Ibid., 262–3.
84. Ritsema and Karcher, *I Ching*, 11.
85. Jung, "Foreword to the 'I Ching,'" 592.
86. Wilhelm–Baynes, 359.
87. Hellmut Wilhelm, "The Concept of Time," 223. See also Stephen Karcher, "Making Spirits Bright: Divination and the Demonic Image," *Eranos* 61 (1992): 27–29.
88. Wilhelm–Baynes, 237.
89. Ibid.
90. Ibid., 237–38; also contained in the Great Treatise, ibid., 305.
91. Audrey Josephs, "Karman, Self-Knowledge and *I Ching* Divination," *Philosophy East and West* 30, no. 1 (January 1980): 70.
92. It should be noted, however, that the Chinese text contains here no equivalent to the English connective "thus"—which has presumably been added by Wilhelm–Baynes to make the implicit relationship between the Image statements clearer.
93. Shchutskii, *Researches on the I Ching*, 169.
94. Wilhelm–Baynes, 382.
95. Ibid., 314.
96. Peterson, "Making Connections," 85. The realm of "heaven-and-earth" refers to "the physical cosmos as a whole" (ibid., 84). Peterson distinguishes four major claims in the Great Treatise, the other three of which are "that cosmological processes are intelligible and humans can adjust their conduct on the basis of that intelligence" (ibid., 91); that "we can know by means of the words of the *Change*, and we can be guided by their counsel" (ibid., 94); and "that by being numinous, the *Change* is the medium giving us access to all that is numinous" (ibid., 110). The last of these claims will prove especially important when I come to discuss spirit in the *I Ching*.
97. Ibid., 89. Cf. Wilhelm–Baynes, 351–52; also Lynn, *The Classic of Changes*, 92.
98. Peterson, "Making Connections," 90. Cf. Wilhelm–Baynes, 302; also Lynn, *The Classic of Changes*, 56.
99. For the second of these, both Wilhelm–Baynes and Lynn use "corresponds."
100. Peterson, "Making Connections," 91.
101. Ibid.
102. Peterson, "Some Connective Concepts," 225.
103. See following paragraph.

104. According to some commentators, the lower trigram represents oneself (or the consulting party) in the situation, while the upper trigram represents the other (or the opposite party). See, for example, Smith, *Fortune-tellers and Philosophers*, 101.

105. Of course, correspondence is considered to exist only when the relevant lines are opposite in nature—one yin, one yang—whereas with the kind of noncontiguous paralleling characteristic of spontaneous synchronistic events it is generally the case that the more similar the related events are, the stronger the impression of synchronicity. However, it is also possible to view the two events composing a spontaneous synchronicity as complementary aspects of a single whole—in Jung's theory, for example, as the psychic and physical aspects of a meaning that at the level of the psychoid is unitary.

106. Wilhelm–Baynes, 357.

107. Ibid., 349.

108. Ibid.; emphasis added. The words translated "cause and effect" are more literally translated by Lynn as "roots and branches" (*The Classic of Changes*, 90–91).

109. See Hellmut Wilhelm, *Heaven*, 116.

110. See C. G. Jung, *Collected Works*, vol. 6, *Psychological Types* (1921), (London: Routledge and Kegan Paul, 1971), 425–27. Though the word "enantiodromia" is Greek—first occurring in the context of the philosophy of Heraclitus—it expresses the same idea as the famous Chinese *t'ai chi* symbol: namely, the idea that any manifestation of a bipolar phenomenon always contains the seed of its own opposite.

111. Wilhelm–Baynes, 350.

112. See, for example, chapter 2, note 37.

113. Jung, "Foreword to the 'I Ching,'" 591.

114. Ibid., liii.

115. See C. G. Jung, "Synchronicity: An Acausal Connecting Principle" (1952), in *Collected Works*, vol. 8, *The Structure and Dynamics of the Psyche*, 2nd ed. (London: Routledge and Kegan Paul, 1969), 450–53; and "Foreword to the 'I Ching,'" 590–94. Also see Marie-Louise von Franz, *On Divination and Synchronicity: The Psychology of Meaningful Chance* (Toronto: Inner City Books, 1980), 8–12.

116. Jung, "Foreword to the 'I Ching,'" 591.

117. Ibid., 593.

118. Ibid., 591.

119. Peterson, "Some Connective Concepts," 216–17.

120. Needham, *Science and Civilisation in China*, 279–91.

121. He mentions especially Marcel Granet (ibid., 280). See Marcel Granet, *La Pensée Chinoise* (Paris: Albin Michel, 1950).

122. Needham, *Science and Civilisation in China*, 280–81.
123. Ibid., 283.
124. Ibid., 286–87.
125. Ibid., 284–86.
126. See Lucien Lévy-Bruhl, *How Natives Think [Les Fonctions mentales dans les sociétés inférieures]*, trans. Lilian A. Clare (Princeton, NJ: Princeton University Press, 1985). Origiously published in Paris in 1910.
127. For an example of how all these systems of categorization can be unified, see Ritsema and Karcher, *I Ching*, 65–83.
128. Needham, *Science and Civilisation in China*, 284.
129. Ibid., 286.
130. Jung, "Synchronicity," 485.
131. Needham, *Science and Civilisation in China*, 302.
132. Ibid., 291.
133. Benjamin I. Schwarz, *The World of Thought in Ancient China* (Cambridge, MA: Belknap Press, 1985), 370.
134. Ibid., 371.
135. See, for example, C. G. Jung, "A Letter on Parapsychology and Synchronicity: Dr. Jung's Response to an Inquiry," *Spring* (1961): 56.
136. Cf. McEvilly, "Synchronicity and the I Ching," 143: "If [these 4,096 possible situations] are indeed sufficiently archetypal it does not stretch the imagination to acknowledge that they would cover rather well each, any, and every phenomenon that might conceivably be experienced, no matter how seemingly unique."
137. C. G. Jung, "The Concept of the Collective Unconscious" (1936), in *Collected Works*, vol. 9i, *The Archetypes and the Collective Unconscious*, 2nd ed. (London: Routledge and Kegan Paul, 1968), 48.
138. C. G. Jung, "Instinct and the Unconscious" (1919), in *Collected Works*, vol. 8, *The Structure and Dynamics of the Psyche*, 2nd ed. (London: Routledge and Kegan Paul, 1969), 135. It is, in fact, not entirely clear that Jung is saying he himself subscribes to this "theory of cognition."
139. It might seem that 4,096 is an *un*manageable number, but it appears less so if it is considered to be built up from the combination of a much more discrete range of elements (for example, 642 hexagram combinations, or even 8^4 trigram combinations).
140. Some of the specific nuances of the Chinese word *shen* are discussed below.
141. Schwarz, *The World of Thought in Ancient China*, 369.
142. Hellmut Wilhelm, "The Concept of Time in the Book of Changes," 219.

143. Jung, "Synchronicity," 451.
144. Jung, "Foreword to the 'I Ching,'" 590.
145. Ibid., 607.
146. David Ruelle, *Chance and Chaos* (London: Penguin, 1993), 36.
147. Ibid., 37.
148. Ibid., 90.
149. Lawrence Rubin and Charles Honorton, "Separating the Yins from the Yangs: An Experiment with the *I Ching*," *Journal of Parapsychology* 35 (1971): 313–14.
150. Michael A. Thalbourne et al., "A Further Attempt to Separate the Yins from the Yangs: A Replication of the Rubin–Honorton Experiment with the *I CHING*," *European Journal of Parapsychology* 9 (1992–93): 17.
151. Jung, "Foreword to the 'I Ching,'" 594.
152. Wilhelm–Baynes, 262; bracketed insertion mine.
153. Jung, "Foreword to the 'I Ching,'" 593–94.
154. Lynn, *The Classic of Changes*, 1–2; see also 18. Hereafter cited as Lynn followed by pages(s).
155. Peterson, "Making Connections," 103.
156. Ibid., 104.
157. Ibid.
158. Wilhelm–Baynes, 301; cf. Lynn, 54. In Wilhelm–Baynes, *shen* is variously rendered as "spirit," "the divine," "mind," "gods," and so forth. In Lynn, the usual translation is "the numinous," though he too sometimes uses "gods" when it is clear that it is a question of agencies.
159. Wilhelm–Baynes, 296; cf. Lynn, 53.
160. Wilhelm–Baynes, 316; cf. Lynn, 63.
161. Wilhelm–Baynes, 338; cf. Lynn, 82.
162. Wilhelm–Baynes, 318; cf. Lynn, 65.
163. Lynn, 81–82. In Wilhelm–Baynes this passage appears as: "Thus the penetration of a germinal thought into the mind promotes the working of the mind" (338).
164. Wilhelm–Baynes, 320; cf. Lynn, 66.
165. Wilhelm–Baynes, 315; cf. Lynn, 63.
166. Wilhelm–Baynes, 313; cf. Lynn, 62.
167. Wilhelm–Baynes, 317; cf. Lynn, 65.
168. Wilhelm–Baynes, 316; cf. Lynn, 64.
169. Lynn's translations, 64, 65, 67. In Wilhelm–Baynes "the sages" are made the subject of all three of these passages with no direct reference to the oracle (317, 322).
170. Stephen Karcher, "*Which Way I Fly Is Hell*: Divination and the Shadow of the West," *Spring* 55 (1994): 95.

171. Ritsema and Karcher, *I Ching*, 8.
172. Ibid.; emphasis in original.
173. Ibid., 14.
174. Karcher, "Which Way I Fly Is Hell," 96.
175. Stephen Karcher, "The Yi Ching and the Ethic of the Image: Reflections at the 1992 Eranos/Uehiro Round Table Session," *Eranos* 62 (1992): 101.
176. Ritsema and Karcher, *I Ching*, 8; emphasis added.
177. Ibid., 9.
178. Karcher, "Which Way I Fly Is Hell," 91.
179. Stephen Karcher, "Oracle's Contexts: Gods, Dreams, Shadow, Language," *Spring* 53 (1992): 87, citing C. G. Jung, "A Review of the Complex Theory" (1934), in *Collected Works*, vol. 8, *The Structure and Dynamics of the Psyche*, 2nd ed. (London: Routledge and Kegan Paul, 1969), 101.
180. Rudolf Ritsema, "Encompassing Versatility: Keystone of the Eranos Project," *Eranos* 57 (1988): xv.
181. See, for example, Adler, "Divination and Philosophy," 24: "Contrary to Kant, says [the contemporary Chinese philosopher] Mou [Tsung san], Chinese thinkers of all schools have consistently claimed that the human mind is capable of 'intellectual intuition' . . . , i.e. it is capable of directly apprehending absolute truth (principle)."
182. Peterson, "Making Connections," 105–6. The realms of "heaven-and-earth" and "all-under-heaven" (see next quote) refer to "the physical cosmos as a whole" and "human society," respectively (see ibid., 84–85).
183. For example, ibid., 106, citing section A10.17 of the Great Treatise in Peterson's numbering; see also Wilhelm–Baynes, 315; and Lynn, 63.
184. Peterson, "Making Connections," 106.
185. Ibid., 107.
186. Ibid., 110.
187. Ibid., 85.
188. Peterson, "Some Connective Concepts," 230.
189. Ibid., 234.
190. Jung, "Foreword to the 'I Ching,'" 594.
191. Ibid.
192. Ibid.
193. Ibid., 595.
194. Jung, "Foreword to the 'I Ching,'" 594.
195. Ritsema and Karcher, *I Ching*, 33–34.

196. Ibid., 34.

197. Ibid.

198. Ibid., 35. Since the Ritsema and Karcher translation did not exist in the late 1960s, we can assume that the experiencer's actual interpretations and responses were based on readings of such versions as did then exist, these versions being sufficiently similar to Ritsema and Karcher's to justify the anachronism here.

199. Lynn, 451.

200. Of course, consciously or otherwise, Ritsema and Karcher could have been influenced in their choice of example by Jung's earlier experience. But this does not detract from the fact that, in response to a similar request for self-characterization, the same hexagram was obtained.

REFERENCES

Adler, Gerhard. "C. G. Jung in a Changing Civilisation." In *Carl Gustav Jung: Critical Assessments*, vol. 4, *Implications and Inspirations*, ed. Renos K. Papadopoulos. London: Routledge, 1992. 11–16.
———. *The Living Symbol*. London: Routledge and Kegan Paul, 1961.
———. "Reflections on 'Chance' and 'Fate.'" In *The Shaman from Elko: Papers in Honor of Joseph L. Henderson*, ed. Garth Hill. Boston: Sigo Press, 1991. 87–101.
Adler, Joseph. "Divination and Philosophy: Chu Hsi's Understanding of the *I Ching*." Ph.D. diss., University of California, Santa Barbara, 1984.
Aquinas, St. Thomas. *Philosophical Texts*, sel. and trans. Thomas Gilby. London: Oxford University Press, 1951.
Auster, Paul. *The Red Notebook and Other Writings*. London: Faber and Faber, 1995.
Avens, Roberts. *Imagination Is Reality: Western Nirvana in Jung, Hillman, Barfield, and Cassirer*. Dallas, TX: Spring Publications, 1980.
Ayer, Alfred J. *Language, Truth, and Logic*. Harmondsworth, UK: Penguin, 1980.
Aziz, Robert. *C. G. Jung's Psychology of Religion and Synchronicity*. Albany: State University of New York Press, 1990.
———. "Synchronicity and the Transformation of the Ethical in Jungian Psychology." In *Asian and Jungian Views of Ethics*, ed. Carl B. Becker. Westport, CT: Greenwood Press, 1999. 65–84.
Beloff, John. "Psi Phenomena: Causal versus Acausal Interpretation." *Journal of the Society for Psychical Research* 49, no. 773 (September 1977): 573–82.
Bishop, Paul. *Synchronicity and Intellectual Intuition in Kant, Swedenborg, and Jung*. Lampeter, UK: Edwin Mellen Press, 2000.
Bloomfield, Bob. *Synchronistic Images*. Cheddar, UK: Charles Skilton, 1987.

Bohm, David. "A New Theory of the Relationship of Mind and Matter." *Journal of the American Society for Psychical Research* 80, no. 2 (April 1986): 113–35.
———. *Wholeness and the Implicate Order*. London: Routledge and Kegan Paul, 1980.
Bolen, Jean Shinoda. *The Tao of Psychology: Synchronicity and the Self*. 1979. Reprint, New York: Harper and Row, 1982.
Brenneis, Sandra, and Frederic Boersma. "Typology and Trance: Developing Synchronicity in Hypnotic Induction." *Medical Hypnoanalysis Journal* 8, no. 2 (June 1993): 45–56.
Bright, George. "Synchronicity as a Basis of Analytic Attitude." *Journal of Analytical Psychology* 42, no. 4 (1997): 613–35.
Brooke, Roger. *Jung and Phenomenology*. London: Routledge and Kegan Paul, 1991.
Brown, Colin. *Miracles and the Critical Mind*. Grand Rapids, MI: William B. Eerdmans; Exeter, UK: Paternoster Press, 1984.
Brown, George Spencer. *Probability and Scientific Inference*. London: Longmans, 1957.
———. "Statistical Significance in Psychical Research." *Nature*, July 25, 1953, 154–56.
Brugger, Peter, Marianne Regard, Theodor Landis, Denise Krebs, and Josef Niederberger. "Coincidences: Who Can Say How 'Meaningful' They Are?" In *Proceedings of the Parapsychological Association 34th Annual Convention Held in Heidelberg 8–11 August 1991*. Heidelberg: Parapsychological Association, 1991. 65–72.
Burniston, Andrew F. "Synchronicity: A Dionysian Perspective." *Harvest* 40 (1994): 118–27.
Cambray, Joseph. "Synchronicity and Emergence." *American Imago* 59, no. 4 (2002): 409–35.
———. "Synchronicity as Emergence." In *Analytical Psychology: Contemporary Perspectives in Jungian Analysis*, ed. Joseph Cambray and Linda Carter. Hove, UK: Brunner-Routledge, 2004. 223–48.
Campbell, Joseph. *The Masks of God*. Vol. 4, *Creative Mythology*. London: Souvenir Press, 1974.
Chambers Twentieth Century Dictionary, ed. A. M. Macdonald. Edinburgh: W & R Chambers, 1977.
Chambers Dictionary of Beliefs and Religions, ed. Rosemary Goring. London: Quality Paperbacks Direct by arrangement with W & R Chambers, 1992.
Cocksey, Brian J. "Coincidence and Divine Revelation." Typewritten manuscript, March 1990. Present writer's personal collection.

Combs, Allan, and Mark Holland. *Synchronicity: Science, Myth, and the Trickster*. New York: Paragon House, 1990. Reprint, Edinburgh: Floris Books, 1994.

Concise Dictionary of Religion, ed. Irving Hexam. Downers Grove, IL: Intervarsity Press, 1993.

Corbin, Henry. "*Mundus Imaginalis* or the Imaginary and the Imaginal." *Spring* (1972): 1–19.

Cousineau, Phil. *Soul Moments: Marvelous Stories of Synchronicity—Meaningful Coincidences from a Seemingly Random World*. Berkeley, CA: Conari Press, 1997.

Cunningham, Adrian. "Structure in Jung and Lévi-Strauss." In *Traditions in Contact and Change: Selected Proceedings of the XIVth Congress of the International Association for the History of Religions*, ed. Peter Slater and Donald Wiebe, with Maurice Boutin and Harold Coward. Waterloo, Ont.: Wilfred Laurier University Press, 1983. 621–34.

Curtis, David. "The Synchronistic Continuum." Typewritten manuscript, February 1994. Present writer's personal collection.

de Voogd, Stephanie. "C. G. Jung: Psychologist of the Future, 'Philosopher' of the Past." *Spring* (1977): 175–82.

———. "Fantasy versus Fiction: Jung's Kantianism Appraised." In *Jung in Modern Perspective*, ed. Renos K. Papadopoulos and Graham S. Saayman. Hounslow, UK: Wildwood House, 1984. 204–28.

Devereux, George, ed. *Psychoanalysis and the Occult*. New York: International Universities Press, 1953. Reprint, London: Souvenir Press, 1974.

Diaconis, Persi, and Frederick Mosteller. "Methods for Studying Coincidences." *Journal of the American Statistical Association* 84, no. 408 (December 1989): 853–61.

Doeringer, F. M. "Oracle and Symbol in the Redaction of the *I Ching*." *Philosophy East and West* 30, no. 2 (April 1980): 195–209.

Donati, Marialuisa. "Beyond Synchronicity: The Worldview of Carl Gustav Jung and Wolfgang Pauli." *Journal of Analytical Psychology* 49, no. 4 (2004): 707–28.

Dulles, Avery. *Models of Revelation*. Dublin: Gill and Macmillan, 1983.

Dyer, Wayne. *You'll See It When You Believe It*. London: Arrow, 1993.

Eisenbud, Jule. "Of Mice and Mind, or The Sorceror's Apprentice: A Cautionary Tale." *Journal of the American Society for Psychical Research* 84, no. 4 (October 1990): 345–64.

———. *Parapsychology and the Unconscious*. Berkeley, CA: North Atlantic Books, 1983.

Ellis, John M. *One Fairy Story Too Many: The Brothers Grimm and Their Tales*. Chicago: University of Chicago Press, 1983.

Encyclopedia of Religion. 16 vols. Ed. Mircea Eliade. New York: Macmillan Publishing Company; London: Collier Macmillan Publishers, 1987. S.v. "Soul: Christian Concept," by Geddes MacGregor.

Erkelens, Herbert van. "Wolfgang Pauli's Dialogue with the Spirit of Matter." *Psychological Perspectives* 24 (1991): 34–53.

Faber, Mel. *Synchronicity: C. G. Jung, Psychoanalysis, and Religion*. Westport, CT: Praeger, 1998.

Flew, Anthony. "Coincidence and Synchronicity." *Journal of the Society for Psychical Research* 37, no. 677 (November 1953): 198–201.

Fordham, Michael. "An Interpretation of Jung's Thesis about Synchronicity." *British Journal of Medical Psychology* 35 (1962): 205–10.

———. "Reflections on the Archetypes and Synchronicity." In *New Developments in Analytical Psychology*. London: Routledge and Kegan Paul, 1957. 35–50.

Freud, Sigmund. "Dreams and Occultism" (1933). In *The Standard Edition of the Complete Psychological Works of Sigmund Freud*, trans. and ed. James Strachey. Vol. 22. London: Hogarth Press, 1964. 31–56.

———. "Dreams and Telepathy" (1921). In *The Standard Edition of the Complete Psychological Works of Sigmund Freud*, trans. and ed. James Strachey. Vol. 18. London: Hogarth Press, 1964. 196–220.

———. "The Occult Significance of Dreams" (1925). In *The Standard Edition of the Complete Psychological Works of Sigmund Freud*, trans. and ed. James Strachey. Vol. 19. London: Hogarth Press, 1964. 135–38.

———. "Psycho-analysis and Telepathy" (1921). In *The Standard Edition of the Complete Psychological Works of Sigmund Freud*, trans. and ed. James Strachey. Vol. 18. London: Hogarth Press, 1964. 175–93.

———. "The Uncanny" (1919). In *The Standard Edition of the Complete Psychological Works of Sigmund Freud*, trans. and ed. James Strachey. Vol. 17. London: Hogarth Press, 1964. 217–56.

Gammon, Mary. "'Window into Eternity': Archetype and Relativity." *Journal of Analytical Psychology* 18, no. 1 (1973): 11–24.

Gatlin, Lila. "Meaningful Information Creation: An Alternative Interpretation of the Psi Phenomenon." *Journal of the American Society for Psychical Research* 71, no. 1 (January 1977): 1–18.

Giegerich, Wolfgang. "The Rescue of the World: Jung, Hegel, and the Subjective Universe." *Spring* (1987): 107–14.

Gordon, Rosemary. "Reflections on Jung's Concept of Synchronicity." In *In the Wake of Jung: A Selection from "Harvest,"* ed. Molly Tuby. London: Coventure, 1983. 129–46.

Granet, Marcel. *La Pensée Chinoise*. Paris: Albin Michel, 1950.

Grattan-Guinness, Ivor. "Coincidences as Spontaneous Psychical Phenomena." *Journal of the Society for Psychical Research* 52, no. 793 (February 1983): 59–71.

———. "What Are Coincidences?" *Journal of the Society for Psychical Research* 49, no. 778 (December 1978): 949–55.

Handel, Sidney. "Mirabile Dictu." In *Chicago 92: The Transcendent Function: Individual and Collective Aspects: Proceedings of the Twelfth International Congress for Analytical Psychology Held in Chicago 23–28 August 1992*, ed. Mary Ann Mattoon. Einsiedeln, Switzerland: Daimon Verlag, 1993. 387–94.

Happold, F. W. *Mysticism*. Harmondsworth, UK: Penguin, 1970.

Hardy, Alister. *The Spiritual Nature of Man*. Oxford: Oxford University Press, 1979.

Hardy, Alister, Robert Harvie, and Arthur Koestler. *The Challenge of Chance: Experiments and Speculations*. London: Hutchinson, 1973.

Heisig, James W. *Imago Dei: A Study of C. G. Jung's Psychology of Religion*. London: Associated University Presses, 1979.

Henry, Jane. "Coincidence Experience Survey." *Journal of the Society for Psychical Research* 59, no. 831 (April 1993): 97–108.

Hillman, James. "An Essay on Pan." In *Pan and the Nightmare*, by W. H. Roscher and James Hillman. Zürich: Spring Publications, 1972. i–lxiii.

Hladkyj, Stephen. "A Comparative Analysis of the Experience of Synchronicity as a Possible Spontaneous Mystical Experience." Master's diss., University of Manitoba, Canada, 1995.

Hogenson, George. "The Self, the Symbolic, and Synchronicity: Virtual Realities and the Emergence of the Psyche." *Journal of Analytical Psychology* 50, no. 2 (2005): 271–84.

Holland, R. F. "The Miraculous." In *Religion and Understanding*, ed. D. Z. Phillips. Oxford: Basil Blackwell, 1967. 155–70.

Honner, John. *The Description of Nature: Niels Bohr and the Philosophy of Quantum Physics*. Oxford: Clarendon Press, 1987.

Hook, Diana ffarington. *The I Ching and You*. London: Routledge and Kegan Paul, 1974.

Hopcke, Robert. *There Are No Accidents: Synchronicity and the Stories of Our Lives*. London: Macmillan, 1997.

Inglis, Brian. *Coincidence: A Matter of Chance—or Synchronicity?* London: Hutchinson, 1990.

———. *The Unknown Guest: The Mystery of Intuition*. London: Chatto and Windus, 1987.

Jaffé, Aniela. "Synchronistic Phenomena." In *Apparitions: An Archetypal Approach to Death, Dreams, and Ghosts*. Irving, TX: Spring, 1978. 187–206.

James, William. *The Varieties of Religious Experience: A Study in Human Nature*. 38th impression. London: Longmans, Green, 1935.

Jenkins, Stephen. *The Undiscovered Country*. Sudbury, UK: Neville Spearman, 1976.

Johnson, Alice. "Coincidences." *Proceedings of the Society for Psychical Research* 14 (1899): 158–330.

Josephs, Audrey. "Karman, Self-Knowledge and *I Ching* Divination." *Philosophy East and West* 30, no. 1 (January 1980): 65–75.

Jung, C. G. "Basic Postulates of Analytical Psychology" (1931). In *The Collected Works of C. G. Jung*, 20 vols., ed. Sir Herbert Read, Michael Fordham, and Gerhard Adler, exec. ed. William McGuire, trans. R. F. C. Hull [hereafter *Collected Works*], vol. 8, *The Structure and Dynamics of the Psyche*. 2nd ed. London: Routledge and Kegan Paul, 1969. 338–57.

———. *C. G. Jung Letters 2: 1951–61*, ed. Gerhard Adler and Aniela Jaffé, trans. R. F. C. Hull. London: Routledge and Kegan Paul, 1976.

———. *Collected Works*. Vol. 6, *Psychological Types* (1921). London: Routledge and Kegan Paul, 1971.

———. *Collected Works*. Vol. 12, *Psychology and Alchemy* (1944). 2nd ed. London: Routledge and Kegan Paul, 1968.

———. *Collected Works*. Vol. 14, *Mysterium Coniunctionis* (1955–56). London: Routledge and Kegan Paul, 1963.

———. "The Concept of the Collective Unconscious" (1936). In *Collected Works*, vol. 9i, *The Archetypes and the Collective Unconscious*. 2nd ed. London: Routledge and Kegan Paul, 1968. 42–53.

———. *Dream Analysis: Notes of the Seminar Given in 1928–1930*, ed. William McGuire. London: Routledge and Kegan Paul, 1984.

———. "Flying Saucers: A Modern Myth of Things Seen in the Skies" (1958). In *Collected Works*, vol. 10, *Civilization in Transition*. 2nd ed. London: Routledge and Kegan Paul, 1970. 307–433.

———. "Foreword to the 'I Ching'" (1950). In *Collected Works*, vol. 11, *Psychology and Religion: West and East*. 2nd ed. London: Routledge and Kegan Paul, 1969. 589–608.

———. "Foreword to Suzuki's 'Introduction to Zen Buddhism'" (1939). In *Collected Works*, vol. 11, *Psychology and Religion: West and East*. 2nd ed. London: Routledge and Kegan Paul, 1969. 538–57.

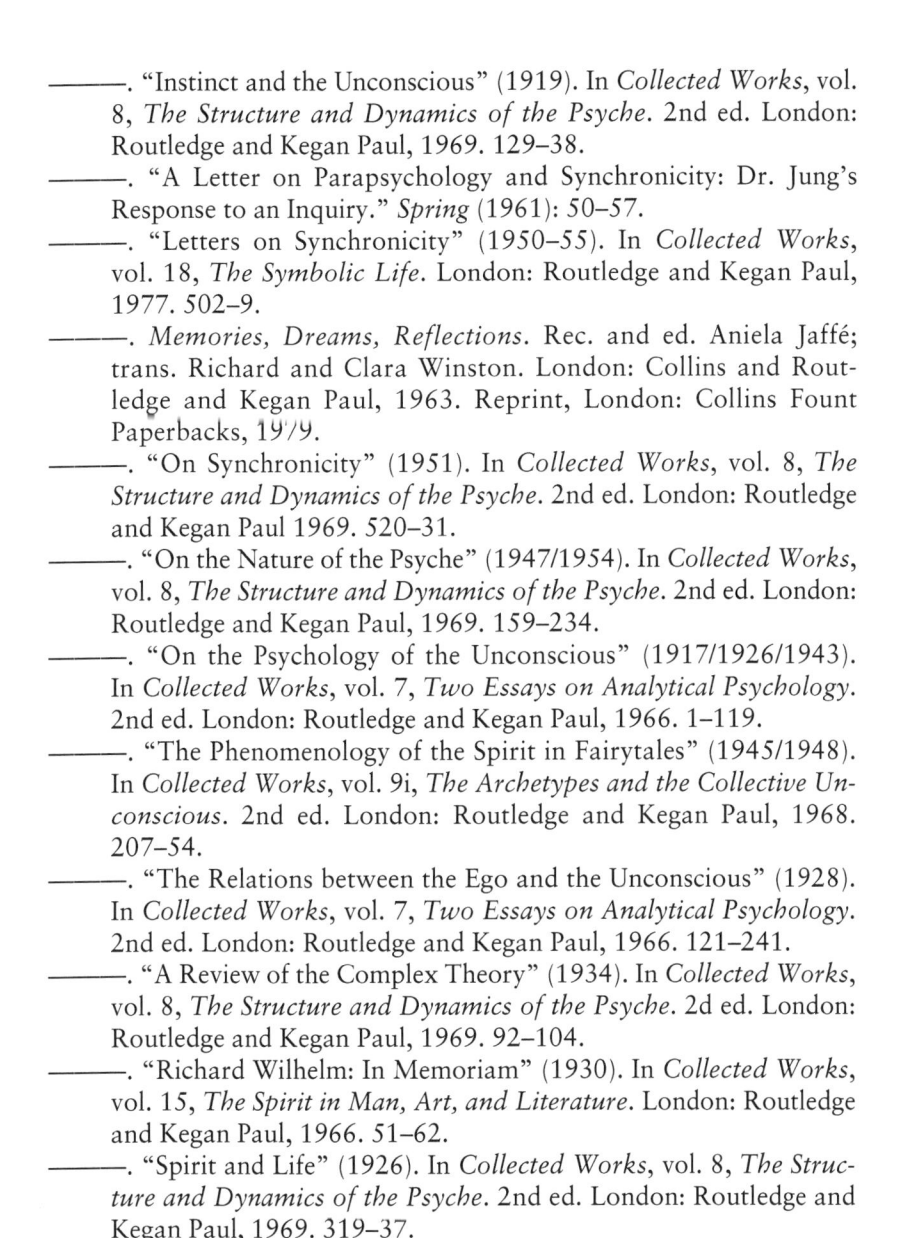

———. "Instinct and the Unconscious" (1919). In *Collected Works*, vol. 8, *The Structure and Dynamics of the Psyche*. 2nd ed. London: Routledge and Kegan Paul, 1969. 129–38.

———. "A Letter on Parapsychology and Synchronicity: Dr. Jung's Response to an Inquiry." *Spring* (1961): 50–57.

———. "Letters on Synchronicity" (1950–55). In *Collected Works*, vol. 18, *The Symbolic Life*. London: Routledge and Kegan Paul, 1977. 502–9.

———. *Memories, Dreams, Reflections*. Rec. and ed. Aniela Jaffé; trans. Richard and Clara Winston. London: Collins and Routledge and Kegan Paul, 1963. Reprint, London: Collins Fount Paperbacks, 1979.

———. "On Synchronicity" (1951). In *Collected Works*, vol. 8, *The Structure and Dynamics of the Psyche*. 2nd ed. London: Routledge and Kegan Paul 1969. 520–31.

———. "On the Nature of the Psyche" (1947/1954). In *Collected Works*, vol. 8, *The Structure and Dynamics of the Psyche*. 2nd ed. London: Routledge and Kegan Paul, 1969. 159–234.

———. "On the Psychology of the Unconscious" (1917/1926/1943). In *Collected Works*, vol. 7, *Two Essays on Analytical Psychology*. 2nd ed. London: Routledge and Kegan Paul, 1966. 1–119.

———. "The Phenomenology of the Spirit in Fairytales" (1945/1948). In *Collected Works*, vol. 9i, *The Archetypes and the Collective Unconscious*. 2nd ed. London: Routledge and Kegan Paul, 1968. 207–54.

———. "The Relations between the Ego and the Unconscious" (1928). In *Collected Works*, vol. 7, *Two Essays on Analytical Psychology*. 2nd ed. London: Routledge and Kegan Paul, 1966. 121–241.

———. "A Review of the Complex Theory" (1934). In *Collected Works*, vol. 8, *The Structure and Dynamics of the Psyche*. 2d ed. London: Routledge and Kegan Paul, 1969. 92–104.

———. "Richard Wilhelm: In Memoriam" (1930). In *Collected Works*, vol. 15, *The Spirit in Man, Art, and Literature*. London: Routledge and Kegan Paul, 1966. 51–62.

———. "Spirit and Life" (1926). In *Collected Works*, vol. 8, *The Structure and Dynamics of the Psyche*. 2nd ed. London: Routledge and Kegan Paul, 1969. 319–37.

———. "Synchronicity: An Acausal Connecting Principle" (1952). In *Collected Works*, vol. 8, *The Structure and Dynamics of the Psyche*. 2nd ed. London: Routledge and Kegan Paul, 1969. 417–519.

———. *Synchronicity: An Acausal Connecting Principle*. London: Ark Paperbacks, 1987.

———. "The Undiscovered Self (Present and Future)" (1957). In *Collected Works*, vol. 10, *Civilization in Transition*. 2nd ed. London: Routledge and Kegan Paul, 1970. 245–305.

———. *The Visions Seminars*. 2 vols. From the Complete Notes of Mary Foote. Postscript by Henry Murray. Zürich: Spring Publications, 1976.

Jung, C. G., and W. Pauli. *The Interpretation of Nature and the Psyche*, trans. R. F. C. Hull. London: Routledge and Kegan Paul, 1955.

Jung, Emma, and Marie-Louise von Franz. *The Grail Legend*. London: Hodder and Stoughton, 1972.

Kammerer, Paul. *Das Gesetz der Serie*. Stuttgart: Deutches Verlags-Anstalt, 1919.

Karcher, Stephen. "Divination, Synchronicity, and Fate." *Journal of Religion and Health* 37, no. 3 (1998): 215–28.

———. "Making Spirits Bright: Divination and the Demonic Image." *Eranos* 61 (1992): 27–43.

———. "Oracle's Contexts: Gods, Dreams, Shadow, Language." *Spring* 53 (1992): 79–94.

———. *Total I Ching: Myths for Change*. London: TimeWarner, 2003.

———. "*Which Way I Fly Is Hell:* Divination and the Shadow of the West." *Spring* 55 (1994): 80–101.

———. "The Yi Ching and the Ethic of the Image: Reflections at the 1992 Eranos/Uehiro Round Table Session." *Eranos* 61 (1992): 97–101.

Keutzer, Carolin S. "Archetypes, Synchronicity, and the Theory of Formative Causation." *Journal of Analytical Psychology* 27 (1982): 255–62.

———. "The Power of Meaning: From Quantum Mechanics to Synchronicity." *Journal of Humanistic Psychology* 24, no. 1 (Winter 1984): 80–94.

Koestler, Arthur. *The Case of the Midwife Toad*. London: Picador, 1975.

———. *The Roots of Coincidence*. London: Hutchinson, 1972.

Krishnamurti, Jiddu. *The First and Last Freedom*. London: Gollancz, 1954.

Kunst, Richard. *The Original "Yijing": A Text, Phonetic Transcription, Translation, and Indexes, with Sample Glosses*. Ann Arbor, MI: University Microfilms International, 1985.

Legge, James, trans. "The Yi King." In *The Sacred Books of the East*, ed. Max Müller. Vol. 16. Oxford: Clarendon Press, 1882. Reprint, Delhi: Motilal Banarsidass, 1966.

Lévy-Bruhl, Lucien. *How Natives Think [Les Fonctions mentales dans les sociétés inférieures]*, trans. Lilian A. Clare. Princeton, NJ: Princeton University Press, 1985. First published in Paris in 1910.

Lindorff, David. "One Thousand Dreams: The Spiritual Awakening of Wolfgang Pauli." *Journal of Analytical Psychology* 40, no. 4 (1995): 555–69.

———. *Pauli and Jung: The Meeting of Two Great Minds*. Wheaton, IL: Quest Books, 2004.

———. "Psyche, Matter, and Synchronicity: A Collaboration between C. G. Jung and Wolfgang Pauli." *Journal of Analytical Psychology* 40, no. 4 (1995): 571–86.

Liu, Da. *I Ching Numerology*. London: Routledge and Kegan Paul, 1979.

Lynn, Richard John, trans. *The Classic of Changes: A New Translation of the "I Ching" as Interpreted by Wang Bi*. New York: Columbia University Press, 1994.

Macmillan Dictionary of Religion, ed. Michael Pye. London: Macmillan Press, 1994.

Main, Roderick. "Magic and Science in the Modern Western Tradition of the *I Ching*." *Journal of Contemporary Religion* 14, no. 2 (1999): 263–75.

———. "Review of *I Ching: The Classic Chinese Oracle of Change*, by Rudolf Ritsema and Stephen Karcher." In *Journal of the Society for Psychical Research* 60, no. 839 (April 1995): 278–81.

———. *The Rupture of Time: Synchronicity and Jung's Critique of Modern Western Culture*. Hove, UK: Brunner-Routledge, 2004.

———. "Synchronicity and the *I Ching*: Clarifying the Connections." *Harvest: Journal for Jungian Studies* 43, no. 1 (1997): 51–64.

———, ed. *Jung on Synchronicity and the Paranormal*. London: Routledge; Princeton, NJ: Princeton University Press, 1997.

Mansfield, Victor. *Head and Heart: A Personal Exploration of Science and the Sacred*. Wheaton, IL: Quest Books, 2002.

———. *Synchronicity, Science, and Soul-Making: Understanding Jungian Synchronicity through Physics, Buddhism, and Philosophy*. Chicago: Open Court, 1995.

Marlan, Jan. "Beyond Projection and Introjection: The Unitary and Archetypal Field of the Transference." Chicago: C. G. Jung Institute of Chicago, 1996.

McCully, Robert S. "The Rorschach, Synchronicity, and Relativity." In *Toward a Discovery of the Person*, ed. Robert Wm. Davis. Burbank, CA: Society for Personality Assessment, 1974. 33–45.

McCusker, Brian, and Cherie Sutherland. "Probability and the Psyche I: A Reproducible Experiment Using Tarot, and the Theory of Probability." *Journal of the Society for Psychical Research* 57, no. 822 (January 1991): 344–53.

McEvilly, Wayne. "Synchronicity and the I Ching." *Philosophy East and West* 18, no. 3 (1968): 137–49.

McHarg, James F. "An Enquiry into the Ostensibly Synchronistic Basis of a Paranoid Psychosis." In *Research in Parapsychology 1972:*

Abstracts and Papers from the Fifteenth Annual Convention of the Parapsychological Association, 1972, ed. W. G. Roll, R. L. Morris, and J. D. Morris. Metuchen, NJ: Scarecrow Press, 1973. 87–89.

Meier, C. A. *Ancient Incubation and Modern Psychotherapy*, trans. Monica Curtis. Evanston, IL: Northwestern University Press, 1967.

———. "Psychosomatic Medicine from the Jungian Point of View." *Journal of Analytical Psychology* 8, no. 2 (1963): 103–21.

———, ed. *Atom and Archetype: The Pauli/Jung Letters, 1932–1958*. London: Routledge, 2001.

Mindell, Arnold. "The Golem: An Image Governing Synchronicity." *Quadrant* 8, no. 2 (1975): 5–16.

Nagy, Marilyn. *Philosophical Issues in the Psychology of C. G. Jung*. Albany: State University of New York Press, 1991.

Needham, Joseph. *Science and Civilisation in China*, vol. 2. Cambridge: Cambridge University Press, 1962.

New Catholic Encyclopedia. 17 vols. New York: McGraw Hill Book Company, 1967. S.v. "Spirit," by A. J. McNicholl.

Nietzsche, Friedrich. *Ecce Homo: How One Becomes What One Is*, trans. R. J. Hollingdale. Harmondsworth, UK: Penguin, 1979.

Otto, Rudolf. *The Idea of the Holy*, trans. John W. Harvey. 2nd ed. Oxford: Oxford University Press, 1958. Original German edition, 1917.

The Oxford English Dictionary. 20 vols. Prepared by J. A. Simpson and E. S. C. Weiner. Oxford: Clarendon, 1989.

Pauli, Wolfgang. "The Influence of Archetypal Ideas on the Scientific Theories of Kepler." In C. G. Jung and W. Pauli, *The Interpretation of Nature and the Psyche*, trans. R. F. C. Hull. London: Routledge and Kegan Paul, 1955. 147–240.

Peat, F. David. *Synchronicity: The Bridge between Matter and Mind*. New York: Bantam, 1987.

Peterson, Willard J. "Making Connections: 'Commentary on the Attached Verbalizations' of the *Book of Change*." *Harvard Journal of Asian Studies* 42, no. 1 (1982): 67–116.

———. "Some Connective Concepts in China in the Fourth to Second Centuries B.C.E." *Eranos* 57 (1988): 201–34.

Plaskett, James. *Coincidences*. Hastings, UK: Tamworth Press, 2000.

———. Earlier presentation of coincidence narrative. Typewritten manuscript, August 8, 1991. Present writer's personal collection.

———. Letter to Roderick Main, Autographed letter signed, August 8, 1991, 5.

———. Revised presentation of coincidence narrative. Typewritten manuscript, July 2, 1992. Present writer's personal collection.

Polkinghorne, John. *Science and Theology: An Introduction*. London: SPCK, 1998.
Progoff, Ira. *Jung, Synchronicity, and Human Destiny*. New York: Dell, 1973. Reprint, New York: Julian Press, 1987.
Quispel, Gilles. "Gnosis and Psychology." In *The Gnostic Jung*, ed. Robert Segal. Princeton, NJ: Princeton University Press, 1992. 239–56.
Redfield, James. *The Celestine Prophecy*. London: Bantam, 1994.
Ritsema, Rudolf. "The Corrupted: A Study of the 18th Hexagram of the *I Ching*." *Spring* (1972): 90–109.
———. "Encompassing Versatility: Keystone of the Eranos Project." *Eranos* 57 (1988): vii–xxii.
———. "The Great's Vigour: A Study of the 34th Hexagram in the *I Ching*, with a Note on Consulting the *I Ching*." *Spring* (1978): 183–206.
Ritsema, Rudolf, and Stephen Karcher, trans. *Chou Yi: The Oracle of Encompassing Versatility*. 3 vols. *Eranos* 58–60 (1989–91).
———. *I Ching: The Classic Chinese Oracle of Change*. Shaftesbury, UK: Element, 1994.
Rose, Stuart. "Transforming the World: An Examination of the Roles Played by Spirituality and Healing in the New Age Movement." PhD thesis, Lancaster University, 1997.
Rubin, Lawrence, and Charles Honorton. "Separating the Yins from the Yangs: An Experiment with the *I Ching*." *Journal of Parapsychology* 35 (1971): 313–14.
Ruelle, David. *Chance and Chaos*. London: Penguin, 1993.
Samuels, Andrew, Bani Shorter, and Fred Plaut. *A Critical Dictionary of Jungian Analysis*. London: Routledge and Kegan Paul, 1986.
Schlamm, Leon. "The Holy: A Meeting-Point between Analytical Psychology and Religion." In *Jung and the Monotheisms: Judaism, Christianity, and Islam*, ed. Joel Ryce-Menuhin. London: Routledge, 1994. 20–32.
Schwarz, Benjamin I. *The World of Thought in Ancient China*. Cambridge, MA: Belknap Press, 1985.
Segal, Robert. *Theorizing about Myth*. Amherst: University of Massachusetts Press, 1999.
Sharpe, Eric J. *Comparative Religion: A History*. London: Duckworth, 1975.
Shaughnessey, Edward. *The Composition of the "Zhouyi."* Ann Arbor, MI: University Microfilms International, 1983.
Shchutskii, Iulian K. *Researches on the I Ching*. Princeton, NJ: Princeton University Press, 1979.
Sheldrake, Rupert. *A New Science of Life: The Hypothesis of Formative Causation*. London: Blond and Briggs, 1981.

———. *The Presence of the Past*. London: Collins, 1988.
Sherrill, W. A., and W. K. Chu. *An Anthology of I Ching*. London: Arkana, 1989.
Smith, Richard. *Fortune-tellers and Philosophers: Divination in Traditional Chinese Society*. Boulder, CO: Westview Press, 1991.
Stiffler, Lavonne H. "Adoptees and Birthparents Connected by Design: Surprising Synchronicities in Histories of Union/Loss/Reunion." *Pre- and Perinatal Psychology Journal* 7, no. 4 (Summer 1993): 267–86.
Swanson, Gerald. *The Great Treatise: Commentary Tradition to the Book of Changes*. Ann Arbor, MI: University Microfilms, 1974.
———. "Introduction to the English Edition." In *Researches on the I Ching*, by Iulian K. Shchutskii. Princeton, NJ: Princeton University Press, 1979. vii–xlviii.
Tart, Charles. "Causality and Synchronicity: Steps towards Clarification." *Journal of the American Society for Psychical Research* 75 (April 1981): 121–41.
Thalbourne, Michael A., Peter S. Delin, Jillian A. Barlow, and Della M. Steen. "A Further Attempt to Separate the Yins from the Yangs: A Replication of the Rubin–Honorton Experiment with the I CHING." *European Journal of Parapsychology* 9 (1992–93): 12–23.
Thornton, Edward. *The Diary of a Mystic*. London: George Allen and Unwin, 1967.
Vallée, Jacques. *Messengers of Deception*. Berkeley, CA: And/Or Press, 1979.
Vaughan, Alan. *Incredible Coincidence: The Baffling World of Synchronicity*. New York: Harper and Row, 1979. Reprint, New York: Ballantine, 1989.
———. *Patterns of Prophecy*. London: Turnstone Books, 1974.
von Franz, Marie-Louise. *Introduction to the Interpretation of Fairy Tales*. Dallas, TX: Spring Publications, 1982.
———. *Number and Time: Reflections Leading towards a Unification of Psychology and Physics*, trans. Andrea Dykes. London: Rider, 1974.
———. *On Divination and Synchronicity: The Psychology of Meaningful Chance*. Toronto: Inner City Books, 1980.
———. *Psyche and Matter*. Boston: Shambhala, 1992.
Watt, Caroline. "Psychology and Coincidences." *European Journal of Parapsychology* 8 (1990–91): 66–84.
Wharton, Barbara. "Deintegration and Two Synchronistic Events." *Journal of Analytical Psychology* 31, no. 3 (July 1986): 281–85.
Wheelwright, Joseph B., Jane H. Wheelwright, and John A. Beuhler. *Jungian Type Survey: The Grey-Wheelwright Test Manual*. 16th rev. ed.

San Francisco: Society of Jungian Analysts of Northern California, 1964.

Whincup, Greg. *Rediscovering the I Ching*. Wellingborough, UK: Aquarian Press, 1987.

White, Victor. *Soul and Psyche: An Enquiry into the Relationship of Psychotherapy and Religion*. London: Collins and Harvill Press, 1960.

Whitmont, Edward C. "Prefatory Remarks to Jung's 'Reply to Buber'." *Spring* (1973): 188–95.

Wilber, Ken. *Eye to Eye: The Quest for the New Paradigm*. Exp. ed. Boston: Shambhala, 1990.

———. "The Great Chain of Being." *Journal of Humanistic Psychology* 33, no. 3 (Summer 1993): 52–65.

———. "Odyssey: A Personal Inquiry into Humanistic and Transpersonal Psychology." *Journal of Humanistic Psychology* 22, no. 1 (Winter 1982): 57–90.

———. "Reply to Schneider." *Journal of Humanistic Psychology* 29, no. 4 (Fall 1989): 493–500.

———. *The Spectrum of Consciousness*. Wheaton, IL: Quest, 1977.

Wilber, Ken, Jack Engler, and Daniel P. Brown. *Transformations of Consciousness*. Boston: Shambala, 1986.

Wilhelm, Hellmut. *Change: Eight Lectures on the I Ching*. London: Routledge and Kegan Paul, 1961.

———. "The Concept of Time in the Book of Changes." In *Papers from the Eranos Yearbooks*, vol. 3, *Man and Time*, ed. Joseph Campbell. New York: Bollingen, 1957. 212–32.

———. *Heaven, Earth, and Man in the Book of Changes*. Seattle: University of Washington Press, 1977.

———. "Preface to the Third Edition." In *The I Ching Book of Changes*, trans. Richard Wilhelm, rendered into English by Cary F. Baynes. 3rd ed. London: Routledge and Kegan Paul, 1968. xiv–xvi.

Wilhelm, Richard. *Lectures on the I Ching: Constancy and Change*. London: Routledge and Kegan Paul, 1980.

———, trans. *The I Ching or Book of Changes*. Rendered into English by Cary F. Baynes. 3rd ed. London: Routledge and Kegan Paul, 1968.

Williams, Mary. "An Example of Synchronicity." *Journal of Analytical Psychology* 2, no. 1 (1957): 93–95.

Zabriskie, Beverley. "Jung and Pauli: A Subtle Asymmetry." *Journal of Analytical Psychology* 40, no. 4 (1995): 531–53.

Zinkin, Louis. "The Hologram as a Model for Analytical Psychology." *Journal of Analytical Psychology* 32 (1987): 1–21.

INDEX

acausality, 5, 15, 139, 167, 168, 173, 199n37; absolute, 21, 23; acausal connecting principle, 14; miracles and, 45, 58; relative, 20–21, 29, 45. *See also* causality; correlative thinking; paralleling: acausal parallelism; paralleling: meaningful acausal

Adler, Gerhard: on significance of *I Ching*, 141, 142; experience of consulting *I Ching*, 148–50, 156, 161; *The Living Symbol*, 220n14

Adler, Joseph, 144, 231n181

Aesculapius, 66; hymn to, 66, 71

Agrippa of Nettesheim, 171

alchemy, 134, 137, 171

amplification, 19, 58, 124, 132, 145

analysis: causal, 21; of *I Ching* hexagrams, 158–59; Jungian, 64; nonpsychological, 147; Otto's, of numinosity, 40; of products of the imagination, 10; rational, 43; symbolic, 119, 120, 121, 175; of synchronicity, 16, 58, 110, 121–22, 132. *See also* interpretation

analytical psychology. *See* Jungian (or analytical) psychology

Aquinas, Saint Thomas. *See* Thomas Aquinas, Saint

archetypes, 13, 15, 22, 35; archetypal image, 34; archetypal patterning; 19; basis of synchronicity, 176–77; cosmic, 60; hexagrams and, 160, 226n77; immanent in their images, 203n99; number of, 177; numinosity of, 15, 16; of rebirth, 16, 176; as such, 34; as transpersonal objects of experience, 36

Arthur, King, 90, 91, 134, 135, 136

Arthurian legend, 84, 99, 126, 130, 132; political dimension of, 136; synchronicities analyzed in depth, 120, 132–40; as theme of synchronicities, 87, 88, 89–91, 94, 118, 129, 132, 133, 213–14n35. *See also* Parsifal; Grail; Round Table

Assagioli, Roberto, 83, 95, 96, 117, 118, 125, 130

astrology, 82, 83, 105, 171, 208n87

Athena: attributes of, 73, 78; birth of, 63, 67, 73, 75, 76, 77, 78; figurines of, 71, 75, 78; owl sacred to, 65, 73, 78; statue on Leeds City Hall, 70, 77, 210n35; symbol of divine wisdom, 73, 78; terrestrial goddess, 68; Virgin Mary associated with, 73, 78

Auster, Paul, 1

autonomy, 5. *See also under* psyche; spirit; synchronicity

Avens, Roberts, 203n99

247

Ayer, Alfred, J., 196n1
Aziz, Robert, 4, 205n24, 221n29

Baker, Stanley, 90, 136
Barth, Karl, 61
Baynes, Cary, F., 146, 147
Beatrice, 87, 91, 92, 115, 127
Beuhler, John, 212n4
Beloff, John, 6, 212n3
Bergman, Ingmar, 106; *The Seventh Seal*, 106
Bhagwan. *See* Rajneesh, Bhagwan Shree
Bishop, Paul, 5, 203n96
Blackmore, Susan, 105, 213n31
blindness, 87, 96–97, 115, 127–8, 215n76
Bloomfield, Bob, 189n3
Boersma, Frederick, 191n16
Bohm, David, 8, 52, 195n55
Bohr, Niels, 52
Bolen, Jean Shinoda, 4, 207n66
Bouvet, Fr. Joachim, 146
Breederveld, H., 212n3, 213n31
Brenneis, Sandra, 191n16
Bright, George, 191n14
Brooke, Roger, 199n36
Brown, Colin, 44
Brown, George Spencer, 7
Brugger, Peter, 194n47
Buddhism, 4, 11
Bultmann, Rudolf, 61
Burniston, Andrew, 190n12

Cambray, Joseph, 191n18
Campbell, Joseph, 137, 220n26
causality, 19, 20–21, 54, 100, 104, 168, 199n37; absence of normal causes, 52, 72, 74, 118, 161, 164, 165, 173, 196n7; *causa sui*, 139; cause and effect, 139, 155, 167–68, 169, 228n108; in Chinese thinking, 168–71, 173; connecting events, 2, 12, 13, 16; formative causation, 8; lower and higher causes, 20–21, 54, 56; normal causes, 14, 18, 19, 45, 131; possible, 65, 76–79, 84; scientific explanation, 7, 141; spirit not bound by, 26, 29. *See also* acausality; skepticism
celestial phenomena, 87, 88–89, 91, 118, 120, 124, 128, 139, 213–14n35, 220n11. *See also* meteorites; moon; stars
chance, 44, 54, 57, 76; in *I Ching*, 153, 161–62, 169; more than, 102, 108
Chang Chou, 172
chess, 82, 84, 87, 106, 106–107, 109–10
China: Chinese language, 153, 222n4, 227n92, 229n141; Chinese science, 170; Chinese thinkers, 144–46, 151, 231n181; Chinese thinking, 153, 168–72, 179, 181, 184; Chinese world, 142; *t'ai chi* symbol, 228n110. *See also I Ching*; Tao
Chou, Duke of, 143, 144, 150
Christ, 60, 134, 136; astrological coincidence with Pisces, 208n87; Grail as evidence of earthly life of, 139; miracles of, 44; as symbol of spiritual reality, 134, 136–37, 139
Christianity, 24, 25, 62, 67, 73; apocalyptic literature, 11; concept of divine in, 201n69; concept of spirit in, 200n48; mystics in, 49; one-sidedness of, 134; spiritual concepts in, 9. *See also* religion
Chu Hsi, 145, 156, 172
Chu, W. K., 225n47
clairvoyance, 17, 41, 195n54
Clarke, Arthur C., 83, 89, 93, 99, 214n42, 215n63, 217n128
Cocksey, Brian, 209n97
coincidence: definition of, 12–13, 18, 19, 212n2; in definition of synchronicity, 16; effect of, 6, 99; as

evidence of greater reality, 88–89, 100, 102–104; explanations of, 5–8, 54; indicating need for new science, 97, 110; interpreting, 81; making meaningful, 100, 108–109; meaning in, 22, 106; meaningful coincidence, 2, 7, 13, 14, 15, 118; meaningful to other than experiencer, 19–20, 57; as miracles, 45–46; nature of, 100–101; recording of, 85, 107; simultaneity in, 17; spiritual aspect of, 5, 6; spookiness of, 42; studies of, 5; survey of, 6; symbolized by meteorites, 88–89; synchronicity as more than, 14, 16, 23; synonymous with synchronicity, 13, 212n2; triggering effect of, 100–101, 110, 133, 173, 174; types of, 6, 17, 20, 83. *See also* coincidence examples; synchronicity

coincidence examples: exploding boiler, 45; Fatima simulation, 46–47; flat tires, 1; Lincoln, 56–57; origami, 18, 20; owl images, 19; praying mantis, 1; scarab, 14–16, 47; Spanish city, 17; Stockholm fire, 17; suicidal patient, 1; synchronized swimming, 18–19, 20; three large bells, 1; train stopping in time, 45; Zechariah's horses, 11–13, 54. *See also* Plaskett's coincidences; Thornton: synchronistic narrative

Combs, Allan, 190n12, 194n46, 220n22

coming up for air, 87, 93, 95, 97, 126, 128, 213–14n35; *Coming Up for Air*, 94, 97, 107

compensation, 4, 16, 22, 34, 134, 221n29

complementarity, 5, 20, 31, 52, 131, 153, 171, 199, 228n105

Confucius, 143, 144, 151, 164

connectedness, 4, 14, 15. *See also* synchronicity: interconnection of themes in

consciousness, 32, 33, 34, 41, 42, 50, 127, 141; dualistic, 29; ego-, 51, 141; higher, 37, 181; higher-level communication to, 57, 61, 62; medieval, 135; numinous, 40; psychophysical orientation of, 29; and reality, 2, 27; ordinary, 64; spectrum of, 201n72; spiritual aspect of, 29, 30, 31, 32, 40, spiritual orientation of, 29; states of, 21, 25, 29, 37, 125; transformation of, 47, 62, 72, 73, 75, 84, 125; unitive, 25, 29, 49, 202n77

coordinative thinking. *See* correlative thinking

Corbin, Henry, 190n11

correlative thinking, 169–72, 181

correspondence, 141, 170, 178, 179. See also under *I Ching*

Cousineau, Phil, 195n52

crater, 88, 91, 95, 129, 132, 136, 137, 138, 139; Plaskett's Crater, 88, 123, 124, 214n37, 214n39

cryptomnesia, 215n76

Cunningham, Adrian, 160, 212n4

Curtis, David, 206n38

Dante, 83, 96, 124, 125, 128; celestial journey of, 124, 125, 129, 130; *Divine Comedy*, 83, 95, 125, 130; *Paradiso*, 87, 91–93, 96, 99, 117, 118, 127, 128, 129, 140, 213n35, 215n76. *See also* Beatrice; eagle; rose; threefoldness

de Voogd, Stephanie, 34, 35

December 22, 87, 88

Delphic Oracle, 175

Democritus, 171

Devereux, George, 6

Diaconis, Persi, 7, 42

Dionysus, 4

divination, 3, 141, 142, 144, 145, 147, 156, 162, 164, 176, 183. See also *I Ching*
Doeringer, F. M., 225n48
Donati, Marialuisa, 191n17
Dorn, Gerhard, 221n28
dreams, 37, 64, 115; interpretation of, 122
Dulles, Avery, 58–62
Dyer, Wayne, 195n56

eagle, 86, 87, 91, 92, 93, 99, 102, 115, 119, 124, 127, 129, 130, 213n35, 215n56, 215n62; Eagle (place names), 92, 127
Eckhart, Meister, 49
ego, 50, 51, 141
Eisenbud, Jules, 7
Ellis, John, 204n125
enactment: of myths and legends, 75, 124–25, 130, 132
enantiadromia, 167, 228n110
Eranos I Ching Project, 10, 147, 183
Erkelens, Herbert van, 191n17
external event, 14, 15, 16, 18–20, 21, 23, 50, 72, 75, 78, 163, 166. *See also* outer event; physical event
extrasensory perception (ESP), 35, 176, 180
eyes and vision, 87, 96–98, 104, 118, 127, 140. *See also* blindness; vision, new; one-eyedness; third eye
Ezekiel, 11

Faber, Mel, 7
fairytales, 37, 204n125
Ferrer, Mel, 90, 136
Fisher King, 132–33
Flew, Anthony, 196n1
Fludd, Robert, 171
Fordham, Michael, 190n14
Freud, Sigmund, 6, 205n18
Fu Hsi, 143, 144

games, theory of, 179
Gammon, Mary, 191n16

Gardner, Martin, 102
Gatlin, Lila, 6
Gauquelin, Michel and Françoise, 105
Giegerich, Wolfgang, 34–35
God, 5, 24, 34, 36, 172, 186, 200n48; Deity, 102; image of, 35; immanence of, 55; and miracles, 46; nonrational and nonmoral aspect of, 40; providence of, 56; revelation of, 57, 59–62 passim; transcendence of, 53; vision of, 128. *See also* goddess; gods
goddess, 65, 67, 68, 71, 72, 78. *See also* Athena; Virgin Mary
gods, 3, 54, 55, 190n12, 172; *shen*, 178, 180, 182, 183, 187, 230n158. *See also* Aesculapius; Athena; Dionysus; God; Hermes; Pan
Golem, 4
Gooch, Stan, 107–108, 110
Gordon, Rosemary, 190n14
Grail, 87, 89, 95, 99, 102, 115, 126, 128, 132–40, 187, 213–14n35; as meteorite, 137; as stone, 136, 138; as symbol of spiritual mystery and power, 136; as vessel, 136, 138, 187
Granet, Marcel, 228n121
Grattan-Guinness, Ivor, 6, 197n9, 198n29, 219n4
Grey-Wheelwright Jungian Type Survey, 212n4

Handel, Sidney, 190n13
Happold, F. W., 206n39
Hardy, Alister, 214n43
Hartston, William, 105–11, 117, 213n31, 219n167; Hartston Case, 100, 101, 105–11. *See also* Plaskett's coincidences
Harvie, Robert, 214n43
Hegel, Georg Wilhelm Friedrich, 172, 203n109
Heisig, James, 203n105
Henry, Jane, 6

Index

Hephaistos, 67
Herder, Johann Gottfried, 172
Hermes, 3
Hillman, James, 190n12, 203n99
Hladkyj, Stephen, 6
Hobbes, Thomas, 94
Hogenson, George, 191–92n18
holism, 8, 29, 48–49, 50, 131
Holland, Mark, 190n12, 194n46, 220n22
Holland, R. F., 44–46
Holy Grail. *See* Grail
Honner, John, 207n49
Honorton, Charles, 180
Hook, Diana ffarington, 223n18, 224n31
Hopcke, Robert, 195n52
Hü Yuan, 145

I Ching (Book of Changes), 3, 8, 9, 10, 141–87; chance in, 153, 161–62, 169; Commentary on the Decision, 151, 156; Commentary on the Words of the Text, 151, 165; correctness of lines, 154, 157; correspondence of lines, 155, 166–67, 168, 228n105; Discussion of the Trigrams, 151, 180, 225; Great Treatise, 143, 153, 155, 156, 165, 166, 167, 168, 181, 182, 183, 184, 185, 227n96; Hexagram 12 (P'i/Standstill [Stagnation]), 161; Hexagram 35 (Chin/Progress), 161; Hexagram 43 (Kuai/Breakthrough [Resoluteness]), 157–59, 165; Hexagram 44 (Kou/Coming to Meet), 149; Hexagram 50 (Ting/The Cauldron), 185–87; hexagrams, 143, 153–54, 157, 162, 176; historical background of, 142, 143–47; holding together of lines, 155; Image text, 151, 152, 156, 165; interpreting, 148, 149; Judgment text, 150, 151, 156, 159; language of, 175; lateral interchange of lines, 167; lines, 143, 148, 154, 157; Lines text, 151, 156, 159; nonspiritual theories of, 177–80; as numinous, 182; position of lines, 155, 157; procedures for consulting, 142, 147–50; provides counsel for action, 175; psychological use of, 147; relationship of text to structure, 155–60; schools of interpretation, 144–46, 224n35; as spiritual, 143, 177–87; structure of, 148, 150, 153, 166–69, 176; synchronistic basis of, 142, 143, 160–72; systematization of synchronicity, 142; Ten Wings, 143, 144, 151, 152, 153, 165; texts, 143, 148, 150–53, 163–66; trigrams, 154, 157, 166; Western study of, 146–47. *See also under* Adler, Gerhard; Jung, C. G.; Wilhelm, Richard
identity, 49, 87, 123–25, 127, 130, 132, 136, 140; spiritual aspect of, 124, 128
immanence, 25, 39, 53, 55, 56, 68, 72, 75, 78, 203n99. *See also* transcendence
implicate order, 8, 52
individuation, 4, 15, 16, 22, 50
Inglis, Brian, 6, 105, 197n10, 206n35, 208n67, 213n31, 217n138
inner event, 18, 19, 20, 49, 50, 65–68 passim, 70, 74–78 passim, 114, 198n32; in relation to *I Ching*, 141, 154, 155, 166, 183. *See also* psychic state
integration, 50, 123, 127, 134, 206n43
intelligence, 56; limits of, 108–11, 218n163; transcendent, 54, 57, 71, 162, 195n54
interpretation, 119–39, 148, 149; spiritual, 123; symbolic, 123, 156. *See also* analysis
intuition, 82, 120, 156, 212n4; intellectual, 5, 231n181

Jaffé, Aniela, 191n16
James, William, 42
Jenkins, Stephen, 11–13, 14, 17, 54, 56
Joachim of Floris, 134
John, Saint, 120
Johnson, Alice, 5
Joseph, Audrey, 164
Joseph of Arimathea, 136
Judas, 134
Jung, C. G., 2, 7, 9, 65, 66, 68, 72, 206n37, 220n14, 228n105, 229n135; on definition of synchronicity, 9, 11, 14–17, 197–98n26; on direct experience of spirit, 32–36; and *I Ching*, 8, 142, 146–47, 160, 171, 176–77, 179, 180, 182, 183, 185–86; influence on New Age, 195n55; introduces concept of synchronicity, 2, 3; method of interpretation, 122; *Psychology and Alchemy*, 122, 196n60; theory of synchronicity, 4, 5, 6, 7, 9; writings on synchronicity, 4, 10. *See also* Jungian (or analytical) psychology
Jung, Emma, 134, 136, 137, 138, 139, 221n32
Jungian (or analytical) psychology, 3, 4, 9, 10, 23, 34, 50, 64, 65, 68, 81, 114, 116, 121, 122, 141, 147, 182, 192n22, 199n36, 203n105. *See also* archetypes; compensation; ego; individuation; integration; psyche; shadow; synchronicity; the unconscious
justice, 91–92, 123, 126, 127; heavenly, 129, 130

Kabbalah, 171
Kammerer, Paul, 192n26
Kant, Immanuel, 181, 231n181; Jung's use of, 33–35
Karcher, Stephen, 8, 147, 153, 162, 182–84, 186, 224n30, 227n87, 229n127, 232n198, 232n200
Kerényi, Karl, 67

Keutzer, Carolin, 191n16, 194n50
Koestler, Arthur, 5, 6, 53–54, 56, 89, 100, 197n9, 214n43
Koestler Foundation, 6
Krishnamurti, Jiddu, 49, 84
Kunst, Richard, 224n29

Lancelot, 90, 128
Legge, James, 146
Leibniz, Gottfried Wilhelm, 146
Lévi-Strauss, Claude, 160
Leviathan, 87, 93, 94, 115
Lévy-Bruhl, Lucien, 170–71
Lincoln, Abraham, 56–57. *See also* under coincidence examples
Lindorff, David, 191n17
Liu, Da, 223n16
looking, new ways of. *See* vision, new
Lotze, Rudolph Hermann, 172
Lynn, Richard John, 181, 223n15, 228n108

magic, 174
Main, Roderick, 189n8, 190n10, 195n53, 213n29, 224n30; *Rupture of Time*, 4–5, 193n41, 194n43, 196n57, 197n25, 198n26, 205n30, 219n8, 222n1
Mansfield, Victor, 4
Marlan, Jan, 190–91n14
matter, 20, 27, 28–36 passim; 39, 44, 50, 51, 183, 199n36, 200n48. *See also* external event; outer event; reality: physical
Maugham, W. Somerset, 94
McCully, Robert, 191n16
McCusker, Brian, 194n46
McEvilly, Wayne, 8, 226n77, 229n136
McHarg, James, 190n14
meaning, 9, 17, 85, 99, 101, 104, 106, 108, 119, 123, 139, 175, 176; archetypal, 120; and content, 22; cosmic, 4; field of, 183; from meaninglessness, 100, 108–109, 218; patterns of, 63,

65, 73, 130, 131, 132, 173, 175; questions of, 82; search for, 133; spiritual, 63; subjective and objective, 121–22; symbolic, 65, 101, 120. See also under coincidence; paralleling
Meier, C. A., 191n15
metaphysics, 35, 83, 192n22, 200n43, 226n77
meteorites, 87, 92–93, 103, 125, 127, 128, 213–14n35; analogy with coincidence, 88–89, 127, 129, 130, 217n130; associated with Grail, 137, 138, 139; reality of, 88–89, 103, 137; symbol of heavenly justice, 130; symbol of spiritual reality, 129
methodology, 2, 10, 119–23, 179
Miles, Tony, 107
Mindell, Arnold, 190n13
miracles, 4, 39, 43–47, 58, 62, 70, 74, 89, 129, 132, 136, 182, 205n30, 207n62; coincidences as, 44; contingency concept of, 45–46; and *I Ching*, 182; violation concept of, 44–45, 46
miraculousness. See miracles
Monoceros. See unicorn
moon, 87, 88, 91, 92–93, 115, 119, 129, 166, 213–14n35; far side of, 88, 125, 136, 214n39; symbol of psychophysical reality, 125–26
Mordred, 134, 135, 136
Mosteller, Frederick, 7, 42
Mou [Tsung san], 231n181
mysticism, 6, 42, 47, 49, 52; mystical experiences, 4, 6, 9, 49–50, 53, 60–61, 64, 68, 72; mystics, 25, 29, 30, 37, 49, 63
myth, 10, 63–79, 77, 78, 79, 127, 130; of birth of Athena, 67, 72–73, 75, 76, 77, 78; characterizing synchronicity, 3; of Holy Grail (see Grail); motifs in synchronicities, 9

Nagy, Marilyn, 192n22
Needham, Joseph, 146, 170–71, 222n8, 222n11
New Age spirituality, 8
Nietzsche, Friedrich, 43–44; *Human, All Too Human*, 43
notability, 14, 15, 22, 23, 41, 57, 58, 196n7
numbers, 92, 93, 144, 146, 178; and synchronicity, 3, 8
numinosity, 29, 39–43, 61, 70, 74, 99, 129, 181, 202n74, 202n75, 204n1; awefulness, 10, 11, 12, 43; *fascinans*/fascination, 39, 40, 43; and *I Ching*, 182, 183, 184, 185, 227n96; *mysterium*/wholly other, 39, 40, 41, 43; overpoweringness, 40, 41, 42, 43; and *shen*, 181, 230n158; of synchronicity, 15, 16, 39–43; *tremendum*, 39, 40, 41, 43; urgency, 40, 41, 43

observation, 52, 85, 111, 133, 169; relationship between observer and observed, 29, 48–50, 102, 131
octopus, 86, 87, 93, 94, 96, 99, 102, 115, 119, 126, 127, 215n69
one-eyedness, 87, 96, 97, 98, 104, 115, 131
operation, 66, 67, 69, 71, 72–79 passim, 209n13
organismic thinking, 170, 171, 172
Orwell, George, 94, 107
Otto, Rudolf, 40, 70, 181, 202n74; *The Idea of the Holy*, 40
outer event, 18, 19, 20, 50, 71, 78, 141, 154, 166, 183, 198n32. See also external event; physical event
owls, 19, 64–67, 69, 70, 72–78 passim, 115, 210n35

Pan, 3
Paracelsus, 171

paralleling, 14, 15, 58, 162; acausal parallelism, 14, 46, 57, 58, 118, 163; meaningful acausal paralleling, 41, 65, 72, 131, 160–61, 173

the paranormal, 5, 8, 41, 82, 83; *The Paranormal*, 107, 110; paranormal causes, 20, 21; proof of, 102–104, 116, 123, 139

parapsychology, 3, 5, 6, 7, 8, 35, 51, 84, 86, 103, 105, 110, 114, 180

Parsifal, 87, 89, 90, 115, 119, 129, 132–33, 134, 213–14n35; failure to occupy *siège périlleux*, 135; *Parsifal* (Wagner's opera), 43, 90; Plaskett's identification with, 124, 130, 132, 136, 140; seeks and finds Grail, 132–33, 136; transformation of, 125, 139

participation, 85, 104, 110, 123, 124, 132, 140, 143, 168, 173, 201n69, 218n165; participative thought, 170; property of symbols, 59

Pauli, Wolfgang, 4, 52

Peat, F. David, 194n50, 197n10

Perceval/Percival. *See* Parsifal

Percival, Lance, 90, 99

Peterson, Willard, 8, 165–66, 169, 181, 182, 184, 185, 223n28, 224n29, 227n96

philosophy, 3, 8, 83, 109, 203n96, 228n110; Chinese, 172; Greek, 171; Western, 172, 226n77

physical event, 18, 19, 20, 65, 72, 74, 75, 77, 115, 116, 130, 163, 169. *See also* external event; outer event

physical reality. *See* reality: physical

physics, 3, 4, 5, 100, 102, 199n37; quantum, 52, 53, 171

Plaskett, James, 81–140 passim, 173, 174, 175, 196n59, 212–19nn1–167 passim, 219–22nn1–58 passim; contact with, 82; nonnarrative collection of coincidences, 213n29; profile of, 82–84; response and interpretations by, 98–104. *See also* crater: Plaskett's Crater; Hartston, William; Plaskett's coincidences; stars: Plaskett's Star

Plaskett's coincidences: (1) far side of the moon, 88, 123, 124, 125, 129, 132, 136; (2) Unicorn, 88, 117, 123, 124, 125, 128, 129, 132; (3) meteorite shower, 88–89, 103, 125, 128, 129, 137; (4) resembling Parsifal, 90, 124, 125, 128, 129, 130, 132, 136; (5) Lance Percival, 90, 99, 124, 125, 128, 130, 132; (6) round table, 90, 115, 133–34, 135; (7) *Camelot*, 90, 134, 135; (8) *Knights of the Round Table*, 90, 134, 136; (9) Ferrer and Baker, 90, 115, 130, 132, 134, 136; (10) grail as *crater*, 90–91, 125, 128, 129, 130, 136; (11) celestial journey, 91, 124, 125, 130; (12) coin counterfeiters, 91–92, 99, 127, 129, 130; (13) red eagle, 92, 99, 124, 127, 130; (14) a question of justice, 92, 99, 124, 127, 130; (15) Eagle Home, 92, 117, 127; (16) Beatrice, 92, 117, 127; (17) nines, 92; (18) meteorites on Eagle, 93, 103, 127, 128, 129, 130; (19) Eagle on the moon, 93; (20) trilogy, 93, 99, 126; (21) Octopus Books, 94, 99, 126; (22) a clergyman's daughter, 94, 107, 126; (23) synchronized swimming, 18–19, 94, 107, 117, 127, 129; (24) great-crested grebes, 94, 117, 126; (25) whale coming up for air, 94, 126; (26) Leviathan, 94; (27) Icelandic fish, 95; (28) submerged treasure, 95, 117, 126; (29) exercises for spiritual psychosynthesis, 95, 117, 118, 125; (30) visualized octopus, 95–96, 117, 126; (31) blind taxi passenger, 96, 104, 115, 127;

(32) triangular cloud, 96, 104, 127–28, 131; (33) blind dates, 96, 104; (34) eye falls out, 97, 104, 115; (35) listeners coming up for air, 97, 126; (36) diabetic blindness, 97, 104, 131; (37) lens falls out, 97, 104, 131; (38) new science, 97, 104, 115, 131; (39) single eye, 98, 104, 131; (40) one-eyed vision, 98, 104, 131; (41) eye patch, 98, 104, 131; Coincidentally Hartston, 107–108, 110; Grandmasterly Castling, 105–107, 110; Limits of Intelligence, 108–110. *See also* Arthurian legend; celestial phenomena; Dante; eyes and vision; sea monsters
Plato, 202n81; Platonism, 25, 171, 208n70, 226n77
Plaut, Fred, 202n75
Playfair, Guy Lyon, 46–47
Polkinghorne, John, 207n62
Portmann, Adolf, 1
prayer, 2, 6, 46, 67, 73, 174
praying mantis, 1
precognition, 17, 18, 41, 116, 195n54
probability, 18, 79, 101, 102, 106, 108, 110, 117, 118, 141, 198n29; evaluating, 7, 12, 76, 99; improbability stimulating inquiry, 101; probabilistic strategies, 180; theory, 7
Progoff, Ira, 56, 191n15
projection, 33, 55, 76, 84, 172, 179, 180, 199n37, 218n165
providence, 39, 56–7, 58, 65, 68, 70, 71; special, 207n62; Thomas Aquinas on, 54
psi, 8, 35, 195n54
psyche, 28, 36, 198n32; as aspect of a continuum, 27, 28, 29, 222n3; autonomous, 35; coloring all experience, 204n118; difficulty measuring, 28; Jung's use of the term, 36; and nonpsychic events,

35–36; psychic and physical, 51, 52, 55, 56, 228n105; psychic processes, 15, 28, 57; psychic wholeness, 16; and spirit, 28–31, 53, 134; transpersonal, 36. *See also* psychic state; reality: psychic
psychic reality. *See* reality: psychic
psychic state, 14, 15, 16, 18–20, 21, 23, 49, 50, 53, 65, 72, 74, 75, 115–16, 130, 163, 169, 197–98n26. *See also* inner event
psychical research, 5
psychoanalysis, 6, 7, 95
psychokinesis, 41, 195n54
psychology, 55, 83, 95, 109, 183; cognitive, 3, 7; Jung's, of religion, 4; mainstream, 84, 116, 219n8; transpersonal, 9, 23, 25. *See also* Jungian (or analytical) psychology; psychoanalysis; psychosynthesis
the psychophysical, 30, 31, 55, 56, 74, 75, 125–26, 129, 139
psychosynthesis, 95, 101, 117, 118, 125, 130

Quispel, Gilles, 189n1

Rajneesh, Bhagwan Shree, 84
randomness, 160, 161, 179, 180
reality: nature of, 102; personal or impersonal nature of transcendent, 55; physical, 2, 21, 27, 30–32, 77, 115, 140; psychic, 2, 27, 32–36, 167, 184; spiritual, 36, 55, 73, 95, 102, 114, 116, 125, 129, 132, 134, 138, 139, 140. *See also under* consciousness
rebirth: archetype of, 16, 176; spiritual, 66, 73, 78; symbolic, 76
Redfield, James, 195–96n56
religion, 11, 81, 83, 114, 186; detraditionalised, 4–5; Eastern, 25, 64; phenomenology of, 4; psychology of, 4, 203n105; Western, 25, 64; world, 25, 57. *See also* Buddhism; Christianity; God; Tao: Taoism

Religious Experience Research Unit (Alister Hardy Research Centre), 50
religious studies, 2, 195n54
revelation, 39, 45, 57–62, 65, 68, 69, 70, 71, 74, 75, 120, 131, 143; collective, 208n69, 208n87; models of, 59–62; personal, 65, 208; *Revelation of St John*, 12; self-revelation of spirit, 37; self-revelation of synchronicity, 113, 143
Rhine, J. B., 51
Ritsema, Rudolf, 147, 153, 162, 182–84, 186, 224n31, 229n27, 232n198, 232n200
ritual, 66, 71, 72–3, 79, 130, 186
rose, 87, 91, 95, 119, 220n11
Rose, Stuart, 195n54
Round Table, 87, 89, 90, 132, 133–36, 140, 213–14n35
Rubin, Lawrence, 180
Ruelle, David, 179

samadhi, 84
Samuels, Andrew, 202n75
Schlamm, Leon, 204n1
Schwarz, Benjamin, 172, 177
science, 4, 5, 6, 32, 52, 53, 82, 84, 171; Chinese, 170; French Academy of Science, 89, 93, 103; mechanistic, 171; new, 97, 102–104, 110, 131; one-sided, 98; Western, 141
sea monsters, 87, 93–96, 118, 126, 134, 140, 213–14n35, 216n81, 220n11. *See also* coming up for air; Leviathan; octopus
Segal, Robert, 189, 200n43
shadow, 50
Shallis, Michael, 104
Shao, Yung, 145, 146
Sharpe, Eric, 189n5
Shaughnessey, Edward, 224n29
Shchutskii, Iulian K., 144, 150, 151, 222–23n11, 224n29

Sheldrake, Rupert, 8
shen, 177, 180–82, 183, 229n140, 230n158; *shen ming*, 183
Sherrill, W. A., 225n47
Shorter, Bani, 202n75
siège périlleux, 134–35
simultaneity, 12, 13, 14, 15, 16, 17–18, 23, 91, 116, 133, 139, 196n7, 198n29
sinology, 8, 10, 145, 147
skepticism, 42, 46, 76–79, 82, 83, 86, 95, 103, 109, 116–17, 149, 219n167
Smith, Richard, 21, 228n104
spirit, 2, 11, 23–37, 131, 177–87; aspect of a continuum, 27–28; autonomy of, 26, 29, 30, 32, 37, 56; definition of present work, 26–27, 76, 181–82; definition of Wilber, 25; definitions in dictionaries and encyclopaedias, 23–25, 200; definitions of Jung, 24, 25–26, 30; differentiating attributes of, 29–30; directly experienceable, 31–36, 182; interpenetrating psychic and physical, 30; materiality of, 200; ontologically and epistemologically on a par with psychic and physical, 31; phenomenology of, 25–26; psychophysical in relation to, 129, 134, 135, 139, 140, 142; purposiveness of, 30, 182; restructuring psychic and physical, 29–30; self-revelation of, 37, 119; spirits, 183; spiritual concepts, 9, 39–62, 63, 129; spiritual reality (*see* reality: spiritual); spiritual search, 124; spirituality, 84, 85, 110, 123, 128–29, 130; and synchronicity (*see* synchronicity); transgressiveness of, 29; unity of, 29. *See also* immanence; miracles; numinosity; providence; revelation; *shen*; transcendence; transformation; unity

Index

spontaneity, 3, 5, 56, 57, 120, 204n125, 228n105; as characteristic of spirit, 26, 30, 37, 56; of fantasy products, 122; of symbolic enactment, 125, 130. *See also* synchronicity: oracular and spontaneous compared; synchronicity: spontaneous
stars, 86, 87, 88, 91, 115, 119, 213–14n35; Plaskett's Star, 88, 91, 117, 123, 124, 125, 128, 214n37; shooting stars, 89, 100
statistics, 3, 7, 107, 116, 231n8
Stiffler, Lavonne, 191n16
Sutherland, Cherie, 194n46
Swanson, Gerald, 145, 224n29
Swedenborg, Emmanuel, 17
symbols, 9, 15, 37, 58, 72–73, 75, 78, 128, 136, 141; meaning and, 101; properties of, 59; symbolic associations, 157; symbolic communication, 59; symbolic content, 114; symbolic death, 70, 76, 78; symbolic enactment, 130; symbolic interpretation, 87, 89, 113, 119, 120, 123, 156, 175; symbolic perception, 36
synchronicity, 2, 35, 123, 129–31, 138–40; absolute, 21; application of, 4; archetypal basis of, 176–77; autonomy of, 56, 57; case material, 3, 5, 9, 10, 63–79, 81–111, 113–40 (*see also* coincidence examples; Plaskett's coincidences; Thornton: synchronistic narrative); content of, 22, 58, 111, 139; contexts informing concept of, 4, 5; contexts of occurrence, 115; definition of, 3, 9, 11–23, 14, 197–98n26, 212n2, 219n5; effects of, 6; enigma of, 48, 111; essential form of, 57–58, 111, 139, 208n70; evidential status of, 118; generated, 141, 142, 143; as Grail, 139, 140; improbability of, 117, 118; indefiniteness in definition of, 23; intelligibility of 79, 114; interconnection of themes in, 79, 114, 118, 216n81, 219n10; interpretation of, 113, 119; manner of occurrence of, 115–16; and myth, 3; numbers and, 3, 8; and numinosity (*see* numinosity); one-off experiences of, 63; oracular and spontaneous, compared, 173–77 (*see also* synchronicity: generated); quantity of incidents, 79, 82, 86–87, 114, 213n29; repetition of themes in, 79, 86–87, 113, 114, 118; self-referring nature of, 110–11, 129, 130, 139; self-revelation of, as spirit, 131; series of, 63, 79, 81, 113, 122, 123; and spirit, 2, 4, 7, 10, 39, 184, 185; spiritual aspect of, 5, 9, 114; spiritual status of, 113, 116–19, 131; spontaneous, 5, 10, 26, 37, 39, 50, 52, 81, 95, 141, 142, 143; systematized in *I Ching*, 142; temporal proximity of incidents in, 118; term, 3. *See also* acausality; coincidence; external event; meaning; notability; paralleling; psychic state

Tao, 39, 55, 158, 181–82; Taoism, 101, 144
Tart, Charles, 6, 21
telepathy, 6, 17, 21, 41, 195n54
Thalbourne, Michael, 8, 180
theology, 3, 33, 43, 55, 102, 109, 171; theologians, 33, 58, 61, 62
third eye, 87, 96, 119, 128, 131, 215n77
Thomas Aquinas, Saint, 54, 56
Thornton, Edward, 63–79, 81, 88, 113–16; 196, 198; *Diary of a Mystic*, 63; operation, 69; synchronistic narrative of, 63–72, 130. *See also* Athena; operation; owls; wound: to the head

threefoldness, 87, 91, 92, 93. *See also* third eye; triangle; trilogy
time, 16, 17–18, 36, 162, 198n29; moment, 143, 145, 152, 161, 162, 173, 174, 175, 187; qualitative, 162–63; relativity of, 16, 21, 29; timelessness, 4, 24, 29; timing, 67, 76, 101, 109, 174. *See also* simultaneity
Tiresias, 127
transcendence, 25, 26, 27, 39, 53–55, 56, 61, 65, 74, 182, 184, 207n57, 211n61; and immanence, 39, 53, 55, 75; self-transcending emotions, 5; transcendent agent, 60; transcendent causes, 20, 21, 128; transcendent intelligence, 54, 57, 65; transcendent reality, 25, 33, 55, 57, 58, 61, 74–75, 123
transformation, 15, 39, 47–49, 58, 68, 69, 61, 62, 74, 75–76, 123, 125–28, 129, 130; of attitude, 71; of consciousness, 47, 62, 125; in *I Ching*, 144, 182, 186–87; of meaninglessness into meaning, 110; of nature, 126; of personality, 48, 49, 69, 82, 109; property of symbols, 59; of society, 126; spiritual, 64, 68, 74, 125, 187
triangle, 87, 96, 215n77
trickster, 3, 54, 190n12
trilogy, 93, 126
Tung Chung-shu, 172
Tylor, Edward, 200n43

uncanniness, 42, 47, 51, 70, 205n18
the unconscious, 15, 16, 51, 134, 179, 183; collective, 13, 15, 22; psychoid, 35, 36, 51, 228n105; symbolized, 125, 127
unicorn, 86, 87, 88, 99; Unicorn/Monoceros (constellation), 88, 91, 117, 124

unity, 20, 29, 32, 39, 49–53, 67, 75, 84, 207n57, 210–11n44; alchemical conjunction, 211n61; and duality, 29, 199n36; empirical indications of, 52, 53; experienced, 50, 51; inferred, 51, 53; mystical, 53, 68; of observer and observed, 29, 49–50, 131; of psyche and matter, 32, 50, 51, 72, 228n105; of spirit, 29, 49; union of opposites, 87; unitary view of reality, 20, 22, 51–53, 55, 58; unitive awareness, 25, 28, 29, 31, 49, 202n77
unus mundus (one world), 52, 211n61

Vallée, Jacques, 194n51
van der Post, Laurens, 89, 100, 104
Vaughan, Alan, 6, 197n10, 205n23, 219n4
Vedanta: Advaita, 49
vessel: Grail as, 136–39; *I Ching* as, 185–87
Whitehead, Alfred N., 172
Virgin Mary, 46, 65, 78; as Divine Wisdom, 65, 68, 69, 73, 78
vision, new, 127, 128, 130, 131
von Eschenbach, Wolfram, 136, 137, 138
von Franz, Marie-Louise, 3, 7, 8, 52, 72, 134, 136, 137, 138, 139, 220n15, 221n28, 221n32, 228n115

Wagner, Richard, 43
Waley, Arthur, 224n29
Wang, Fu-chih, 145, 178
Wang Pi, 145, 187
Watt, Caroline, 7
Wên, King, 143, 144, 150
Wharton, Barbara, 190–1n14
Wheelwright, Jane, 212n4
Wheelwright, Joseph, 212n4
Whincup, Greg, 222n11

White, Fr. Victor, 64, 200
Whitmont, Edward, 33, 35, 36
Wilber, Ken, 30
Wilhelm, Hellmut, 150, 152, 162, 178, 222n8, 223n24, 224n29
Wilhelm, Richard, 142, 146–47, 149, 151, 152, 156, 158, 159, 161, 162, 164, 168, 186, 222n3, 225n60; Wilhelm-Baynes *I Ching*, 3, 146, 185, 222n3, 222n6, 223n28, 224n32
Williams, Mary, 190
Wilson, Colin, 103, 213n31, 215n74
Wilson, Ian, 83
wound: Christ's, 90, 136; Fisher King's, 132; to the head, 66–69 passim, 72, 73, 75, 76, 77, 78, 79

Zabriskie, Beverley, 191n17
Zechariah, 11, 197n8
Zeus, 67, 78
Zinkin, Louis, 194n50

Printed in Great Britain
by Amazon.co.uk, Ltd.,
Marston Gate.